The Divorce Experience

The Divorce Experience

Morton Hunt and Bernice Hunt

McGRAW-HILL BOOK COMPANY

New York • St. Louis • San Francisco

Book design by Barbara Hall.

1 2 3 4 5 6 7 8 9 0   F G F G   7 8 3 2 1 0 9 8 7

Library of Congress Cataloging in Publication Data

Hunt, Morton M, date
  The divorce experience.
  Bibliography: p.
  Includes index.
  1. Divorce—United States.   2. Remarriage—
United States.   I. Hunt, Bernice Kohn, joint
author.   II. Title.
HQ834.H83   301.42′84′0973   77-5910
ISBN 0-07-031301-6

Acknowledgments

This book and we, its authors, owe a very considerable debt to the people who contributed information and insights to its pages, and to those whose lives, as formerly married persons, are its very substance. *The Divorce Experience*, even more than most books, could not have been written without the generosity of the many experts who freely gave of their time, knowledge, and expertise, and the great number of separated and divorced people who took us into their private lives and shared with us their anguish, their hopes, their joy, and their tears. We are immensely grateful to them all.

Probably no two individuals deserve more special thanks, both for their dazzling command of demographic data and their willingness to answer our innumerable queries, than Paul C. Glick, Senior Demographer, Population Division, and Arthur J. Norton, Chief of the Marriage and Family Statistics Branch, of the U.S. Bureau of the Census. They received us cordially in Washington and made sense, for us, of a great many published—and not-yet-published—data. So did Alexander A. Plateris of the National Center for Health Statistics of the Department of Health, Education, and Welfare.

Barbara Chase, editor of *The Single Parent*, the national publication of Parents Without Partners, did us the incalculable service of running our questionnaire in that magazine; the many hundreds of readers who filled it out form the larger part of our national survey sample.

C. Ray Fowler, Executive Director of the American Association of Marriage and Family Counselors, was extremely helpful in enlisting the aid of thirty members of his organization, throughout the country, in distributing additional copies of the questionnaire.

Some two dozen other people, most of them sociologists, also helped distribute questionnaires and deserve our thanks; among them (we apologize for omitting academic credentials here, in the interest of brevity) are Alan P. Bell, Barbara Jo Chesser, Jack R. and Joann S. DeLora, Howard E. Freeman, Kent Hall, Kathy K. Hamill, Harold M. Hodges, Jr., Mel Krantzler, Roger Libby, Barbara Lovenheim, Joseph W. Maxwell, Donald S. Milman, Janis Newton, Robert D. Patton, Alice Thornton, Philip Selznick, Paul S. Weikert, James D. Weinrich, J. Gipson Wells, Robert N. Whitehurst, and Linda Wolfe. Several others who distributed questionnaires also provided us with information and are thanked in a later paragraph of these Acknowledgments.

When we were overwhelmed with data and realized that only an electronic brain could make sense of it all, we were rescued by a computer, or rather, by the extraordinary intelligence and dedication of the people operating it—the computer team at Longwood High School in Middle Island, New York. Supervised by John Caracciola, the computer programmers were Jack Millrod, Richard Conde, and Stephen Aurelio; they were ably assisted by Teresa Arasi, Jeanette Barsi, Sheryl Morson, and Lynn Sellers, who prepared the punched cards. The entire team was able to do what it did because of the painstaking and insightful coding of thousands of pages of human experience into digits, a herculean labor performed admirably by Judith Wolman, with the assistance of Louise Sussin.

Those who have shared with us their special information or recent research findings (and some of whom, in addition, distributed questionnaires) include Betty Berry, editor and publisher of *Marriage, Divorce and the Family Newsletter*; Paul Bohannan, University of California at Santa Barbara; Ruth

A. Brandwein, School of Social Work, Boston University; Ferol Breymann, Paulist Center Community, Boston; Emily M. Brown, director, Divorce and Marital Stress Clinic, Arlington, Virginia; Jim Buchan, Office of Public Affairs, Public Health Service; O. J. Coogler, president, Family Mediation Center, Atlanta; Dennis Corriveau, Office of Child Support Enforcement, Department of Health, Education, and Welfare; Betty Daggett, director, Portland (Oregon) Solo Center; Esther Oshiver Fisher, marriage and divorce counselor, New York; Paul O. Flaim, Bureau of Labor Statistics, Department of Labor; Patricia A. Gongla, Case Western Reserve University; Rev. Andrew M. Greeley, National Opinion Research Center, University of Chicago; Louis B. Hays, deputy director, Office of Child Support Enforcement, Department of Health, Education and Welfare; Edwin M. Long, Jr., Alcohol, Drug Abuse, and Mental Health Administration, Public Health Service; Leonard R. Mellon, National District Attorneys' Association; Helen J. Raschke, Norfolk State College, Norfolk, Virginia; Ethel L. Mendelsohn, Women's Bureau, Department of Labor; Philip F. Solomon, president, American Academy of Matrimonial Lawyers; Lenore J. Weitzman, principal investigator, California Divorce Law Research Project, University of California at Berkeley; Robert S. Weiss, The Laboratory of Community Psychiatry, Harvard Medical School; Daniel C. Williamson, rare-book bibliographer, Samuel Paley Library, Temple University; and Rev. James J. Young, director of ministerial studies, Weston School of Theology, Cambridge.

Millie Becerra was our diligent and flawless typist.

Those to whom we owe the deepest thanks are the ones whose names we may not reveal: they are the 1,300 separated, divorced, and widowed people who took the time and trouble to complete our lengthy questionnaire, or who gave of their time and themselves and trustingly permitted us to interview them on tape.

And last, we are deeply grateful to Fred Hills, who has, quite possibly, spoiled us for all other editors.

Contents

A Word About This Book

The Divorce Experience is a contemporary portrait of separated and divorced Americans, a study of their customs, problems, experiences, and life-styles. It is an examination in intimate detail of the world of the formerly married, and a critical appraisal of the place divorce occupies today in the larger world of American society.

The book is the end product of an intensive research program that included field observation, roughly 200 depth interviews, a survey of recent lay and professional divorce literature, consultations with experts, and, most important of all, a national questionnaire survey that we designed and carried out in 1976. We received and computer-analyzed questionnaires from 984 separated and divorced persons (details of the sample can be found in the Notes on Sources), and, for comparative purposes, 113 more from widows and widowers. To the best of our knowledge, this is the largest and most up-to-date body of information extant about the formerly married and the special world they inhabit.

It is not a compilation of statistics, and not a "how-to" guide, but a book of human experiences. Data are given where the numbers are particularly surprising, enlightening, or fascinating, but in the main our significant findings are presented through case material and descriptions of behavior; these are far more accessible to most people than are tables, charts, and graphs, and the voices of divorced people are far more persuasive than our own.

We have avoided step-by-step advice because both of us believe that such advice, offered wholesale to unknown individuals, is like medicine prescribed for unknown patients; it could, by chance, cure their ills, but it could easily make them much worse. And yet, since both of us have been through divorce ourselves, we know how eagerly one looks for help, for guidance, for reassurance at this painful and bewildering time. We think that the best help we can give is to describe what is happening in the world of the formerly married today, and to depict how various kinds of people deal, in various ways—some successfully, and some not—with separation, divorce, and postmarital life. Having lived through all this vicariously, the reader can judge which forms of behavior to take as models that fit his or her own needs and situation. It is not we, the authors, but rather the reader, using this book as both medical manual and pharmacopeia, who can best function as physician to him or herself, the patient.

Finally, although this is a new book in every way, it is an outgrowth of Morton Hunt's *The World of the Formerly Married* (1966), and borrows freely from its ideas. Much that was true more than a decade ago is still true; much more, however, has changed, and we will, from time to time, point out the most dramatic differences between what we find to be the case today and what was the case then—before divorce had become an integral part of the institution of marriage and an essential means to its survival in modern society.

All direct quotations and case histories are drawn from our own interviews or questionnaires unless otherwise indicated in the text or the Notes on Sources; to protect the persons involved, we have altered identifying details and assigned fictitious names.

Sources are given in the Notes; for the limitations of our sample, and other caveats, see discussion on pages 271–273.

I

Another World, Another Life

1. CROSSING THE BORDER

Emily McDowell groped for the bedside lamp and flooded the room with light. Her heart was pounding as if she'd been running, and as she sat up, sweat trickled down her sides and left wet streaks on her nightgown. She looked at the clock and saw that it was 2 A.M. Only three hours had passed.

Three hours since her husband had set down his suitcases at the door for a moment while he pulled on his gloves, then nodded silently to her, and left. They had been talking about a separation for weeks, and both of them knew it was necessary; yet, as soon as the door closed behind him she felt a sudden unreasonable sense of panic. She had taken a strong sleeping pill and gone to bed, and had slept after a while—but now the panic had broken through and she was wide awake again.

Emily got up and padded softly down the hall past the children's room, and into the kitchen. She took some grapes out of the refrigerator, ate a couple, felt slightly nauseated, hurriedly put the rest of the bunch back into the crisper. She went to the living room, and turned on the television set, but found it impossible to pay attention to the movie.

What's the matter with me, anyway? she thought. *Why am I acting like such an idiot? I wanted him to go. What am I afraid of?* Emily McDowell, thirty-five years old, registered nurse, saw frightened people every day, sick people afraid of pain, afraid of death. And she, Nurse McDowell, was strong and competent, always able to comfort and to cheer. Now who would comfort her? Who would *ever* comfort her?

She picked up a novel she'd been reading but after five minutes realized that her own obsessive thoughts crowded the story out of her mind. *This is crazy*, she thought. *I must be out of my mind. I'm acting charge nurse tomorrow, how will I ever get through the day? What will I do if I begin to cry at the hospital? Suppose the kids cry when I tell them? How will I get them off to school?*

Emily took another sleeping pill, got back into bed, and resolutely turned off the light. After a while she fell asleep and dreamed that she was all alone, lost, wandering through the dark and deserted streets of some unfamiliar city.

Ralph Lipman was planting the sixth of a dozen young fruit trees, late of a spring afternoon, when an oil-delivery truck pulled into his driveway. The driver stopped to chat for a moment on his way to the fill pipe, but he cut short his recital of neighborhood gossip and edged away as he realized that Lipman looked distinctly peculiar: there was a disturbing frenetic glitter in his eyes, he seemed unaware that his bare back and bald head had been badly sunburned on this unseasonably hot day, and he never stopped his furious digging even while talking.

Lipman had been in non-stop motion since before dawn. He and his wife had had one of their raging all-night quarrels, and at last she was screaming that she wanted him to get out and stay out. Eager to escape her voice, he began packing at 4:30, loaded the station wagon with his essential possessions, and drove to their vacation home, eighty miles away. There he unloaded and put away several cartons of books and records, a small file containing business papers, several suitcases full of clothing. He was all finished by 10:30; then he drove to the village for a great batch of groceries, beer, frozen pizza. On the way back, he stopped off at a nursery and pestered the owner into making immediate delivery of six peach trees and six apple trees. As soon as he got home, he began digging, and in between lunch and more plantings, he had a series of rambling telephone conversations with his business partner, his lawyer, and his brother. As long as Ralph kept going, he felt all right.

But by 8 o'clock, he had watered his new orchard, taken a shower, and sunk down in the living room with a cold beer. Then the anxiety attack swept over him and, with some astonishment, he watched his hands tremble as if they were motorized. *What's going on? How could I have been ordered out of my own home, my own life? Why am I sitting here, all alone in a dark room, at the age of fifty-one—on a weekday in May? What am I going to do tonight? And tomorrow, and the day after tomorrow? Will I ever be able to get up and go to work in the morning? What am I going to do with the rest of my life?*

"So long," said Arnold Atkins to his wife, Jane. "I'll call you later, to see how you are." She looked puzzled. "Well, we *are* still friends, aren't we?" he asked. "And we do care about each other's welfare, don't we?"

"Sure," she said, smiling. "I really like you a lot—except when I can't stand you." They both laughed and then Arnold was gone.

She waited by the window until she saw him turn the corner; then she went straight to the bedroom, stripped the sheets off the king-size bed, and made it up with fresh linen. Next, she arranged the closets and drawers, expanding her things into the newly vacated spaces; finally, she put her night-time reading material on what had been his night table, the one with the better reading lamp. She chuckled at herself for marking out her new territory (just like any jungle beast, she thought), but as soon as she finished, the bad feeling began to seep in.

It was Saturday, and she had no office to go to, no idea of what to do next. For four years she had been part of something that had just ceased to exist; she'd been a—what had that sociologist called it?—a *with*, and now she was something else, a *single*, alone, disconnected, and . . . *lost* was the word that came into her mind.

Should she call her parents or friends, tell them, talk about it? Not yet; they would ask too many questions, and she wasn't ready, might become tearful and incoherent, or say things she would later regret.

Should she go shopping? She usually liked to shop, but strangely, she didn't feel like buying anything; there wasn't anything she wanted or cared about—and she felt that she looked strange, too, so strange that people in stores might stare at her, at her frozen face, tight mouth, blank eyes.

Should she go for a walk? The apartment was ominous and oppressive in its emptiness—but outside, a winter wind was driving sleet with a force that made pedestrians hold their hands in front of their smarting faces.

She seized the telephone as if it were a life preserver and she, a drowning swimmer; she dialed her mother's number, and hung up after the first ring, then dialed again, hung up again, and burst into tears of shame. *I'm acting like a frightened child, a little girl who's lost her Mommy in the crowd. I'm being ridiculous, stupid, immature. Why should I feel like a lost kid when I'm twenty-eight and a successful career woman in the big city? Damned if I know, but that's how I feel, anyway.*

Just as it was to these three people, the moment of separation is a severe shock to most people—even to those who wanted it or expected it. It stuns, disorients, and frightens, because it is a wrenching transition from the known past into an unknown future. The newly separated person has just stepped across the border from the familiar land—no matter how bad—of marriage, into the *terra incognita* of postmarital life; he or she must set foot upon what appears as a blank space on the map, ignorant of what its inhabitants are like, how newcomers are expected to behave, what dangers lie in wait, where to turn for comfort and help. No wonder the newly separated so commonly experience the nightmarish feeling of unaccountably finding themselves in a strange place with no idea of where to go or what to do to save themselves.

Yet, they will learn that the unknown territory is not a featureless void or a savage wilderness after all. It turns out to be a surprisingly "civilized" place with its own beliefs, customs, and values; it has ample opportunities for friendship, social life, sexual partnership, and love, and its own ways of indoctrinating the newcomer. Of course it isn't entirely beneficent—it has its own special dangers and deprivations, too. But, seen as a whole, it has a distinct culture—or more accurately, a *subculture* of the American culture we all share. Throughout this book we will often refer to that subculture as *the world of the formerly married*, and for convenience, to its members as the formerly married, or FMs—those who are informally separated, legally separated, divorced, or whose marriages have been annulled.

Like members of other subcultures—racial or religious minorities, homosexuals, members of high society—FMs belong to two different worlds. They are part of American society and spend most of their time living within its institutions and interacting with its people, most of whom (roughly 70 per cent of those eighteen and over) are married. But in their hearts, and in their private lives, they are separate and apart from the married, and are drawn together by their very difference and apartness. Together, a people within a people, they are no longer misfits, outsiders, but people who *belong*; to the initiates, it is the never-divorced married people who seem to be the Others, the Outsiders.

Less than a generation ago, married people knew little about the world of the formerly married; it was a semi-secret society. Its members were close-mouthed about their feelings and experiences because, in the larger society, divorce was still considered a tragedy and, in many quarters, something of a disgrace; FMs were uneasy about telling the married—whose ranks they had so recently left—that there was much that was positive and rewarding in their new world: relief, freedom, a sense of rebirth, and often, a great emotional and sexual flowering. They were quite right in thinking that none of this would have gone down too well with the married, who could sympathize wholeheartedly with the sinners—but only as long as they were suffering.[1]

But in recent years, divorce has become so common, so much more approved, and so widely discussed, that one would hardly expect separation to be as terrifying as it used to be. In the past fifteen years, for example, well over 500 books and articles about divorce have been published. Every person who can read a newspaper knows that by 1976 there was one divorce for every two marriages—an all-time high;* the divorce rate, rising since 1962, has more than doubled since then.[2] Not only were there over eleven million people in the world of the formerly married in 1976, but thirty to forty million had passed through it and rejoined the world of the married.[3] Divorce, once seen only as a failure, has come to be regarded as the creative solution to a problem. In view of these changes, how could the subculture still be so unfamiliar, so alarming? It hardly seems possible that the newly separated don't know what to expect—and yet they don't.

Even a professional social worker who should know the territory may feel terrified, unready. Mel Krantzler, a family counselor, describes in *Creative Divorce* his own early reactions to separation; they included acute loneliness, self-pity, "emotional shakes and sweats," and a view of the future as a "vortex of emptiness, fear, and uncertainty."

Strange? Not really. The explanation is cultural lag—the time needed for some elements of our culture to catch up and adjust to changes or innovations in other elements. The behavior patterns and ideals of the FM subculture have become public knowledge only within the past dozen years, and that knowledge has not yet been assimilated by the married.

To most of them, divorce is something that happens to others; few couples, at the time of marriage, accept the fact that their marriage has a one-in-two chance of breaking up either temporarily or permanently—for who would get married except in the belief that it is "forever"?[4] So not expecting it to happen, they don't bother to learn what becomes of people who separate and divorce, and if it *does* happen, they are ignorant, unprepared, and frightened. Some of our secondary schools have only just begun to give instruction in family life and marriage; it will probably be a long while before instruction in divorce becomes common. But in any case, the conditions of life for the formerly married have been changing so swiftly that even those who remarried as recently as a dozen years ago, and who now face a

---

* Although the ratio of divorces to marriages is a favorite headline for journalists, a more sensitive index of the growth of divorce is the divorce rate per thousand population. This increased by 127 per cent from 1962 to 1976.

second separation, recognize that they are out of touch with the present realities and will have much to relearn—but they will never be as ignorant or as terrified as they were the first time.

The paradox of the increase and acceptance of divorce versus the unpreparedness of the divorcing will disappear as cultural lag is overcome. There is ample evidence that the lag is already diminishing rapidly, for divorce is no longer regarded as curious, exceptional, or deviant. Everyone knows—or at least rubs elbows with—someone who has been divorced. They can hardly avoid it since for every nine married people there is one FM plus three FMs who have remarried.[5]

Eventually, the married will find it possible to tell their friends, families, co-workers, and neighbors of an impending divorce without shame or fear of stigma. It is already considerably easier than it was ten or fifteen years ago.

That still doesn't mean that divorce will become easy. In a world that is increasingly impersonal, in a society whose people are on the move and so form few permanent bonds of friendship and community, marriage is—and will remain—emotionally more important than ever. The much-publicized decline in the marriage rate is no contradiction of this: the rate continues to be higher than it was from 1957 through 1967, and the present decline may be only a short-term phenomenon due to such factors as the recent recession, the delay of marriage by women who go to college or work, a temporary imbalance between the number of marriageable young women and marriageable young men, and so on. Indeed, in 1976, the three-year decline leveled off.[6] Because we value marriage, today and for the foreseeable future, its breakup will continue to be one of the most distressing, bewildering, and painful emotional traumas we can undergo.

2. THE ELUSIVE "TYPICAL" FM

Who and what is this typical FM we have been speaking about? Most FMs would probably deny that they are typical, for people resent and resist being classified or categorized. We all treasure our individuality and are quick to reject any suggestion that we can easily be fathomed, *a priori*, as specimens of known types. "Yes," we say, "but my case is somewhat special," or "I'm not like most people in my category," or "I don't fit into any of the usual pigeonholes." And, in truth, every individual *is* unique: no two people, even twins, are absolutely identical, for no two people have identical life experiences.

Yet we all recognize that we do resemble certain people in various ways, or that we differ markedly from others. We categorize ourselves whenever we use that familiar kind of shorthand that helps strangers understand us: "I'm a sort of Catholic—the kind who goes to Mass on Christmas and Easter"; "At heart I'm still an upstate farmboy"; "I'm the type that wouldn't be caught dead at a costume party."

In the same way, while there is no one typical FM, there are many *categories* of FM that might be called typical because they represent the behavior of a large number of people. None of the following persons can be called a "typical" FM, and yet, each is typical of one segment of the FM population.

—Asparagus Beach, the singles' meeting ground at Amagansett, on New York's Long Island. Bob G. is busy at his favorite weekend pastime: beach-hopping. Bob is twenty-nine, a trifle too plump, but genial, curly haired, and outgoing; with his disarming affability he manages to move the length and breadth of the beach greeting and chatting with woman after woman—but deftly avoiding any commitment for the evening until he has decided which woman looks like the best of the lot. Only a year and a half ago, suffering from an ulcer, Bob began psychotherapy and discovered that he really hated being a lawyer and still mourned his original plan to become a commercial artist. He promptly quit the law, and when his status-minded young wife greeted the news with scorn and fury, he quit her, too.

After the first few bad months, Bob began to feel better than he had in years, and as his spirits rose his ulcer healed and disappeared. He has been enjoying himself ever since, even though as a beginner in the art department of an advertising agency his salary is modest and he has to live in a tiny, dingy, ground-floor apartment on a noisy Manhattan cross-street. But feeling that he might make art director some day, and that all life lies ahead of him, he has been working hard, going to parties, dating around (as far as his money will carry him), and relishing his second chance at everything. His rare moods of depression stem not from regret for the broken marriage, but from a sense of oppression and loneliness when he is alone in his bleak quarters, and from an occasional fit of concern that he might *never* care about any woman but always flit from one to another.

—Jennifer G., in a large dance studio in downtown Philadelphia, is doing pirouettes as if she were practicing for opening night at the Bolshoi. She is in a late-afternoon ballet class for people who, like herself, just want some exercise and body training. Jennifer, thirty-six, is rather plain looking, wears thick glasses, and is a bit dumpy—nobody's ideal Giselle. But ballet class does make her feel physically good and even graceful.

After class, in a fine mood, she rushes home, where the mood soon dissipates; her children, nine and eleven, are impatiently awaiting dinner, and though they help (grumbling), Jennifer has to hurry to get the cooking done, clean up the kitchen when dinner is over, and look over the homework before the children's bedtime. Afterward, thoroughly weary, she still has to put a load of laundry through the washer and dryer, pay some bills, make up a shopping list, and write to her lawyer—once again—about her vanished husband and the equally vanished child-support payments. Sometimes, it's all just a little too much, and she cries a bit; at other times, she gulps down a half a tumbler of vodka instead.

The vodka tends to blur the problems and that's a help since Jennifer has learned to keep her problems to herself. She used to take advantage of her dates to unburden herself, but while most of the men listened sympathetically, few called again. Now Jennifer knows better. She has learned to be "fun." She has also learned how to make herself look reasonably glamorous when she goes out; she wears contact lenses, chic clothes, and makeup she learned to apply in a special course. Along with the makeup, she puts on an expectant manner that is new since her divorce; it's genuine, though, for one of the surprises of her life was to discover that recently, men seem to think she's great in bed. She thinks so, too, and is tremendously excited by new-found joy in sex such as she never knew with her husband. But she has almost given up hoping or expecting that any man will be more than a pleasant date and, if she's lucky, a good lover. It seems wiser to hope for nothing than to hope, again and again, only to be disappointed each time.

—Harry T., sitting in his elegant walnut-paneled library, has been on the telephone for nearly two hours; he has called half a dozen men and women friends, including one in Mexico and one in Hawaii. This is what Harry does on those one or two evenings a week when he's alone and disheartened by his life as a divorced man. Few would understand Harry's misery: at fifty-one, he's flat of belly, has all his hair, makes $80,000 a year as a management consultant and investor, lives in a spacious duplex apartment furnished with antiques; he frequently goes to the opera or the theater, and always has an active list of two or three attractive women who are delighted to spend time with him in companionship or lovemaking—and none of whom expects anything more of him. Harry is the envy of his friends, and he doesn't tell them that their envy is misplaced because he finds it hard to explain why his life seems so barren.

The truth is that Harry hates not being married. He has been married twice, once for twenty years (there were two children), once for four years (no children). Both marriages ended in divorce, and after the second time, disillusioned, Harry told everyone who would listen, "Never again!" He made it plain to the women he dated he would flee from the first sign of involvement and, indeed, he did just that several times.

But inside himself, Harry feels incomplete in the unmarried state. Intellectually, he wants to remain single, emotionally he hungers for a woman to share his life, his thoughts and feelings, to be part of him; he longs for a wife. Harry doesn't know how to resolve his conflict—and until he does, he talks to his oldest and closest friends on the telephone so that he can feel *connected*.

—Susan M. is proud of the Swedish meatballs she made for dinner, a favorite of her two teenagers and her husband; they have all just shown their appreciation by taking second helpings. The four of them, sitting around the table in a lovely Malibu home, make a friendly, chatty family scene.

Beneath the pretty picture, however, is a curious reality. Susan's husband left her two years ago, set himself up in a

bachelor apartment, and has had a string of women friends—
some of them even on a live-in basis for short periods. Yet, he
has consistently arrived at Susan's for dinner a couple of times
a week, taking it for granted that it is his right to "visit his
family."

Susan makes no protest. She is a pleasant-looking but fluttery
and timid woman in her forties, who admits that she has a
problem and doesn't know how to solve it. Her lawyer assures
her that she can get a divorce at any time—but she doesn't want
one. Her sister and friends tell her she must be crazy—and at
times, Susan is sure they're right—but she knows that she secretly
wants her husband to keep visiting and staying for dinner, and
dreads the time when he might stop; she is both revolted and
alarmed by attention from other men.

—A gay bar in San Francisco. Roger R., aggressively masculine in boots, tight jeans with studded belt, a tee-shirt that makes
much of his tattooed and powerful upper arms, has turned his
back on the crowd and chats with the bartender.

Roger is forty, barrel-chested, and has a bushy mustache
which, like his outfit, is part of his new image. But there is far
more than these externals that is new in Roger's life. Until a
couple of years ago, he was a married man with two children;
by day he drove a delivery truck, and during his free time he
was a model husband and father—except for one or two evenings
a week. These were the nights when Roger ostensibly played
poker with the boys, but actually went cruising for homosexual
sex—often consummated in the back of his parked truck. And
then one night he was arrested in the act; when his wife found
out, she was horrified and filed for divorce at once.

Roger decided to come out; he dropped all his old friends and
doesn't even dare to visit his children because he doesn't know
if they can understand, doesn't know how he can explain. He
rents a large, dreary room and kitchenette in a rooming house,
but does not feel confined since he is rarely there. He still drives
a truck and now spends all his leisure time cruising in gay bars,
baths, parks, and other forums; he has never had a roommate or
a lover for more than a single night.

Nowadays, more and more often, he gets spells of deep
depression; it seems to him that something changed with his

fortieth birthday, for it is increasingly difficult to pick up the young, beautiful partners he likes best. Despite his tough confident look, Roger often thinks of suicide. One night, not long ago, the thought was so insistent that he grew frightened; he took his pistol down to the wharf and dropped it into the water.

—A walk-up cold-water apartment in a slum in the Bronx, New York. Hattie G., after a long, hot day of work in a clothing factory, labors up the steps to the fourth floor lugging a large bag of groceries. The hallways stink of urine, the paint is peeling from the walls, plaster has fallen in chunks from the ceiling, roaches scurry for cover as she approaches.

Hattie, in her early thirties, is a shapely, light-skinned black woman, still attractive though her face is set in lines of discontent and fatigue. She unlocks three locks on the door and enters her shabby, stifling apartment. There's no one home. Her sons, aged twelve and fourteen, are chronic truants who probably skipped school again today and are out somewhere with a street gang. When they come home, late, they will lie to her—skillfully and fluently—about where they've been.

Still, Hattie means to cook dinner in case they do come home in time; she tries to be a good mother although there isn't much she can do. There isn't much she can do about anything, she muses, except work, and sleep, and worry. What she really needs is a man to live with her, comfort her, love her, help her with the bills and the boys, a man who is not a drifter and a drunk like her husband. Over the years he has left her countless times for a few days or a few weeks, but the last time, he seems to have disappeared for good. Hattie wishes she knew if he were dead or alive, for even if she did find the right new man, how could she know the old one wouldn't walk back in some day? She has no idea how to protect herself from him, no idea how you get a divorce when you have no money, are scared to death of courts and judges, and can barely read and write.

Are any of these people typical FMs? They certainly aren't typical of *all* FMs, yet each is typical of one kind of FM. There are many more kinds, too. The sexually promiscuous middle-aged man-about-town, living out all the fantasies he stored up during a long, arid marriage; the attractive young woman who perceives herself as a femme fatale and gets even with her ex-husband by having one affair after the other; the woman in her sixties who has done little but drink, shop, go to doctors, ever since her husband left her to marry a woman in her thirties; the assorted habitués of singles bars, resort ships, adult camps, pick-up beaches.

The list could go on and on indefinitely, and while we would find out a great deal about the many kinds of FMs, we would never find out what a typical FM is like. To do that, we have to shift our focus away from single cases and take a broad view of the entire FM population; there, right in the center, is a composite of all the kinds of FMs we have talked about and all those we haven't mentioned—the *average* FM. To find the average, we must use numbers, and although people are more interesting than numbers, figures don't lie and people do; therefore, we resort to statistics in order, at last, to define the typical FM.

3. TRUTH IN NUMBERS OR: THE TYPICAL FM

The typical FM is twice as likely to be divorced as separated. Put another way, two-thirds of all FMs have been divorced— up from little more than half in 1962 when the divorce rate began its steep climb.[7] The change is a striking example of both the increased availability and acceptability of divorce. Relatively few people linger in the limbo of separation because they are afraid or unable to take the final steps; they take them quickly, too; the average lag is under one year from separation to divorce, whereas it was two years in 1960.[8]

For every five FM women there are three FM men. Divorced men marry sooner and in greater numbers than women, so that more unremarried women than men accumulate in the FM population; in 1976, the figures stood at 6,826,000 women to 4,138,000 men.*[9]

* Most of our data on the total number of divorced persons in the United States do not include those whose marriages were annulled, since the Bureau of the Census classifies these people as "single" (i.e., never married). But the figures for the number of divorces granted in any given year are compiled by the National Center for Health Statistics, which does include annulments in its totals. The discrepancies this makes for are minor, however, since annulments currently amount to well under 2 per cent of total marital dissolutions.[10]

Half of all divorces are granted within the first seven years of marriage. Contrary to popular belief, marriages do not break up much sooner than they used to: the average divorce takes place only about two-thirds of a year earlier than it did in 1962, and about a year and a half sooner than at the end of the last century. The highest rate of divorce takes place during the second year of marriage, but less than a tenth of divorces take place in that year, and though the percentage declines steadily for each succeeding year, it never drops off sharply. People continue to divorce in every year of married life; over a third of all divorces occur after ten or more years, over a tenth after twenty or more.[11]

The median age of men at the time of the final decree is a little under thirty-three, of women, thirty. (Median means that half are younger, half are older.) The median age at separation is one year less than at divorce. Though the divorce rate declines with age, a surprising number of persons divorce fairly late in life: 12 per cent of divorcing men are fifty or over, 14 per cent of divorcing women are forty-five or over, and, in 1972—the last year for which estimates can be made—some ten thousand men and five thousand women got divorced at sixty-five or over.[12]

These data shatter another popular myth: there is no divorce boom in middle age; there are more divorces at mid-life today only because there are more divorces at every age today.

The median age of a male FM is the early forties, of a woman, the late thirties. The average age of FMs is considerably higher than the average age at time of divorce, and the reason is obvious: Most FMs spend several years or more between marriages, and some (out of choice or chance) never remarry. The older people are, the longer it takes them to remarry and the less chance there is that they will ever do so; accordingly, older FMs accumulate in the population.

The typical FM is a few years younger than the typical FM of 1962, but the world of the formerly married is neither basically young nor middle-aged; the bulk of FMs are distributed throughout the years from twenty-five to sixty-five, in much the same proportion as the American population is. The following table shows the complete distribution:

Age	Separated	Divorced	Total FMs[13]
14 to 24	584,000	542,000	1,126,000
25 to 34	1,088,000	1,978,000	3,066,000
35 to 44	761,000	1,607,000	2,368,000
45 to 54	634,000	1,446,000	2,080,000
55 to 64	408,000	1,015,000	1,423,000
65 and up	296,000	601,000	897,000
	3,771,000	7,189,000	10,960,000*

* The slight discrepancy between this total and the figures on p. 13 is due to rounding.

The chance that you are currently divorced, if you are black, is about a third higher than if you were white; the chance that you are currently separated, if you are black, is nearly six times as great as if you were white.,[14] Blacks constitute about a quarter of the FM population but only about a tenth of the national population.

The lower in the socioeconomic scale you are, the greater your chance of divorce if you are a man or a non-working wife. Many people think that divorce is most common among the relatively affluent, sophisticated, discontented, spoiled darlings of our society; the families of working-class people are supposed to be noisy and brawling, but rock-solid. The truth is just the reverse, and has long been so. Studies made from the 1930's through the 1950's showed that unskilled or semi-skilled laborers were about three times as likely to get divorced as professional and business people.[15] This figure probably understated the case, for at that time (even more than now), the poor had a much higher rate of informal desertion or separation without divorce than the middle and upper classes.

But since 1960, according to Bureau of the Census demographers Arthur J. Norton and Paul C. Glick, the gap in divorce rates between the different social levels has been closing; this is due, chiefly, to a more rapid increase in the rate for upper-level men than for lower-level men.[16] One might view this as a "democratization" of divorce, with the lower-class pattern seep-

* Comments in this book on black FMs and poor whites are based chiefly on government and sociological studies, not on our own survey and interviews; these, as explained on p. 272, included only an insignificant number of blacks and poverty-level whites.

ing upward—quite the opposite of the usual mode of cultural diffusion.

High-income women are more apt to divorce than low-income women, reversing the male pattern. If you are a woman earning $15,000 or more, you are three times as likely to be currently divorced as a woman earning under $3,000. Yet again, democratization is taking place: even though divorce rates have been increasing for all women who earn money, the rates for those at the low end of the income scale have increased more than for those at the high end, narrowing the gap between them.[17]

There is no longer any significant difference in the divorce rate among the major American religious groups. Prior to 1960, the Roman Catholic divorce rate was very low; divorce was forbidden by the Church, and Catholics obeyed the rules. Today, Catholic and Protestant divorce rates seem to be converging. There are no government data on this point, but we have reports from sociologists and public-opinion researchers. On the basis of this evidence, the Reverend James J. Young of the Paulist Fathers in Boston and the leader of a national movement to minister to divorced Catholics, wrote us, "I think one can safely say that whatever resistance to divorce existed in the Catholic community a decade or two ago has now disappeared; Catholics have become as American as apple pie, for better or for worse, and now divorce as much as everybody else."

There is no longer a significant difference between the divorce rates of the devout and the non-devout. The devout in every major religion used to be far less likely to divorce than those of weak or no belief. There are no recent definitive studies of this matter, but in our own survey sample, the percentage of regular churchgoers is only a little smaller than that in the American population; since regular church attendance is one indicator of devoutness, the data suggest that devoutness has little to do with willingness to divorce.

The typical FM lives in a city. It used to be thought that the typical divorced person was always a product of the wicked city—but today, we aren't so sure. Census data do show that somewhat smaller percentages of rural and village people than city people are separated or divorced,[18] but our own survey data and interviews lead us to believe that this may be because when their marriages begin to crumble, many suburban and rural people flee to the city where there are better job opportunities (particularly for women) and far greater possibilities for FM social life.

While FMs are scattered all over the nation, the West seems particularly conducive to divorce rather than to separation. Compared to the Northeast, for example, the West has lower percentages of separated persons, but double the percentage of divorced ones.[19]

The rate varies from state to state, too, and it is hard to say why. In 1975, the divorce rate in Nevada was more than six times as high as that in New Jersey, North Dakota, or Pennsylvania.[20] Some of the variation is due to differences in divorce laws, but far more complex factors must account for the variations among the counties within one state. In California, for instance, Imperial County had one divorce for every 14 marriages in 1972, while San Mateo County had one divorce for every 1.2 marriages.[21]

The typical FM is more likely to be a parent than not. And this, unlike so much else, represents no change in recent years. In 1962, close to 60 per cent of all divorcing people had children under eighteen; in 1973 (the latest year for which data are available), the figure was about the same.[22]

In the face of the facts, not many people still believe that children hold a marriage together. Yet, it is true that childless marriages, though they contribute a minority of divorces, do have a higher rate of divorce. In part, this is because couples with poor marriages avoid having children. But even after many years of marriage childless people are more apt to divorce. At Dr. Glick's suggestion, we looked at the data on women thirty-five to thirty-nine who have been, or still are, married to see what difference children make. In this group, 12 per cent of the childless are currently separated or divorced as compared with only 7 per cent of those who have children.[23] This may very well mean that in at least some cases, people stay married for the children's sake.

Although roughly 40 per cent of new FMs are childless, most of these have been married only a short time and are quite young; they are apt to rejoin single society rather than the society of FMs, and most of them remarry sooner than older FMs with children. The net result is that although 60 per cent of divorcing people have children, the percentage of parents within FM society is much larger than that.

In sum, then, we can envision the typical FM in terms of the overall composition of, and averages within, the FM population. That sub-society of Americans is made up of people from all social levels, though somewhat more from the working class and lower-middle class than the higher strata. It is distributed unevenly throughout the nation, but can be found everywhere. It is concentrated in cities, their suburbs, and larger towns. Most of its members are parents who bear the special problems and worries of having disrupted the family life of their children. The society includes people of all ages from the upper teens to the nineties, but the great majority are between twenty-five and fifty-four. It is, all in all, a world not of carefree hedonists who have flung away marriage to live more freely—the "gay divorcee" of earlier times, and her male counterpart—but a world largely made up of mature, responsible adults in search of a satisfying way of life, in pursuit not just of pleasure, but of real happiness.

4. WHAT WENT WRONG?

What explains the epidemic of divorce that is sweeping through American marriages? What has happened to make the average married couple's chance of divorce more than double that of fifteen years ago and nearly twenty times that of four generations ago? What went wrong for eleven million people?

Having asked the question, we admit that we cannot fully answer it here. Since this is a book about what happens to people whose marriages *have* broken up, we must content ourselves with a superficial inquiry into what the major causes of divorce seem to be.

We say "seem to be" for there is far less known about the cause of divorce than appears on the surface; what we read in the newspapers or learn from other popular media is a report on what people swear to in the divorce courts—and people cite as causes whatever the law allows as cause for divorce. As laws change, so do the complaints.

Until a decade ago, almost all states required that one spouse, ostensibly blameless and wronged, had to sue the other spouse for some serious breach of marital behavior. Several generations ago, these were, commonly, drunkenness, desertion, brutality, or adultery, usually on the man's part. But during the present century, as many states came to allow the more "civilized" grounds of mental cruelty, or mental suffering, those became the popular charges in divorce cases.[24] More recently, as simple incompatibility and breakdown of the relationship have become admissible grounds, they have rapidly crowded out the older "causes."[25]

Obviously, legislators do not change the causes of divorce, but they change what people say in court. Incompatibility and breakdown are both "no-fault" grounds, and are valuable developments for they permit people to divorce with dignity, without combat, scandal, or lying under oath; no matter what has happened in a marriage, if it has failed, it is truthful for the partners to claim that it has broken down or that they are incompatible. However, after we know that, we still don't know what went wrong, or why things are going wrong for so many people today.

Sociologists, unlike the courts, can tell us a great deal about the real causes of marital breakdown, but in terms of probabilities rather than the specifics of any one couple's woes. Sociologists tell us which sociological and economic changes cause the divorce rate to rise, but they do *not* tell us why some marriages fail and others remain intact under the same conditions.

For example, after World War II and until the mid-60's, there was a distinct increase in teenage marriage. Statistics show that females who marry before eighteen and males who marry before twenty are at least twice—and perhaps three to four times—as likely to divorce as those who marry in their twenties.[26] What the statistics don't divulge is why some teenage marriages thrive while so many others fail.

But teenage marriages account for only a small part of the rise in divorce. A broader sociological explanation is that the easing of divorce laws creates a milieu in which divorce becomes more acceptable as a solution to the problem than the old alternatives of passive suffering, mutual avoidance, de facto separation, adultery, and so on. It is true that as divorce laws ease, the rate goes up—but the laws only permit people to divorce with less difficulty and therefore at a lower level of discontent; it still doesn't explain the nature of their discontent.

So it is, too, with those other aspects of permissiveness toward divorce that are often cited as causes: the greater tolerance by churches, the generally increased social acceptance, the "domino" effect (the more divorces among one's friends, the easier it becomes to envision it for oneself), and the greater readiness to divorce of those who had divorced parents as their adult models.

We are told, too, that the increased employment of wives leads to a rise in the divorce rate. It is true, as we have already seen, that greater earning power increases a woman's likelihood of divorcing if she is dissatisfied with the marriage—though once again, we do not know the source of her discontent. But the divorce rate among non-working women, while lower than among working women, has been rising steadily, too; clearly, some more basic answer remains yet to be given.

And sociologists have given it, although it is so large and so general that it will seem like no answer at all to most people who are separated or divorced. It pins the blame on industrialization, a process that began two centuries ago and has transformed the functions of marriage and family life. Basically, the wife used to be the producer of goods (bread, cheese, clothing), the performer of essential services (educating the young, ironing shirts, nursing the old and ill); the husband was the provider of food or money, the defender—and ruler—of his wife and children.

But factories, transportation, schools, hospitals, and modern merchandising changed all that. Man and woman no longer need marriage in order to survive, and marriage has ceased to be basically practical and productive but has become instead a special kind of friendship. When it fails to provide us with companionship, sex, and the satisfaction of our individual emotional needs, we are deeply dissatisfied—no matter how many goods and services the spouse provides.

The struggles within many marriages over equal rights, and

over the equitable division of roles and tasks, are often blamed for the rising divorce rate: they play a part, but ultimately responsible is our expectation that marriage will be an emotionally satisfying relationship—an unattainable goal if there is frequent conflict or lack of mutual interests.

And so a high divorce rate is the outcome of the technological developments that have altered the functions of marriage and our expectations of the benefits it should yield. No wonder society has become more accepting of divorce, the churches more tolerant, the laws more liberal; these changes *had* to take place or marriage itself would have died out, for without divorce, marriage would be grossly unsuited to modern life. The epidemic of divorce in our time is only our adaptation of marriage to the social changes of recent years—which are, themselves, only the furthest advance of a process that began two centuries ago.

But no one in the agonies of marital disintegration thinks of his or her suffering as having been due to the industrial revolution and the changed functions of marriage. It doesn't *feel* like that, and people who hurt don't care about sociology or its explanations anyway. What they want to know is simply, "What went wrong in *my* marriage?" They need answers that make order and sense out of their personal chaos; in an effort to find them, they often seize upon some wrongdoing—usually by the other spouse—and there isn't anything new about that.

What *is* new is a major trend toward equal-fault and even no-fault explanations. Most people view the marital failure in relatively sophisticated and complicated terms of multiple, interrelated causes, of mistakes on both sides. And a growing and significant minority speak of poor interaction or misfit personalities, without assigning guilt to either party.

It is time to hear what FMs themselves say, but a caveat is in order: people frequently have a distorted and selective view of what happened. When we have been able to interview or hear from both ex-spouses, we have found that although the same major events (a job change, an infidelity, a child-related problem, and so on) are named by both, they are generally interpreted quite differently. As for intangibles such as faulty communication, emotional conflicts, and sexual difficulties, the ex-spouses often give accounts that are not even recognizably related. Yet, if what they think went wrong is not necessarily objective reality, it is certainly subjective reality; it is what went wrong within the narrator. Perhaps this is more important than the objective reality, for the same words or events, if interpreted differently by the person telling the story, might not have been reason enough to end the marriage.

A relatively small number of today's FMs, in an outmoded, naive fashion, still attribute the marital breakdown to one or a few isolated events or causes in which the ex-spouse plays the villain. Those who speak in such simplistic terms are somewhat more likely to be high-school educated than college educated, and of the working class rather than the middle or upper class.

A blue-collar woman said her marriage broke up because, "I came home one night to find my husband engaging in a sexual act with another male." She had never suspected this tendency in him, nor had she ever felt there was anything wrong with the marriage. But from then on, she occasionally learned that he was having other homosexual experiences and she became enraged; when, after five years, the anger was too great for her to bear, they separated.*

One woman believes that her marriage was fine until her mother-in-law moved into town; then, she said, "My husband spent his free time with her discussing me, his business, and other things that a man should discuss with his wife."

Another woman told us her marriage failed because her husband was a gambler and a liar even from the start, and after a while he also became a heavy drinker and started seeing other women.

---

* Homosexuality by the spouse is named as a cause by only a handful of women and by none of the men in our sample, but it is a more common factor in marital breakups than this indicates. Nine per cent of the FM men and two percent of the FM women in our survey said they themselves had had some homosexual experience while they were married. And throughout the country, some hundreds of thousands of formerly married men and women have joined the gay community rather than the world of the formerly married; according to several surveys, one out of every five men and four women leading a committed homosexual life has been married.[27]

Still another said that her husband was a nervous, high-strung type with a tendency toward physical violence; for years she lived in fear that he would harm her or the children with his fists or his many guns, until one night "he smashed my face and gave me a broken nose; that released me from my contract feeling."

A man wrote, "My wife was such a good mother to the children that she never had time to be a good wife."

Another complained that his wife left him for another man, and this move was so unexpected and without reason or explanation that he "flipped out" from the effort to understand it and had to be hospitalized for a month. Notice that not one of these respondents suggests that he or she might have, in any way, contributed to the spouse's undesirable behavior.

Some of those who think in simplistic terms name a whole series of wrongs—nagging, fighting, frigidity, and sloppy house-keeping, for instance—again, without any insight into the inter-personal sources of such behavior. Occasionally, this kind of person may even take all the blame himself instead of placing it on the spouse, as this statement by a skilled machinist shows:

> It came as a complete shock to me. I came home from work one day and she had taken off with the children with no indication that anything was wrong. I didn't know anything until a few days later, when her attorney called to give me the word.
>
> I have to say in her behalf that I had given her ample reason to divorce me, although I never cheated on her or beat her. I was a drinking alcoholic, I worked nights and she worked days, and we had financial problems because of a business failure of mine involving real estate. I guess I was pretty callous and she was inarticulate, so I couldn't see what I was doing to her.

In contrast, the majority of FMs explain their marital breakups not in terms of bad behavior by one spouse, but in terms of in-compatibility of tastes, habits, and especially of emotional and sexual needs. Yet, though both partners are seen as having played a part in the interaction, the chief burden of the fault is still laid on the ex-spouse. (Although the report may be correct, it often sounds like a self-justifying distortion; but even if it is, it still represents the way it was experienced by the teller.)

Typically, a professional man who had married for the second time in his late thirties said that he had seen his wife as an independent person with a strong personality. Instead, she proved to be extremely dependent and to make continual and increasing demands on him for money, companionship, reassurance, and affection, until he felt invaded and drained. He admitted that he is a "workaholic" and that he is given to feelings of martyrdom, but in the end, he felt that it was not these traits but his wife's inability to deal with her own insecurity that made the marriage fail. This is a minor variation on a large genre of complaints about a spouse so totally immersed in job or profession as to completely neglect the mate and children; most often, the "hard worker" counters with the accusations that the high degree of industry should have been appreciated instead of reviled, and that the neglected spouse should have been "doing his (or her) own thing."

Infidelity, for people in this category, is most often seen as the outgrowth of a defective relationship, with the ex-spouse largely to blame for the imperfections. One man explained that his wife looked for a father-figure in him, and this spoiled their sexual relationship: "She never had an orgasm, and either avoided sex altogether or suggested that I get it over with as quickly as possible. Eventually, I turned to sexual fulfillment outside."

A young woman said that her husband's sexual interest in her waned inexplicably after they married, though it had been adequate before. She began to have affairs, and at one point he grew suspicious and hesitantly queried her. "Don't ask me any questions you don't really want to know the answers to, because I'll answer honestly," she told him—thereby, in effect, answering him, although he did not press the point. This kind of exchange went on, with increasing indirect disclosure, for several years. Then, one day he quite unexpectedly told her, a calm smile on his face, that he had filed for divorce. She found his action shocking, sadistic, and unjustified.

Some FMs attribute their marital breakups to open-marriage experiments which, contrary to expectation, created jealousy, or led to one spouse's falling in love with an outside partner; the other spouse was blamed either for instigating the experiment in the first place, or for having been the one to fall in love, or to become jealous. Only rarely did the narrator make any effort to search his or her own motives in cooperating to subject the marriage to the risks involved. One man, who did blame himself for suggesting mate-swapping and also, for having been stingy and unaffectionate, saw himself as blameless in the end. When the sexual experiments produced a crisis (his wife fell in love), the couple called a halt to swapping and went into counseling. The husband corrected his previous faults and the marriage lasted two more years, "during which time," he said, sounding more and more aggrieved, "I was almost perfect. I gave my wife complete freedom with the money and showed more affection than I used to. But unknown to me, she was running around on me, and later asked for the divorce. I'll never understand how she could have done what she did!"

Many men and women recognize that their marriages, which had worked smoothly at first, began to malfunction when the balance of power or the distribution of roles between the partners changed; most of them put the bulk of the blame on the ex-spouse for not adjusting to the change. One woman told us that her marriage was quite successful for several years while she and her husband were childless and relatively independent of each other. But then they had a child and "I tried to change the rules, asking for more emotional support. Not only wasn't he able to give it, but he resented the attention I paid our child and felt I was intruding on his independence." The man became increasingly jealous, hostile, violent, and domineering—and got even worse when his wife became pregnant for a second time. She had the baby, and on the same day that she saw the gynecologist for her six-weeks' checkup, she "stole" the family car and a credit card, took the children, and left.

Very few FMs, men or women, directly blame the women's movement for their marital breakups, but a fair number do say that the marriage failed after the woman changed things by furthering her education, beginning a career, or demanding that wife and husband have equal roles in making decisions and dealing with daily tasks. Those who had such experiences identify the role changes as part of the problem, but still see the spouse as largely to blame. A man said, "My wife went back to college and then got a job. When she discovered a world out there, our marriage came to look dull to her, and she decided to leave. I had warned her that this might happen, but she wouldn't listen."

And a woman's point of view: "I went back to school and became a lab technician. I loved it. But my husband couldn't stand the fact that my life didn't revolve around him as it had in the beginning of the marriage, and he became impossible to live with."

The third, and certainly the most intriguing, category includes those who explain their marital failures in equal-fault fashion—a 50-50 division—or even without invoking the concept of fault at all or assigning guilt to either partner. This represents the emerging ethos of the divorce subculture. A dozen years ago one heard very few such explanations, while today, a large minority of FMs offer no-fault accounts (although most of them, in time-honored tradition, throw in one or two of the old kinds of reasons, too). In general, no-fault explanations have to do with incompatibility, defective or neurotic interactions between the partners, or changes in one or both due to personal growth. This kind of thinking is far more common among the highly educated, especially those who have had psychotherapy, than among those with only high-school education and/or no therapy; accordingly, it is more common among middle- and upper-class people than among working-class people.

One common no-fault explanation is that both spouses were immature when they married and so chose unwisely or had personal problems they couldn't handle. A woman says, "We were too young, too inexperienced. Sex was a disaster, and neither of us knew how to make it better. We leaned on each other and couldn't stand on our own feet, but later, when we could, there was nothing to hold us together."

Others say that they and their ex-mates had different life goals, different faiths, or different interests, but that they simply hadn't realized how these things would interfere with the relationship when, because of pregnancy, or peer pressure, or out of defiance of their parents, or to escape from home, they married too young.

Another genre of no-fault explanation does see fault—on *both* sides—but since it is perceived with psychological insight, there appears to be more compassion than anger; neither partner is actually blamed for the neurotic interaction, since neither chose to be neurotic. One man says, "I admit that I was an egocentric bully, but at the same time, my wife was an insecure goody-goody; I wanted a doormat and she accepted the role." They came to grips with their interaction when the wife joined a women's discussion group, and shortly after, the marriage fell apart.

A particularly good statement illustrating the recognition of problem behavior on both sides comes from a thirty-four-year-old woman, a county legislator in a western state:

> I knew that I would divorce my husband the day I married him, but it took me eight years to accept the responsibility that goes with that decision. He was an alcoholic, and since I also have an addictive personality, our need to persecute, rescue, and victimize each other again and again was well satisfied. He drank, and I persecuted. He would promise to stop, and then embarrass me in front of my friends. So the cycle continued for years. The marriage would probably still exist if I had not gone into therapy.

By far the largest number of no-fault explanations can be classified under the heading "drifted apart"; roughly four out of ten men and women in our survey gave "drifting apart" explanations of what went wrong in their marriages. Drifting apart can be evidenced by such symptoms as sexual boredom, a loss of emotional intensity or warmth, a gradual divergence of interests and tastes, a diminishing pleasure in each other's companionship, a growing tendency to find trifling things about each other annoying, and so on. In practical terms, when two people no longer enjoy the same friends, the same movies, books, music, activities, general lifestyle, they can be said to have drifted apart. And yet, all these outward signs of the drift are only symptoms; the underlying process is, most often, a matter of significant growth in either one spouse or both. In itself, this is a desirable and positive development, but it can be harmful to the couple relationship when it is one-sided, or when the growth is of a distinctly different nature for the two people involved. If this happens, what was once a "good fit" between the two becomes a poor one. As anthropologist Paul Bohannan puts it, "Married people, like any other people, must continue to grow as individuals if they are not to stagnate. . . . That means that no one, at the time of marriage, can know what the spouse is going to become. Moreover, it means that he cannot know what he himself may become."[28] Unfortunately, spouses sometimes become people who just don't like being married to each other any more.

The husband's career used to be cited as a major cause of couples drifting apart. The man went out into the world each day and was continually drawn into new areas and experiences while the homebody wife was soon left behind and outgrown. She usually complained of being neglected. Although this still sometimes happens, now it is often the wife's (perhaps belated) career and personal development that causes the couple to diverge.

A forty-year-old physician said that he and his wife "gradually realized how different we had become after we had finally gotten the family established and my career set, and had time to look at ourselves." During his years in medical school, she had been his main source of strength and her secretarial job was their only source of income; she enjoyed being the caretaker, he appreciated her care, and they were ideally suited to each other. Now he was a busy doctor, and although he no longer needed her salary, he still wanted her physical and emotional care. But she, no longer doing a routine job that she could forget at five o'clock, had become a lawyer and had a challenging, time- and thought-consuming career; in addition, she had the job of mothering two children. Not only could she not devote much attention to her husband, she often wanted to lean on him rather than be leaned on. There was frustration on both sides, and the doctor felt chronically furious with his wife for having become "different." When, after ten years she demanded a divorce, he felt betrayed and angry—but today, more than a year later, he recognizes the extent of his own dependence and has recently come around to a no-fault view: "We each had some personal growth to accomplish and just couldn't do it while married to each other. We are still very close, and cooperate completely on our parenting."

Another kind of no-fault explanation sees the drifting apart as stemming from basic personality differences. This one is a half-way stage; it is *basically* no-fault, but the speaker is obviously highly critical of her ex-spouse. She is a thirty-five-year-old assistant professor in a western university.

We were both emotionally unstable when we married, and were looking for "protection" from the outside world; we hoped, unrealistically, that we could make up for each other's miserable childhoods. We were both high-school teachers when we met and married, and in balance with each other. But a number of episodes led to our renegotiating the terms and concept of our marriage. The first disaster occurred when my husband lost his teaching job. We moved to another state and tried over.

Then I had a miscarriage and suffered a severe depression. In pulling myself out of it, I decided to do something constructive with my life, and went back to graduate school to work for my Ph.D. We had a baby son, and Al and I both cared for him, taught, and took graduate courses. These were happy, involving years.

But then he began to expect me to help him with his papers even though I had my own work to do. At first, I did it, but after a while I grew resentful and began to realize that I wasn't really helping him but only making him more dependent. As I neared the completion of my own work, he began staying in beer joints every night, and just as I got my first college teaching job, he flunked his comprehensives.

We went to the city where I had my new job, and he got a position in a high school. But he went from heavy drinking to heavy use of marijuana. I plunged deeper and deeper into work on my dissertation. Al stopped contributing to household expenses, and he finally quit his job, claiming that he was going to write a book.

Then I was offered a better-paying job in a western university, and he agreed to look for work there. But instead, he became a recluse, devoting himself to reading mystical literature and to making experiments in a darkened room with black light and symbolic drawings. I began to fear for his sanity. I asked Al to leave, and he did—although I admit I was gravely concerned that he might crack up. But he didn't; he went back home to his mother.

It seems as if the marriage broke up because as I developed more independence, Al became more and more dependent.

This final no-fault explanation is "pure" in its content; the speaker, a forty-year-old woman who has just completed her master's degree in computer science, assigns no blame whatsoever.

Basically, we were just too different, our life-styles were incompatible. He was very successful and money was very important to him; personally, he was withdrawn, didn't like people. I am very extroverted. At first he enjoyed this trait vicariously, but after a while, it drove him crazy. I get all involved in social causes, something he cared little for. Our personalities canceled each other out. It always seemed that I was competing with him —or at least he felt I was. After a while I felt like a zombie, and he was my jailer. I don't mean to imply he's a villain; I still respect him more than anyone I've ever met. He never promises what he can't deliver, is ethical and honest.

But he nearly bored me to death and I nearly drove him crazy with my exuberance, something I didn't see while we were married. In a sense, the death of the marriage was so gradual I can't remember when it started—but by the time we buried it, there was very little emotion left on either side. He didn't want it when I first asked for a divorce, cried, and asked if there was someone else. (There wasn't.) However, I think he was secretly relieved when he saw that he could survive without the highest-priced housekeeper in town.

5. THE UNMAKING OF MARRIAGES

Such are the causes, as FMs see them, of their marital breakups. But how long are these causes at work, and in what ways do they lead up to the final rupture? It's important to know, for the ways in which marital relationships deteriorate have much to do with the ways FMs feel about the separation, how they adjust to it, and what they make of their lives afterward.

The lucky ones are the few whose marriages merely fade away like old photographs left in sunlight, until there is nothing left but a pale ghost of the original relationship. Some young, childless couples find that what began as a youthful and exciting adventure gradually, and without sharp conflict, becomes bland, dull, and anemic. The partners come to be, as one young woman put it, "more like pals or roommates than married lovers." Such a marriage, although it shows no cracks or signs of stress, becomes so tenuous, so fragile, that almost anything that touches it—

a flirtation, a job offer in another city, a chance meeting with some former lover—is enough to make it crumble into dust. Afterward, the ex-spouses look back on it as little more than a summer romance, and after some years each may find it difficult to remember exactly what the other looked like, or why they ever loved—or ceased to love.

For certain other people, the breakup of a seemingly good marriage comes suddenly and without forewarning, and is as shattering as the death of a mate in an automobile accident. A woman who is happily in love with her husband finds a love letter in his pocket. A man who is proud of his serene, smoothly running marriage comes home to find his wife strangely grim; she asks him to sit down, tells him she must leave to try to find some happiness in life before it is too late. A woman and her husband have a lovely Christmas week in Bermuda; the first day home she returns from work, laden with groceries, to find a note on the kitchen table. Her husband tells her he has left on the advice of his lawyer. *His lawyer!* Oh, yes, there had long been the usual kinds of disputes about money, friends, children, but for the past year things have been relatively good; what could have happened, how was this possible? (Much later she finds out: he has been having an affair for a year, and was keeping things smooth at home both out of guilt, and in an effort to protect her.)

How could these people have known nothing, sensed nothing? Perhaps they feared to feel, feared to look—and there is none so blind as they that will not see. Or perhaps their marriages had been, in sociologist John Cuber's term, *utilitarian*—practical rather than intimate, useful rather than personal; in such a relationship, one might well remain ignorant of what was happening within the partner's feelings until the revelation.

But the great majority of FMs arrive at the moment of separation only after a prolonged and agonizing process of which both partners are well aware. The popular notion that many people divorce hastily, after a few bad quarrels, is baseless; most FMs say that anywhere from several months to several years elapsed between their first serious thoughts of separation and the moment when it finally took place.

And how could it be otherwise? Marriage is not just a legal

merger, but an intricate interweaving of two personalities, two lives, by love, habit, shared thoughts and experiences, commonly owned property. Partners in marriage are like Siamese twins, joined by flesh and blood and nerves, and the process leading up to marital separation approximates a hesitant, amateurish hacking away at the bleeding filaments and tissues of the point of union. No wonder many men and women, according to sociologist William J. Goode, come to feel that homicide is cleaner and neater than divorce.[29]

Whatever the causes of the process—even those we lumped together under the rubric "drifting apart"—the partners alternate between tearing further at the wound and frantically trying to repair it. A terrible quarrel, lasting for hours, ends in exhaustion, tears, compromises, promises, surprisingly bittersweet lovemaking that seems to set all to rights again; it is followed by a period of calm and hopefulness. And then the next quarrel leads yet further into the impermissible, the savage, the never-before-uttered "truths": "The truth is, I've never really enjoyed sex with you—I've just pretended, for your sake"; or, "The truth is, I've tried to talk you out of a career because I don't think you've got either the brains or the guts for it"; or, "The truth is, I was attracted to John (Mary) because he (she) is twice the man (woman) you are."

They say of each quarrel that it has been a good thing, that they've been more "honest" and "real" than ever before, that they've "got to the bottom of the trouble" and now they can devote themselves to fixing whatever is wrong. But long before the wound has knitted together, the next fight tears it open again; each time the join grows weaker, and there is less than ever holding them together.

As the partners approach the inevitable severance, they seek makeshift ways to halt the process, to reduce the chances of further damage. They agree to get along for the children's sake —and for a while, treat each other with deliberate courtesy. They sleep in separate beds, or even separate rooms. They busy themselves with visiting, partying, movie-going, night work, organization meetings, so as not to be alone together. They experiment with separate vacations, a few days away from each other "to get things straight," "to let things cool off."

But still the attacks become ever fiercer, more shocking. A man has been laid off; his wife, who is supporting both of them, comes home to find the house dirty, the marketing not done. She is furious and tells him that he's crazy to call himself a man; his manhood is a bad joke, and he knows it; that's why he has to avoid anything he thinks of as women's work. He calls her a "ballbreaker" and says she loves seeing him down and out. She picks up an ashtray overflowing with his day's dead butts and hurls it at him. He slaps her across the face and a trickle of blood appears on her chin. Each feels horrified, and yet, perversely, dreadfully pleased at being able to say, "See what you've done?" "See what you made me do?" and all the time knowing that they have come closer than ever before to the goal. Most people, especially in the middle class, do not resort to actual violence. One recent study finds violence in about one out of six divorce-bound marriages.[30] But the verbal violence may be worse than the physical; a damaged ego heals more slowly than a blackened eye or a split lip.

At some point, one partner is apt to suggest marriage counseling; in our survey sample, an astonishing six-tenths of all FMs said they had had at least some psychotherapy or counseling, either individually or jointly, during the period of marital turmoil. But as is well known in the profession, counseling has the best chance of preserving a marriage if begun before the relationship has undergone serious deterioration; later, counseling has little chance to repair the damage, and is chiefly helpful in easing the way out. This is one function of the new specialty within marriage and family counseling known as *divorce counseling*, of which we will say more later.

And finally, there comes the moment of decision. Sometimes it is an abrupt one-sided announcement: "I'm getting out!" or "I want you out of here, out of this house and out of my life!" More often it comes as an agreement: one or the other mentions the dread word "separation" or the even worse one "divorce," the other agrees that this is what they have come to, and one of them packs up and leaves; usually it is the man. When there are children, this is often the practical choice, but in part, it is a tradition, a piece of leftover male gallantry.

The crucial decision—or actual leave-taking—may come at

the end of a discussion, a battle, or some especially memorable episode, not necessarily worse than many that have preceded it, but merely the one that is one too many, the one that severs the last shred of connective tissue. One man gathered his things and moved out after his wife, a proper Bostonian and college teacher, rushed at him during an argument about his infidelities and raked his cheeks with her nails. Another man's wife had been nagging him about their having a child even though (or because) they were in serious marital trouble; he moved out one night minutes after she drunkenly bragged that she had secretly pulled out her IUD and might even now be pregnant. (She wasn't.)

A fifty-year-old woman who is a life insurance agent tells of a deteriorated marriage that had dragged on for several years:

> I began to paint the house inside and out, I spaded up the garden again and again, I remember standing in the shower banging my head against the wall in frustration. I developed asthma, arthritis, back pains, and a variety of other ailments, and one day while I was at the doctor's, he asked me some simple question and I suddenly started to weep. I went on for an hour and a half and unloaded the whole bag. He asked me what I was going to do about it and I knew then and there that the answer was divorce. All my physical ailments vanished overnight, and in a couple of days, I asked my husband to leave.

Another woman says that after ten years of a good marriage there had been a four-year decline into incompatibility, constant conflict, and very little sex.

> One night after a particularly bitter quarrel, I demeaned myself by almost begging him to make love to me. His response was, "How can I, after the way you talked to me?" I got out of bed, got dressed, and told him not only that I was going to go out and get laid but that "Someday I'll have you on your knees begging for it!"
>
> It was 3 A.M., but I drove around the rest of the night fuming, stopping at restaurants, drinking, and feeling totally humiliated—especially since I didn't have the guts to *get* laid.
>
> The next day I filed for divorce.

Thus, in one fashion or another—unexpectedly or with advance planning, violently or peacefully—husbands and wives arrive at that moment when they knowingly and purposefully separate; they look at each other and turn away, the door closes, the deed is done. As of that moment they have become expatriates, refugees from the world of the married, ignorant newcomers to the world of the formerly married.

II

The Newcomer

1. FIRST FEELINGS: MIXED

The door closes. It's over.

Every day, across the nation, thousands of doors close, thousands of men and women become newcomers in a strange land. Some have had separation forced on them and arrive as unwilling exiles. Some wanted out, themselves forced the separation, and arrive as hopeful immigrants. The ones who were abandoned expect to feel bereft, frightened, and depressed; the ones who wanted out anticipate that they will feel liberated, confident, and euphoric—but rarely is it so simple.

One of the most surprising things to many newcomers is that they are subject to enormous mood swings that may continue not just for the first few hours, but often for many days or even many weeks. The unwilling exiles are dismayed to find themselves relishing their aloneness at times, the ones who wanted the separation are astonished when they find themselves in tears.

Like Jane Atkins who cheerfully arranged the bureau drawers before she collapsed into misery, one forty-year-old woman who had struggled intensely for a separation was jubilant the night her husband finally moved out. Her first act was to rearrange the bedroom furniture, laboring mightily to move the heavy pieces, so that when she awoke in the morning she would have a clear view from the bed out of both windows.

For several nights she slept soundly and awoke each day with a rush of pleasure to admire the cherished view. But one morning she awoke to quite another feeling. Her first thought was that her husband was gone, and her marriage broken; she felt "weak and drained, as if I had awakened from surgery." Looking around the room, so different now from the one she and her husband had been happy in, she burst into bitter sobs. *Why had it seemed so important to drag the furniture around?* she asked herself. *Who cares about the damned view? Who cares about anything? I'm all alone!*

Unexpected mood swings also take place in the other direction, from down to up; discarded newcomers steeped in despair may abruptly be caught up by feelings of freedom and exhilaration. A well-to-do middle-aged real estate agent, who had begged his wife to reconsider the separation, finally gave up. He signed a lease on a furnished apartment and moved in over a weekend. He mechanically arranged his books, put away his shirts, and hung up his suits; he wrote his new telephone number on a business card which he put into his wallet because he was sure he couldn't remember it. He felt numb, disoriented, and in shock. Later, he walked to a neighborhood restaurant and mechanically picked at some tasteless food, wondering how soon he could get up and leave without attracting notice.

During the week, back at the office, he had trouble paying attention to clients or even to his employees when they spoke to him. His eyes filled with tears time and again, and he hastily mopped at them when anyone neared. But one day, dreading the hated visit to the restaurant, he stopped at an employment agency on his way to work and asked if they could send a part-time housekeeper-cook who would prepare his dinner each evening. He left his apartment key.

That night he opened the door and sniffed the delicious aroma of vegetable soup and roast lamb. He was astonished when he walked into the kitchen and saw his housekeeper—an attractive, red-haired woman in her early thirties. He suddenly felt excited by his independence, and his cleverness in arranging to have his own dinner in his own home. The meal was excellent, and in his unexpected expansive mood, he engaged the cook in a long chat when she served his coffee, urged a glass of wine on her, and could hear himself becoming more and more charming and delightful; before the evening was out, he had taken the lady to bed. He was almost bursting with exuberance.

But in the middle of the night he awoke from a bad dream, sweating and gasping, and overcome by guilt. *I must be a really vile person*, he thought; *I'm sorrowing for my marriage, I love my wife and want to win her back, and what am I doing, for God's sake, screwing some woman I don't even know—just because she happened to be here?*

A few days later he went to his wife's house to visit his daughters. As he waited at the door to be let in he could feel his heart race, his hands become cold and clammy. After a brief, unsatisfactory meeting with the girls (his wife did not appear), he left, thoroughly confused, and as he got into his car he had trouble remembering, for a moment, where he was going. Then it hit him, and he felt the depression wash over him like a tidal wave.

But once again, when he returned to his apartment, he felt a surge of freedom and a rush of excitement as he engaged the housekeeper in conversation. Then he invited her to join him in a drink, and in a while they were on their way to his bed. When she left, he was delighted with himself for having been so light-hearted, so witty, such a clever lover.

Like him, many of the rejected, at first sunk in self-pity and grief, are snatched up by events that produce short-lived bursts of well-being. A young graduate student, the mother of three children, recalls:

I withdrew from friends, cried alone for hours and hours. I was supposed to go to a party a week after the separation, but instead, I took the phone off the hook, turned all the lights off, locked the door, and sat and cried for about two hours. Then there was a loud knocking on the door and two friends literally forced me to get a babysitter and go to the party—where I had a *super* time. The next period was a paradoxical one because along with crying I was very high, relieved, and excited, especially because attention from males was immediate. So after a while I stopped crying—but then I overloaded myself with courses and became chronically anxious, and had a long depression and zero sex drive.

Even for the minority in our survey who were in full agreement with their spouses about wanting the divorce,[1] mood swings were common. The sight of a lovingly chosen birthday gift of yesteryear, the record album they used to play while making love, are enough to make the limbs go weak, the stomach knot, the tears begin.

It is not always the pull and haul of love and hate that causes conflicting emotions, but frequently the intrusion of mundane realities that remind the novice of the loss, the costs, the waste inherent in the situation. The happy discarder who has left a comfortable home and is temporarily encamped in a sleazy sublet can easily be plunged into gloom and doubt by the dripping faucet, the lumpy bed, the roach-infested kitchen. Thoughts turn to the years of effort spent in creating and improving a home—and now it is all lost, all gone. How to start again? How to find the energy, the hope, the enthusiasm, the motive?

Or, for that matter, the money? For it is financial worry that bursts the first bubble of euphoria time and again. A young teacher, after four years of an agonizing marriage to a latent homosexual, writes:

> I felt like I could breathe again, like I had been holding my breath for years and could finally let go. The first time I walked back into the house, I looked around in all the closets and corners to reassure myself that I was alone at last; it was too good to be true. But I also felt a wave of despair at being left with a partially renovated house overrun with rats and littered with lumber. And it got worse when I discovered he had withdrawn all the money we had paid on our home-improvement loan and had cleaned out our savings account. I cried intermittently for days as I saw the mess I was in. But at night I would cry for joy, because I didn't have to cover my body to avoid his comments, or hide my poetry so he wouldn't pour out his scorn for me.

And the woman with children to care for (or the fewer than 10 per cent of men with custody) may be cheerful during the busy days but beset with worries during the quiet nights. How is it possible to juggle a job, the children, the household? The only thing that seems less possible is changing things for the better.

Mood swings are particularly troublesome because newcomers can't figure out what they *should* feel. Most of the time our society provides us with ready-made emotional scripts for life crises: we learn, as we grow up, how to feel at weddings, funerals, births, disasters. In the case of marital separation, the old script is out of date—and the new one hasn't been written. It makes for a great deal of uncertainty and confusion. But the inconsistency of feelings that most newcomers find so bewildering is the very embodiment of the newly emergent social evaluation of divorce: a wounding act, but eventually a restorative one; a destructive solution to a problem—but one which is ultimately creative.

2. FIRST FEELINGS: DOWN

If the majority of the newly separated are astonished at the bright shafts of relief and exhilaration that keep breaking through the emotional storm, many are equally astonished at how dreadful they feel most of the time. And those who feel nothing but misery are doubly astonished: they had expected to feel bad, but not *this* bad.

Who suffers the most, who the least? Any answer based on popular belief is bound to be wrong, for the beliefs are largely out of date. The public has not yet adjusted its beliefs about divorce to conform to its own massive shifts in attitude toward a number of interrelated matters—women's rights and place in society, the morality of divorce, the sexual behavior of unmarried people, and the nature of middle age, among others.

Consider the last point first. Almost everyone believes that middle-aged people are harder hit by marital breakup than the young. But this notion is based on an outmoded view of middle age as a period of rigidity, withdrawal, and decline. Actually, middle age has begun to emerge as a time of continuing emotional and sexual capacity, of high work potential, and of new personal freedom resulting from the end of parenting.[2] That doesn't mean that divorce is *easy* for the middle-aged—it is no easier than it is for the young—but according to our survey results, it is no harder, either. While the reasons for their misery may be different, the intensity of distress for the young and the middle-aged is identical. "I wished I would die!" states a twenty-two-year-old; "I felt as if I couldn't go on living," says a fifty-year-old. It is true that the young will slip back into single life sooner and more easily, and are more likely to remarry than the middle-aged. But in the first agony of separation, the young scarcely think of this—nor would it comfort them if they did.

It is also widely believed that the longer a marriage has lasted, the more severe the impact of its breakup, but this belief, too, is based on outmoded ideas. It is left over from an era when a woman who had been married for any length of time (and was therefore no longer in the first bloom of youth) had almost no way of ever entering either the job or social market; her life was virtually over and hence her divorce was a calamity. (Today, she will have a harder time in the marketplace than the young woman, but not an *impossible* time.) In the contemporary milieu, the initial impact of divorce is no worse for the long-married than for those married a short time—or rather, it is just as bad for the latter as for the former. Those whose marriages fade away after only a few months are excepted, for they have hardly had time to send a thousand tendrils of thought and feeling deep into each other's beings.

The most widespread beliefs about who suffers more when marriage ends involve a cluster of obsolescent clichés. In fiction, drama, and much non-fiction, the wayward male, hungering for his bachelor freedom or for his young mistress—yes, that archaic word is suitable in this context—abandons his wife and children and goes off to lead a hedonistic, self-indulgent life. Such men are referred to by some as "wife-shuckers." Meanwhile, the wife, bereft, shamed, and burdened by endless cares, trembles and shakes, can hardly speak to a soul without bursting into tears, takes sleeping pills, and nips at the bottle.

But both halves of the picture are badly out of date. For one thing, while the man is still more often the one who physically moves out, the woman is more often the one who has wanted the separation. In about half our cases, the wife was the discarder; in about a third, the man was the discarder; in about a fifth of the cases, the two were equally eager to end the marriage.

For another thing, about as many men as women feel terrible—and *just* as terrible—in the early phase. They tell, in equal numbers, of being unable to sleep, to eat, to concentrate on their work, of using alcohol to dull their pain, of smoking heavily, of suffering from a strong sense of failure and worthlessness. Later on, the woman's practical problems—especially if she has children to care for—often make her life harder than that of the man, but at the outset, the emotional impact is much the same.

The clichés that have to do with women are particularly tenacious even though they are no longer supported by facts. It is true that until recently, when a woman lost her husband, she lost security, social position, and her *raison d'être*. She was defined—and she defined herself—in non-person terms: she was a woman without a husband, an abandoned wife, an ex-wife. But a decade and a half of the women's movement has done a great deal to change the average FM woman's view of herself, her ability to support herself, her ability to make a good life and to be *someone*—without a man.

And there's one more thing wrong with the old picture. The idea that the one who wanted the breakup feels happy, and the one who didn't feels miserable, is a gross oversimplification. It's true that the discarders tell of sleeplessness, loss of appetite, and general depression only about half as often as those they discarded—but that still means that roughly one-third of discarders have such symptoms, and feel bad all or almost all of the time, at first. A self-inflicted wound can be as grievous as one inflicted by another. This is how some who favored the separation talk about the early period:

[Woman, forty-five]   I would wake up with attacks of uncontrollable chills and shivering. I had terrible nightmares about yawning cliffs and rushing rivers.

[Woman, twenty-nine]   My only thought was to get from one day to the next without cracking up. Every move was an effort.

[Man, forty-four]   I had great difficulty waking up in the morning, but was restless and nightmarish all night. I felt broken, physically and emotionally.

[Man, twenty-nine]   I went out and got smashed regularly, and spent money like crazy until I was deep in debt. For two months I was like a bull in a china shop.

A thirty-six-year-old woman, a college instructor, had experienced both good and bad years in her marriage, the bad ones being the last ones, during which her husband drank heavily, was unpredictable, irascible, and violent. After she became increasingly terrified of him, she finally got a court order forcing him to move out and to leave her alone. This is how she felt:

> I was relieved to have him gone—but I also felt dreadful anguish. It couldn't have been worse if he were dead. I was intensely unhappy; I had loved my life, and loved him (when he wasn't drinking), and simply couldn't bear to have all that torn asunder. Also, I couldn't bear the feeling of failure. Even when dear friends tried to sympathize, I couldn't endure their sympathy. I was like someone with no skin, to whom every touch was sheer agony.

Those who have been discarded are more apt to feel pain than those who discarded them, but the pain they feel is much the same:

> [Woman, thirty-six]   I was in shock. It felt like the end of my life (though I was only thirty-four). I stared out of the window hour after hour, for months.
>
> [Man, twenty-nine]   I felt despondent and helpless, a failure at being worthy of someone's love.
>
> [Woman, forty-three]   It was like death to me. I couldn't eat, I couldn't cry. My emotions were frozen. My mother died and I couldn't even cry for her.
>
> [Man, forty-two]   I drank, I cried, I felt like ending my life.

When the break is unexpected, a shock, the discarded one often sounds a special note of hurt: *How could he (she) do this to me?* A mature and successful professional man had not married until his thirties. After seven years, his wife said she was stifled and hemmed in by the marriage and thought she wanted out, but would be willing to try counseling. We'll let him tell about it:

> It happened like this. Wednesday afternoon we had just left a meeting with a marriage counselor.
>
> SHE: I'm feeling much better about us. I think we should spend more time together, take walks on the beach, get to know each other all over again.
>
> ME (My heart singing: My God, perhaps there's a chance!)

That night: Holding hands, walking together, same ambiance, same smile. Sweetness, caring. God, it felt good.

Thursday morning, in my office. Man appears at door.

HE: I guess you were expecting this.

ME: What?

HE: This subpoena. Weren't you expecting it?

He hands it to me. It's an order to appear in court. She is suing me for divorce.

I have never forgotten this. I never will. It almost destroyed me. I felt awful. Terrible. Horrible. Betrayed. Lied to. Alone. Deserted. Fucked over. Screwed over and screwed up. Disbelieving. How could anyone do this to another human being?

The fact is that whether one left or was left, separation is a major change in one's way of life—and *all* major changes, even those that are thoroughly joyous, cause stress. In 1967, Drs. Thomas H. Holmes and Richard H. Rahe, psychiatrists at the University of Washington Medical School, published a "social readjustment scale" which ranks 43 life events from 0 to 100 according to how much adjustment they require.[3] The greater adjustment needed, the greater is the stress on the human organism; and as the doctors showed from survey data, the greater the stress, the greater the likelihood of illness, or even death. Tragic events have the highest ratings on the scale, but even happy major events which call for a great amount of readjustmetnt, such as marriage or pregnancy, are stressful. Marriage was rated at 50 points—3 more than being fired (47). Marital separation, at 65 points, is the third most stressful event on the list; it is worse than a jail term (63) and is exceeded only by divorce (73), and the death of one's spouse (100).

No wonder, then, that rejecting spouses are so often not only relieved but afflicted, and that some have only bad reactions. No wonder FMs have higher rates than the married of suicide, accident, and physical illnesses.[4] No wonder separated women and men are eight and twelve times as likely, respectively, as married women and men to be hospitalized for mental illness.[5]

So many things come as a painful surprise to the newcomer— but who would anticipate that loneliness could be worse than the presence of a hostile or silent spouse? Even when there are children to create a hubbub, the new FM is lonely within. It is not just *aloneness* that is hard to handle, it is the loneliness that comes from knowing that one's partner is not just away on a trip, to return in a few days, but really *away* in every sense of the word. When married people separate, every outer sign of absence makes the inner absence manifest; the "we" is now only an "I," the other half of one's self is gone. Bedtime is the worst time, and they put it off as long as possible with television, magazines, and books. Bed is where the loneliness is most acute because, on a level that is almost infantile, one misses the warm breathing body nearby, another beating heart. Many a newcomer sleeps tidily on his or her half of the bed; to move across to the other side, even in sleep, would awaken one in panic to the absence of the other.

> [Woman, forty-six, mother of six children] During the night I tossed fitfully, then from sheer exhaustion would go unconscious —only to wake up flailing my arms frantically over the bed, looking for my lost companion. I would gasp, my heart would pound, then fully awake, I would cry until I was soppy wet and clammy cold. I finally piled his side of the bed with boxes of things, pillows, whatever I could find, so it would feel heavy, as if there were someone there.

While the days may be less panic-filled than the nights, they bring different problems, for it is in dealing with others that the new FM must assume the new identity: not "we," but "I." One must learn to say to friends, salespeople, babysitters, not "We'll be in after six," but "*I'll* be in after six," not "We always go to my sister's for Christmas," but "*I* always go." The habit comes hard.

The newly separated person wonders about doing things for this new self: is it worth the bother to shave, to bathe, to wash one's hair, to make the bed? For whom? Then, angry: *For me, of course!* And weary: *But what for?*

No wonder the newcomer so often thinks of going back, or of asking the spouse to return and make a new start. Discarders, just like the ones they discarded, miss the well-known voice, face, presence; feel strange, incomplete, unnatural; are overcome by rushes of yearning for the other, by a feeling that everything would be all right again if only they were together. They are smitten by doubts, by a weakening of resolve, by fantasies of reunion. More than half the men in our sample and four out of ten women had thoughts of reconciliation.

Sometimes, the very desire for reconciliation makes one angrier than ever with the ex-spouse. But those who feel rage are the fortunate ones, for when rage is not directed outward, at the source of hurt, it becomes depression. A case in point:

[Woman, thirty-nine] I had longed all through my childhood to be grown up and happily married, to have a man to understand me and to share my life. I was simply unable to accept the fact that this fantasy had been shattered by my husband's continuing infidelity. I had forced the separation because of it, and I felt devastated by his absence—but I really believed that the separation would make him come back to me, changed. I could think of nothing but my husband and my dream of his return. As the days and weeks went by, I began to realize that my dream would not come true; I saw no hope for the future and I really didn't want to be alive.

The new FM suffers not only from loneliness for the spouse, but from a disconnection and partial isolation from the known social world. It begins with the grim chore of telling people the news, not much different from telling them of a death. Like a death, a separation both saddens and alarms others: who can say for whom the bell will toll next? The chore is awkward, too, since there is no recognized etiquette either for delivering the news or for receiving it. If the newcomer simply blurts out, "We've separated," or "We're getting a divorce," close friends and relatives will be offended; not to be told anything at all makes them feel shut out, excluded. So he or she feels obliged to tell them something, but it is an embarrassing and self-denigrating task; it puts one at a disadvantage to be explaining, justifying, blaming ,whining, begging for sympathy. Or to pour out grief and anger in a gush as unceasing as a waterfall, knowing that it's all a horrible mistake, sure to be regretted later—and yet, the need to pour it out is there. The sympathetic friend with the listening ear may suffer, too, for often, those who have told all the tawdry intimate details to a dear friend are uncomfortable or even angry with that friend ever after; one feels naked and resentful before the friend who knows too much.

Pulled one way and the other by conflicting needs and motives, only about one man in four and one woman in three explains what went wrong to most married friends. The large majority of just-separated people explain to a few dearest friends, and a small number reveal nothing to anyone.

Whatever they do about married friends, it becomes very clear, very fast, that the relationship between them is different now; in some way they have become partly alienated. The closest couples will invite the newcomer over for an evening of dinner and sympathy—an awkward evening if the subject of what went wrong is glossed over, an exhausting evening if it is not. The guest may be grateful for a chance to dwell on his or her miseries, and while the friends may feel virtuous for being such sympathetic listeners, it is not a role they want to play repeatedly. Once or twice is enough. The newcomer senses their weariness and draws back.

As for more normal social occasions with married people, he or she feels awkward and out of place—half a couple in a roomful of couples. The married, too, feel disturbed by this familiar person who is no longer familiar but suddenly strange. If the newcomer is a man, they may wonder if he has already begun to sample the fleshly delights of single life; the thought makes husbands jealous or pruriently curious, wives fearful. If the newcomer is a woman, the married men often feel an unexpected libidinous interest in her, assuming that any woman who was "used to it" must "need it." Usually they guiltily stifle the thought, sometimes they pursue it; most female newcomers are subjected to several unsettling surprise overtures from what one of our respondents called "Helpful Husbands." Wives, consciously or not, are sensitive to the threat. "She shouldn't have too much trouble finding someone else," a woman will say to her husband on the way home from the party. "She's still quite attractive, don't you think?" And her husband, unless he is a fool, will keep the peace by mildly disagreeing, rating the newly separated woman as rather plain and looking older because of the recent strain, or conceding that she's attractive but unfortunately unsexy.

With relatives, the distancing is less severe in some ways, more in others. The in-laws may drop their soon-to-be non-relative—unless there are children with whom grandparenting is to continue; even so, contacts may become infrequent and strained. (There are exceptions, of course; occasionally, the in-laws prove to be firm allies.)

The newcomer's own parents and siblings are, on the other hand, bound by family loyalty—and family loyalty is generally at its best in a crisis. Yet, it is usually much harder to break the news to family than to friends, knowing that they will be deeply grieved, pained, upset, trying desperately to understand. And the fear that they will be disapproving makes one feel like a child, waiting to confess a misdeed and be judged. One woman asked the husband she was leaving to call her parents for her and tell them about it; she simply could not do it, she said, and she begged him to tell them that she would call as soon as she could talk to them without bursting into tears.

These fears of judgment or disapproval are almost always unfounded, though not long ago they were often realistic. In 1960, to pick a convenient benchmark, the separated and divorced were faced with a certain amount of suspicion or contempt.[6] Families, especially if they were Roman Catholic, were often strongly disapproving or even shocked. FM men in business were sometimes passed over for promotion or appointment to desirable posts; women in suburban neighborhoods might find themselves excluded from female society and their children snubbed by their playmates on orders from home. In small towns in the Bible Belt and other conservative areas, FMs were sometimes harshly ostracized; in some places, people crossed the street to avoid a face-to-face meeting with a separated woman.

Today, only about one in six separated people experiences distinct disapproval from relatives. Virtually none is harmed or penalized in any way at work and very few acquaintances show moral disapproval. Only a minority of friends now "take sides," which represents a change; taking sides, of course, was in part a moral judgment as to who had been the wronged and who the wrongdoer—a way of thinking which, as we have seen, is obsolescent.

The new tolerance and acceptance is most prevalent among better educated and middle-class or upper-class people. But we are still in transition: at every level of American life a few FMs continue to experience rejection and hostility on the part of some friends, family members, and people in the community.

Fairly often, however, those who expect to be harshly judged are only judging themselves harshly and projecting these feelings onto others. One man, a forty-one-year-old sales representative for a machinery company, described this vividly:

> I felt the following words were emblazoned on my forehead for all who passed to read—and that people's reaction to them was a mixture of pity and disgust: "This man has left his wife and children; he couldn't keep his family together; there's something wrong with him."
>
> I avoided meeting old friends, fearing their rejection and condemnation; I shopped at out-of-the-way stores; I did my laundry furtively in the laundromat at strange hours, fearing to be seen there. At work, or at the rare social gatherings I went to, if talk turned to family matters I felt disoriented, isolated, not knowing whether to stand there silently with a silly grin on my face or to blurt out, "I'm not married any more."

Only after some time did this man realize that although many of his friends were surprised and saddened, few disapproved or condemned him.

Finally, as if all this were not enough, there are the many practical problems we have already referred to. The novice is unprepared for countless dilemmas that generate feelings of anxiety and helplessness. A man of thirty-nine recalls the worst moment of his days as a newcomer:

> That first week, I went to see old friends, a couple I've known since my college days. At first, they were great; they listened to my story, they sympathized, they helped me let off steam. But after an hour or two, they started asking me how I was going to handle things. What did I think would be the effect on the kids, especially since their mother was so often away on field trips now, and left them with the housekeeper? How could I divide our community property without wrecking my business? What would I do about my mother, who had been hoping to live with us when

my father died—which would be in a couple of months, at most? What kind of place did I mean to live in, and how would I be able to afford anything decent, if I were as open-handed with my wife as I felt I ought to be? Finally, I couldn't stand it. I yelled, "Stop! Please stop!" I said I felt crushed by all these problems, I couldn't deal with them all at once. I would have to take things one at a time. I couldn't stand any more of this discussion.

They said they were sorry, but I had the feeling they were deeply offended. I left in a little while, but all night long I kept thinking about the questions they had raised, and I couldn't decide whether to go back and beg my wife to give it another try, or to hope that I'd have an accident in the car and end all my problems.

That night was the low point of my life.

3. FIRST FEELINGS: UP

In contrast to the majority, about one tenth of FMs in our sample had only positive emotions and feelings of well-being at first. Nearly as many more, while they had some admixture of negative emotions, felt generally much better in all ways than they did before the separation.

Such people soon, or even immediately, are restored to normal physical health, and regain—or exceed—their former work capacity and their libido. Some of them can be wonderfully precise about the dimensions of these improvements, as is this fifty-five-year-old history professor:

> When I finally decided to leave, my blood pressure was 190/140. Within two months it had returned to normal. (I had it taken yesterday and it was 110/70.) I think that says what it says. Ever since the earliest post-marital period, I have been able to sleep seven hours a night without drugs. I eat well and sensibly, have lost about ten pounds and now weigh what I ought to. I no longer drink after dinner. Sexually, I gave myself carte blanche, and realized that I was as good as ever, and that I had been missing a lot and performing at far less than capacity.

Who responds to marital separation with swift or even instant well-being? Some of the answers are not particularly surprising; more are.

NOT SURPRISING:

—If, when you are separated, you are having an ongoing

extramarital affair, or if you immediately begin having sexual relations or a new involvement, you are more likely to feel good than those who don't.[7]

—You are more likely to feel good if you did the rejecting than if you were rejected. About a third of all discarders and those in mutual agreement feel wholly or mostly good; fewer than a tenth of those who were discarded do.

—If you are a man, the better educated you are, and the higher your socioeconomic status, the more chance there is that you'll feel good—perhaps because you have many other sources of ego-reward. Curiously, though, it doesn't work that way if you are a woman; our study shows that neither education nor high social status increase a woman's chance of feeling good.

SURPRISING:

—If you are a woman, you are more likely to feel good than if you are a man. Over a quarter of the females but only a fifth of the males in our survey felt wholly or mostly good.

—If you are a man under twenty-five, you are less likely to be swiftly restored to physical and emotional health than if you are in your upper twenties, thirties, and forties. If you are a woman under twenty-five, however, you are about as likely to do well as women in older age groups.

—If you have children, you are more likely to feel good than if you are childless. This seems to contradict what some other researchers reported,[8] but their studies didn't focus on the immediate post-separation period; childless FMs do make an overall adjustment more quickly than parent FMs, and after the early period are more likely to report well-being.

—If you are a woman with custody, you are more likely to feel good than your ex-husband. But if he had custody, he would be likely to feel better than you.

—Your degree of religious belief has little or nothing to do with how you feel as a newcomer: about the same percentage of religious people as non-religious people feel good after separation.*

—As noted earlier, if you were married for twenty or thirty years, you have as much—or more correctly, as little—chance

* A recent study by sociologist Helen June Raschke includes a similar finding.[9]

of feeling good as those who were married for only two or three years.

—If you are separating from a second marriage, despite your familiarity with what lies ahead, you are, if anything, less likely to feel generally good than you did the first time. Second-timers may not be as fearful, but the great majority are thoroughly dejected, feeling like "two-time losers."

These several surprising findings point up once again how little our beliefs have caught up to the democratization of divorce, the improvement of women's status, and the changing nature of marriage—and the effect of all of these on the immediate impact of marital dissolution.

Several overlapping but distinguishable components contribute to the sense of well-being in that minority of the newly separated who experience only well-being.

The most common reason for feeling good is simple relief; relief from personal conflict, from one's own ambivalence, from fear, and from the tension of uncertainty about whether the marriage will or will not break up. Such relief can be more than a mere ending of pain; it can be an almost intoxicating experience:

[Woman, thirty-seven] Hallelujah! I heaved one big sigh of relief. All the adjustments, the turmoil, the emotional upheaval, the painful self-searching—they were all worth it just for that sigh of relief.

Similarly, a psychologist in his fifties says that when he finally moved out, after a number of years of an acutely miserable relationship with a domineering and belittling wife, for the first few weeks he spent every night alone in his new apartment; he was utterly content with books and television, luxuriating in relief, not wanting or needing human contact. Still other men and women speak of the vast release of being able to sleep soundly once again. Sometimes, this is so for physical reasons, as is the case with women whose husbands beat them or pushed them out of bed in the middle of the night. More often, it is so for emotional reasons, as is the case for those who quarreled at night, or who lay awake waiting for the return of a spouse who was out late; one man says, "The very presence of my enemy, my wife, created a palpable tension that filled the darkness between us, and ruined my sleep for months so that I was on the brink of nervous exhaustion."

Other newcomers stress not so much relief as a feeling of regained freedom. They often speak of themselves as "being out," "newly out," or having just "broken out," as if they had long been imprisoned and had just escaped or been released. Prison is the most common metaphor, but FMs use many others: A woman who lives in farm country says she felt as if she had been "let out of the bottom of a dark silo"; a man alludes to "being freed from the jaws of a terrible trap." Other men and women speak, without metaphors, of being "free again," "free at last," and "a free person for the first time." The "free again" motif is even the basis of several of the divorce greeting cards now on the market; one of them, predictably, is illustrated with a jocular cartoon of an escaping prisoner.

The regained freedom is more than just freedom of movement. It is a freedom granted not by the spouse, but by one's own self *to* one's own self; it is a freedom from emotional commitment. Until one has made it plain to the spouse—or has had it made plain—that the contract of emotional union that has existed between them is now invalid, one feels morally bound, even though the agreement may long have been moribund.

Some FMs find the relief and the freedom of separation exhilarating; they don't just quietly wallow in it, but are frenetic and hyperactive. They rejoice to have themselves back in their own possession, they lavish love and kindness upon themselves as assurance that the hostility or indifference they so recently felt were a wrongful appraisal of their worth. A childless woman with only $170 in the bank goes on a shopping spree and spends $160 of it on a long dress, lingerie, and perfume. A middle-aged man spends his first free day getting his hair styled, buying two new sports jackets, and having the first massage of his life at an expensive health club. Men and women alike tell of taking long relaxing baths (without fear of tying up the bathroom too long); of feeling their bodies fondly in bed at night, as if to reassure themselves that they still feel good and are worth being touched; of granting themselves little pleasures at unconventional times—a dish of ice cream at 4 A.M., a midmorning movie, a Late Show followed by a Late, Late Show—just to be self-indulgent. They allow themselves to skip all sorts of unpleasant chores and tasks that now, in their new freedom, they can leave undone with no one the wiser—making the bed, doing the dishes promptly, balancing the checkbook, making dinner, washing the car. They grant themselves permission to do all kinds of things that symbolize freedom from obligation to any other person.

[Man, forty-five] Once, during the early days after the separation, I helped a friend rig his sailboat. We took it to the lake to try it, and wound up sailing all evening—because it had suddenly occurred to me that I didn't have to call anyone and explain or argue about being late. *I didn't have to go home at all!* For the first time in all those years I had a tremendous feeling of exhilaration and freedom.

Another and particularly important component of the novice's euphoria is the feeling some have of competence and self-sufficiency that either they never knew they had, or had ceased to believe in during the ego-destructive final phase of marriage. Some newcomers, filled with energy and enthusiasm, become freshly dynamic and creative in their work, or confidently change jobs or go into different businesses in order to live up to their newly sensed potentialities. A feeling of new-found competence is especially common in those women who have not had a career, or have been away from it for years, and who now look for work, find it, and do well at it; they are exultant to discover that they can take care of themselves and are not dependent on a man—or on anybody. One young woman who went back to graduate school and a part-time job upon separation, tells of her "elation and fulfillment. Even with the hassles of single parenthood, lack of money, and family disapproval, I felt really proud of myself and my accomplishments for the first time in several years."

Another woman, separated at thirty-seven, began looking for free-lance assignments in advertising, her former field. She got a few small jobs within the early weeks and discovered a hidden self. She sounds as if she's joking, but jocularity is part of her style; she is perfectly earnest about this:

I realized that I could truly be anything, go anywhere, *feel* anything, and that I was able to *choose*. I was dizzy with joy at the choices I had. I felt omnipotent. I was happy, smiling, able to enjoy the fun aspects of everything—I could even enjoy a "bad" movie. I could be beautiful, slim, rich, I could travel, collect. I was a child in a candy shop with a blank check!

One other component that contributes to the overall mood of this minority of FMs is a reborn libido. Most newcomers are not sexually active for a while, but a certain number of those with very positive feelings about the separation begin sexual activity almost at once. Much of it is self-indulgent, like their eating, dressing, and other self-pampering. Most commonly, these early sex experiences are brief encounters with little emotional involvement; they serve chiefly to express the newcomers' freedom and self-love. "I was feeling so great," a twenty-eight-year-old woman told us,

> that I started to feel very sexy—something that hadn't happened to me in months. It was so good to feel that way again I didn't want to waste it, so I simply went out looking; I went to a big singles tennis club, met a guy, made a date for that night, and had a ball. He and I didn't have much in common; to tell the truth, I was using him—and enjoying it. But it wasn't so bad for him, either.

And a man in his early thirties said:

> In my first week of freedom I was like the well-known sailor on shore leave. I called an old girl friend and spent the night with her. A couple nights later, I dated a secretary in my own office—not a very smart thing to do, really—and I made it with her, too. I even went to a meatrack bar and wound up taking home a fairly good-looking gal. What I kept feeling all the time was: After ten years of being faithful to a wife who didn't like it much, I deserve to treat myself good!

Fairly often, however, the well-being that some newcomers experience at first proves to be transient; the sense of confidence and optimism collapses after a while and gives way to a period of depression. This is different from the mixed-feeling syndrome, the continuing alternation of gloom and cheer; for the Ups, the initial period of good feeling lasts for days or weeks, and then the balloon of happiness is punctured by a recognized event.

Commonly, it is the ending of the first post-marital relationship. A thirty-seven-year-old woman, a hospital administrative assistant, tells just such a story:

> Right after the separation I felt great—Wonder Woman! Super Achiever! No problem I couldn't solve. I worked, took care of my home and kids, dated, went out and basked in male attention, and for a while got involved with a man I'd known at work.
>
> But when he began to call infrequently, I said I wanted to end it—and suddenly found myself with nothing. By then it was the peak of summer: 100° heat, my house air conditioner not functioning, changes in my job that caused me great insecurity, and nothing but *nothing* going on in my city. (The sane singles get out of town in the summer!) I hit rock bottom and stayed there for several months, filled—stuffed!—with self-loathing and feelings of inadequacy in all areas of my life. My colleagues at the hospital gave me much support (I avoided actual therapy), and gradually I came out of it.

The descent from the initial high can also be the product of inner processes rather than external realities. One woman felt free, happy, and content for some time, but this mood gave way to a severe six-month depression when she wrote the autobiography that was necessary for her to obtain an annulment in the Catholic Church. "My whole life was staring me in the face," she explains, "—not a pretty picture. I found coping with the facts intolerable." And a forty-six-year-old man, a government employee, who at first felt thoroughly liberated and cheerful, owed a large part of his good humor to the anticipation of triumph: he had walked out on his wife to "teach her a lesson" and he had every confidence that she would soon beg him to return —on his terms. After some time, however, it was clear that she had come to enjoy being separated from him and was eager to get on with the divorce. At this, he says, "I deteriorated completely, feeling I had made a drastic mistake, had behaved like a young child instead of an adult; I was dismayed to realize that I had acted purely on emotions, without a shred of reason."

But for these late-comers to sorrow—and indeed, for nearly all initiates, whatever their early reactions—another kind of future is close at hand. It is not humanly possible to function in perpetual depression, and almost as difficult to live in perpetual euphoria. Nor is it tolerable to oscillate continually from up to down and back again, for the stress is insupportable. And so the great majority of FMs soon make their first adaptation and begin to level off. Only then are they able to start real work on the broader and more sweeping adjustments they need in order to live in the world of the formerly married.

4. LEVELING OFF

After a while, most newcomers begin to settle down emotionally. The minority who were on a free-at-last high descend to more ordinary levels and most of those who were in the Slough of Despond crawl up to more livable ground. The majority, who oscillated between depression and elation, tend to level off as their fits of gloom become less black, their spells of joy less dazzling.

How long the leveling-off process takes depends on a number of obvious factors—the way the marriage disintegrated, the individual's desire (or reluctance) to separate, the degree of financial hardship for one or both, one's inner resources, the presence of friends, the establishment of comfortable living quarters, and so on. Those who begin to see that the welter of problems *can*, in time, be solved, are well on the way to solving them and to settling down.

Some people manage it very quickly. One forty-four-year-old woman, a university administrator, says it took her only a week: first she had a couple of days of panic, then a few of blossoming good feeling, and then a comfortable sense of adjustment. Such speed is extraordinary. In contrast, a man of fifty-five says that he went through months of relief, then months of despair, then a couple of years of successive periods of anger, high spirits, jealousy, and regret; at last, he says, "I began to mellow in the third year." This timetable, too, is unusual—although not unheard of.

The vast majority fall somewhere between the extremes: to achieve genuine emotional stability takes most FMs two or more years.[10] Most commonly, however, the first signs of leveling off appear within a matter of months.

Many of the symptoms reported by newcomers—the exhilarated as well as the depressed, the ones who wanted the breakup as well as those who did not—resemble those of people with severe neuroses; yet, unlike neurotics, most of the newly separated soon begin to get better, with or without professional therapeutic help. They do so because, as a number of psychologists and sociologists have pointed out, most of them are *not* neurotics; they are reacting normally to tremendous situational stress, the enormous upheaval that separation has caused in their lives. Less than a generation ago, much of the general public as well as some psychologists believed that all divorcing people had "something wrong with them." Within the last decade, this opinion seems to have all but vanished.[11] Most newcomers support the newer view by doing what all reasonably healthy human beings do under situational stress: they begin to cope with their problems in realistic ways in order to lessen the pressures upon themselves.

The first step for most newcomers, and one they take almost immediately, is to start to deal with their own feelings of inadequacy and failure. They mull over the past endlessly, replay each scene again and again, wonder what would have happened if ... if ... ; fix some part of the blame here, some there, perhaps finds some no-fault explanation that seems to fit; tell the tale to a friend or two, later to another, each time wording and rewording it, and finding, with each telling, a more tolerable version. Thus, bit by bit, they develop the "story," a subjective history of the marriage, its trials, and its collapse, that makes sense of, and gives order to, the sequence of events.

Whether the story is factually accurate or not, whether it is made up of insights or only of excuses, it is indispensable to the newcomer, for it is a vital tool in coping with self-doubt, shame, and guilt. Those who lack the ego-strength to develop a story are in trouble; five or ten years later they are still saying things like, "I'll never understand what happened," or "I keep asking myself what I did wrong," or "I'll always believe that if A, B, or C had (hadn't) happened, we would have made it—but I guess I'll go to my grave not really knowing." Such people, by and large, rarely make a good adjustment to postmarital life or enter into satisfying new relationships.

A second kind of coping, also concerned with one's feelings about oneself, is the conscious effort to learn the new lines, to rehearse the new role. We have noted the immediate problem of learning to say "I" rather than "we"; however, leveling off requires not just the ability to speak and behave like an FM instead of a married person, but actually to *think* of oneself that way. It takes some time to achieve this, to learn to be one who was part of another, and is no longer. Anthropologist and divorce researcher Paul Bohannan thinks that this may be the most difficult of the several major adjustments to divorce.[12] But most newcomers, like most widows and widowers, learn that to cope with the change in identity, however difficult, they must begin using the right words, playing the part, redefining themselves both internally and in the eyes of the world. They force themselves, at first, to say to others, "I'm separated," or "We've split," or "My husband (wife) and I have broken up—we're getting a divorce." But after the first few practice tries accompanied by blushes, stammers, or awkward movements, the task begins to get easier; the words grow familiar, the announcement slips out in a calm, detached voice, the feeling of awkwardness disappears.

Novices also have to practice deciding and choosing for themselves—what to eat, when to go to sleep, where to go, how much to spend, how to dress. After their early indulgences and excesses comes the serious business of making formerly shared decisions alone. What they decide or choose is their own affair, and as they grasp this, they begin to *feel* like singles, and hence they *become* singles. They learn to respond easily and naturally to the outside world's recognition of this new identity. A recently separated man, invited by married friends to a dinner party, may be asked, "Will you be coming alone, or shall I invite another woman—not a date, you know, just someone to balance out the table?" The first time, he is embarrassed, doesn't know what to say, and mumbles something incoherent. But soon, as he levels off, he becomes used to the question, even expects it, and answers firmly and surely, "Yes, do invite someone," or "Thanks, I've just met a woman I'd enjoy bringing along." The recently separated woman, too, learns to deal with this situation in the same way —and in addition, she has now become expert at fluffing off Helpful Husbands with a tolerant smile.

Most of the early efforts to cope, of course, revolve around practical problems. Normal life cannot begin until these are dealt with because they concern such essentials as housing, money, and children. Newcomers will have to struggle with some of these problems for months, some for years. The first efforts to cope result only in the construction of a temporary framework, but it is the framework on which a whole new life will be built. The building may take a long while, and the framework may need repairs in the meantime, but the important thing is that it is *there*, and with it, life can go on. The very act of finding some early solutions lessens the initiate's depression, for he or she is busy doing and creating, not just sitting there helplessly, sunk in pain. It lessens exaltation, too, for it soon becomes clear that the new freedom bears a price; only much later will the newcomer know whether it was exorbitant or a bargain.

Housing is the first and most urgent problem, at least for the one who moves out. Newly separated people often stay with friends for a few days, or check into a hotel or motel—all depressing moves, because they leave the newcomers still, in fact, homeless. But soon, most mobilize themselves enough to make somewhat more permanent arrangements: a rooming-house if they have little money, a small furnished apartment if they have more, an unfurnished apartment (or even a house) and new furnishings for those who are relatively well off. What the newly separated rarely do is "go back home to mother." A common expedient a generation ago, it is no expedient at all now, except for some of those who are under twenty-five. Of FMs in this youngest age group, half the men and nearly 40 per cent of the women choose to go home.[13] As for those twenty-five and up, even of the women with children and severe money problems, very few elect to give up their independence; quite apart from the question of whether or not there is room in the parental home, newcomers recoil from a move that would rob them of autonomy and adulthood and plunge them back into pseudo-childhood.[14]

At the moment of separation, many couples have not come to any understanding or agreement about money. Nor is there any customary way to deal with a financial settlement on an informal basis. At the lowest economic levels, where the family income cannot possibly be stretched to cover two households, men often desert their wives and children and make no financial contribution to them at all. At the working- and middle-class levels, husbands are more likely to recognize an obligation to their children, or to wives who have not been employed outside the home. But hardly ever do husbands and wives reach an instant meeting of the minds on the money question, and as long as it remains unresolved, both are likely to remain anxious and depressed. For this reason, it is a problem they attempt to solve sooner rather than later, and if they are too hostile to work it out together (as is often the case), they engage intermediaries (friends or relatives) to establish at least some makeshift arrangement so that everyone involved can pay pressing bills. The discarder, often guilt-laden, may be more generous, and the discarded one, hoping for a reconciliation, may be less demanding, than either will be later, after turning the matter over to lawyers; but temporary though the first arrangement may be, it is yet another step to help them pass through the crisis.

Whatever the terms of the first informal money arrangement, both husband and wife (unless they are wealthy) are bound to be deeply concerned for the financial future. The income that supported one household must now support two, and two establishments cost between a quarter and a half more than one. For the majority, it is not possible to support two homes in the old life-style. Early efforts at coping may involve looking for a better job, moonlighting, and making such cutbacks as ending the payroll savings plan, switching to low-cost term insurance, giving up summer vacation plans, moving to a place with lower rent, and trading the large family-size car for a smaller, cheaper model that gets better gas mileage. The heaviest burden of coping falls on the mother who has been staying at home with her young children. Most of the time, she must now look for work, and this involves making day-care or other arrangements for the children; it also means job-hunting, never the most pleasurable of tasks, and even less pleasant when harsh necessity creates an aura of desperation around the search. Once it is under way, however, many women feel emotionally relieved just to know that they're out there looking, and that sooner or later they are bound to be successful. And most of them are: almost two-thirds of separated and divorced women hold jobs, far more than the married.[15] Even among FM women with preschool children, well over half manage to work; only about a third of the married women with preschool children do so.[16]

Going to work, even though it puts a staggering burden on the FM woman with young children, helps her to level off because it gives her yet another new status, and this one, *the working woman*, is both positive and ego-building. She has come a long way from the wife who derived her social status only from her husband's occupation. Even though she may bring home a meager paycheck from an undistinguished job, and the total task of working, homemaking, and mothering is almost too much to manage, she feels buoyed up by the new status she has gained for herself. Obviously, if her job is a good one, and the pay high, she will be relieved of her financial worries and have a soaring self-image besides. In any case, she can no longer be refused credit by stores, banks, and credit-card companies merely because she is a separated or divorced woman. Federal regulations that became effective in 1975 forbade such discrimination except in the case of women wholly dependent on alimony.

Even the woman with children whose husband skips out, or has little or no income, is in a less disastrous situation than formerly. In the old days, such mothers had to fall on the mercy of relatives or place their children in institutions; now, they are more apt to rely on the Social Security program known as Aid to Families with Dependent Children (AFDC). The non-working separated mother in the lower economic brackets has usually heard about AFDC and heads for its nearest assistance office. While the help is usually only a subsistence-level amount, it does serve to make the woman less panicky about the immediate future.

Along with these mundane but critical matters, the newly separated husband and wife make early efforts to cope with their new relationship to each other. The first few phone calls to inquire about the children, visits to pick up possessions, or chance encounters in church or the supermarket elicit sweats, stomach cramps, or palpitations, and it becomes clear that there will have to be a better way to do it. But there is no norm to follow; everyone knows that "civilized" behavior is much admired by some—but so is the expression of legitimate anger, hostility, and aggressiveness by others. With such contradictory guides to FM conduct, newcomers must invent their own ways of dealing with each other as part of the leveling-off process.

Some do cultivate the civilized, friendly manner, though anger often leaks through in the form of a sarcastic phrase or two, silences, or flushed faces. Others are straightforwardly and fiercely hostile, refusing to speak to each other at all, or committing numerous misdemeanors or even felonies by way of revenge. One woman sweetly agreed to send her husband his custom-made suits and shirts; when he received them, each item had been neatly sliced with a razor blade. One man repeatedly broke windows and entered his wife's house when she had the locks changed on the doors.

Still other separated people alternate between hostility and seductiveness. The seductiveness may stem from genuine yearning, or it may come from a need to maintain a hold over the other. But the antagonisms that drove the two apart keep breaking through—sometimes in the middle of a more-than-friendly chat, sometimes an hour after they've gone to bed with each other. The seductive-hostile relationship is probably the least successful mode of coping with the postmarital relationship since it is generally only a continuation of the one that existed toward the end of the marriage.

But any other consistent deportment—icy detachment, overt hostility, artificial politeness—will feel like something of an accomplishment, and indeed it is, for even if this early solution is not the permanent one, at least the separated spouses know what to expect, how to act with each other; they have established a stratagem for the present. "We're able to talk to each other calmly," an FM will tell a friend with some pride. Another, with equal pride, will say, "We've had to turn it all over to the lawyers—it's just not possible for us to communicate with each other."

And then, of course, there are the children. Newcomers must

begin to cope with the children's hurt, bafflement, and anxiety, tears and tantrums, bedwetting, reversion to bottle or babytalk, school failures, withdrawal, behavior problems. And the absent parent's visits must be staked out. Most separated couples cope, at first, by reaching some temporary understanding, much as they do about money; the arrangement, like the financial one, will very likely undergo much change as the two labor through the embittering steps of divorce. But even though the first arrangement may be a stopgap, like the other stopgaps it helps the leveling-off process. It is a boon to both children and parents to understand that Thursday afternoon (or Saturday, or every other weekend) is Daddy day; once a routine is established, it is something to count on.

The most unfortunate newcomers are those who cannot bring themselves to cope with these problems at all: the mother or father who can't or won't discuss the matter with the children, the father who starts a savage custody fight out of a desire for revenge, the couple who are so angry that they cannot make any visitation arrangement by themselves and so keep the children isolated from one parent while the lawyers try to work it out, the maddened ones who hide or run away with their children, or kidnap the children from each other. It is, of course, the children who suffer most, but the parents suffer too, because until they begin to solve these problems, they can't begin to level off—and until they level off they are immobilized, unable to function, unable to live.

5. HELPING HANDS

Although the emotional impact of separation seems as severe today as it ever was, there has been a dramatic change, within recent years, in the way separated people handle that impact. Most of them no longer try to deal with their problems all alone, but instead seek help from a variety of sources; some of these sources have become available only in the last half-dozen years or so. The assistance is valuable; most newcomers begin to adjust sooner and more successfully than their counterparts of a decade or more ago.

For one thing, almost everyone now has friends who either

are or were FMs, and are empathetic and understanding. The novice is quick to turn to a few such friends for reassurance, comfort, guidance, and practical advice. Those who have "been through it" listen, ask questions, offer interpretations, and so help in the development of the story. Beyond that, they begin the novice's acculturation and orientation by passing on folkways of the FM subculture that relate to the very emotions and problems he or she is experiencing, and that offer some of the solutions that have been tried and found workable.

For another thing, there are available to the newcomer a number of books—some trivial or doctrinaire, others genuinely informative and helpful—for separating and divorcing people. Some—like this one—are primarily descriptive and interpretive, and serve much the same function as well-informed friends, but with a broader scope. Others, books of the how-to genre, are prescriptive. Some focus on financial and legal bargaining with the ex-spouse; others are guides to divorce law, and do-it-yourself (lawyerless) divorce; still others deal with such matters as running a single-parent household, survival cooking for men who have never cooked, and solving emotional and sexual problems.

But the revolutionary change in facilitating early adjustment has been the recent establishment of a whole array of social mechanisms designed to provide support and help to the recently separated. Some of them have been created by unpaid volunteers, others by professionals or business people with commercial ends in mind, and still others by civic organizations and government agencies. It seems likely that all this was brought forth by the large growth of the FM population, but particularly by its growth among the middle class—that part of our society that is the best "market" for such social services.

One of the new mechanisms is the voluntary divorce organization. In America, any group of people with a common interest—especially a minority or deviant* group—is likely to form its own support organization. In the world of the formerly married, the first, largest, and best-known of these is Parents Without Partners (PWP), which is open to separated, divorced, and

* The term "deviant" is used here not in any pejorative sense, but in its strict sociological meaning: deviating from the accepted norm.

widowed persons with children of any age. Founded in 1957, its size has quadrupled within the last decade, and by late 1976 it had nearly 1,000 chapters in the United States and Canada and a membership of over 140,000. Scores of similar organizations exist, most of them small by comparison and usually limited to a single city or megalopolitan area; many, unlike PWP, are open to childless FMs and the never-married.

While the major appeal of these organizations is social—a subject we'll look into in the next chapter—many of them also offer discussion groups, classes, and lectures by professionals on various aspects of FM life; these include ways to contend with the initial emotional and practical problems of separation. "The Period of Readjustment," for instance, is one of the topics regularly scheduled for group discussions in the homes of Washington, D.C., members of PWP; similar group discussions are held regularly by all PWP chapters.

Other organizations, both voluntary and professional, offer much the same mix of social activities and supportive-educational services. For example, in Portland, Oregon, Solo Center is a community center for unattached adults that was created by Betty Daggett, a social worker. For a modest fee, people can come to the center's large, comfortable old house to take part in social activities, discussion groups, workshops, and classes; one of the class topics is "Divorce: a Transition," and most of those who come to Solo Center are FMs. Although we know of no national directory of such organizations, the proliferation of listings in weekend newspapers, magazines, and divorce-group newsletters suggests that there must be many scores of them throughout the nation.

In a number of cities and towns, feminist organizations have begun to offer their own programs of assistance and information to FM women. These include consciousness-raising discussions, workshops, referral services—and of great value—the fellowship and support of other women in like circumstances.

Another answer to the needs of the burgeoning market of troubled FMs is a brand-new profession—or at least a brand-new specialty within the old profession of marriage counseling— namely, divorce counseling. It is less than a decade since marriage counselors began to add divorce counseling to their list of services, but now, according to C. Ray Fowler, executive director of the American Association of Marriage and Family Counselors, about 10 per cent of the members of that organization identify themselves as "marriage and divorce counselors," and virtually all the rest do some divorce counseling. There are probably many hundreds of other divorce counselors outside of this organization.

Some divorce counselors are private practitioners, but others are associated with yet another new phenomenon, divorce counseling centers. Such facilities are springing up everywhere; some are operated on a low-fee non-profit basis and sponsored by service organizations like the YWCA, while others charge somewhat higher fees and are run as professional businesses. An example of the latter category is the Creative Divorce National Counseling Center in San Rafael, California, founded by Mel Krantzler, author of *Creative Divorce* and himself a divorce counselor. Physically, it consists of a modest suite of offices—two small rooms for individual therapy and a larger one for group therapy and training sessions—in the business section of the city. A staff of three counsels adults and their children, and trains other professionals to do the same kind of work in their own communities.

According to Betty Berry, editor and publisher of *Marriage, Divorce and The Family Newsletter*, many other organizations are now beginning to offer divorce counseling. They include some of the 600 women's centers on and off college campuses, some of the chapters of the National Organization for Women, and, increasingly, mental health centers and family agencies throughout the country.

The churches, which for the most part tried not to notice the formerly married a few years ago, now appear to be sharply aware of them. Churches of various denominations in a large number of communities have set up "support groups" for separated and divorced people; the groups offer a variety of discussions, counseling, and social events. And some individual churches that were traditionally hostile to divorce have changed their positions; in Iowa City, Iowa, for example, the First Baptist Church now has a divorce group initiated by its minister, the Reverend Paul Sandin—himself divorced and remarried, but able to let that fact be widely known only three years ago. In 1975, in Galveston and two other Texas cities, Baptist, Lutheran, and Presbyterian pastors joined with the Family Service Association and the County Bar Association to sponsor a series of divorce seminars open to the public at $2.00 each.[17]

Even the Roman Catholic Church, still categorically opposed to divorce, has begun (unofficially) to take an interest in divorced Catholics. Father James Young (quoted earlier in this book) of the Paulist Center in Boston, started the Divorced Catholics Group movement in 1972. Since then, more than 100 similar groups, all offering support, have sprung up throughout the country. The movement is, of course, formally outside the Church, but by 1975, at least a dozen dioceses had set up their own "ministries to the divorced and separated."[18] (In December, 1976, the bishops of the Memphis diocese and the Newark diocese actually allowed Catholics who had divorced and re-married to partake of communion, at special services, despite the official Vatican position that such people may not receive the sacraments.)[19]

Finally, a number of city and state agencies that work with low-income families now operate advisory services for single parents (usually women with children), to help them get on AFDC, or to get other kinds of assistance such as food stamps and Medicaid.

It is not possible to include any comprehensive listing of services for FMs in this book, for the list would be hopelessly incomplete before the words were even in print. But the scope and character of the development should be clear: there are now a number of supportive and advisory mechanisms that new-comers can turn to for help in coping with their problems. Ser-vices are not yet available everywhere, and the help offered is sometimes of dubious value, but by and large, the proliferation of helping hands has greatly ameliorated the shock of entering the world of the formerly married.

Or so we strongly believe. There is no rigorous proof of this as yet, but there are preliminary indications of it. Two small-scale studies, both by sociologists, have found that FMs who interact in support groups definitely make quicker adjustments, and experience less stress, than those who remain isolated.[20] In our own survey, over four-tenths of the men and about half the women had some kind of counseling or therapy after separation; this ranged from a few hours to many months, and from pastoral counseling to classic individual therapy, TA, and encounter groups. Two-thirds of the men and three-quarters of the women who had any therapy rated it as helpful, the majority even rating it very helpful.

To be sure, "very helpful" can mean many things. For one respondent it meant only five or six meetings with a counselor to "be sure I wasn't to blame and that I wasn't unworthy or un-attractive." Others have spent months or years uncovering their hidden conflicts, altering their feelings about themselves, and pursuing emotional growth. For most, "very helpful" means finding ways to cope with the external as well as the internal problems of separation. A thirty-eight-year-old woman who had spent a year in therapy while still married and another year afterward says:

> It was time-consuming and expensive, but worth every bit of it. I could not afford *not* to have gone through it. It helped me in all phases of life—from dealing with my children daily, to my job, to involvements in clubs, dating, understanding men—I could go on and on.

And a forty-year-old professional man says:

> I didn't work for two weeks, and spent many hours alone, crying and feeling sorry for myself. I felt alienated, inadequate, lost, unloved. I didn't know where to turn. Then I got into group therapy at a divorce counseling center. My feelings went from shock, to denial, then to anger, then guilt; I had to go through the whole mourning process—but after less than half a year I really got it together.
>
> Even in the beginning, though, I felt a lot better to see that I wasn't the only one who felt rotten and who couldn't deal with everyday problems. There were plenty of others like me—and plenty who had already worked out some of the snags—from whom I could learn a fair amount. Once I got into the group and knew I wasn't alone, I figured I might just make it after all.

III

The Bazaar

1. IS ANYONE THERE?

Linda Grey, grading a batch of student papers for her Introduction to Psychology course, belatedly realized that she was being unduly caustic in many of her comments, and felt ashamed. *I seem to be angry with them, but why am I?* she thought, and instantly knew the answer: *Because they're not alone like me, because they belong and I don't.* Every day she saw them huddled in conversational groups in the lounges, or on the grass in the spring sunshine, smiling, talking, laughing together. But she, Associate Professor Grey, didn't laugh because she belonged nowhere and to no one.

Two months had passed since her husband left, the night she had awakened terror-stricken from a nightmare in which she was all alone in a tiny boat, drifting in the ocean. Since then, she had fought off the nightmare mood and gotten her life into passable order. Even before the separation it had always seemed like a small triumph to be able to juggle teaching, faculty meetings, housekeeping, and mothering, with the help of only a part-time housekeeper, and she was relieved to see that she could still make it all work. But one aspect of the nightmare remained: she was alone. It didn't help that she saw her students and fellow faculty members every day, visited married friends for dinner from time to time, had taken the children to spend two weekends with her parents; her loneliness remained untouched.

Still, when a close friend offered to introduce her to an attractive man, Linda took instant fright. What could she talk to him about? How should she act? How could she—age thirty-two, an associate professor, mother of two—play the ingénue meeting a new man without being totally ridiculous? She begged off, telling herself that she wasn't ready for that sort of thing, had no need for men anyway, that her life was fine as it was. But the last time she dined with married friends she felt listless and bored; worse, she suspected that they were just as bored as she but were trying hard to be kind. On the way home she admitted to herself that she didn't belong with them; she had become a displaced person, an outsider.

And this evening, looking at her cranky remarks on the student papers, she knew it was time to act. *If I were playing tennis, I'd know enough to change a losing game, and this losing game is my life. I've got to get out and meet some new people, not married people, people like me.* The very thought that she was going to change her life made her feel better. She went back through the papers, erased her most acerbic remarks, and finished her work in a determined, hopeful mood.

Bill Novak, separated for six months, felt that his whole life was a muddle. To keep himself too busy to think about his troubles, he had discharged his secretary and begun handling his own business correspondence and billing; unfortunately, he made numerous errors and alienated some of the firm's customers.

Nor was he doing well emotionally. Although he had left the suburbs and rented a tiny apartment in the city, he was reclusive and apathetic. In the past, he had spent summer weekends and his vacation at his beach house, but this year it was barred to him because his wife was there with the children. The city seemed deserted on Saturdays and Sundays, and alien and hostile on weekdays. He felt so isolated and depressed that, at his brother's urging, he began to see a divorce counselor, who assured him that there was a busy social world full of people just like himself, and gave him some ideas about how to go in search of them. Tonight, poring over a local magazine and the weekend edition of the newspaper, Bill is surprised to see how many ads there are for social clubs, open parties, and nearby resorts that cater to singles—some of them clearly intended for formerly married, middle-aged people like himself. While his interest is piqued, the idea of going to any such place alone makes him deeply uneasy, but that's something he'll have to talk to the counselor about at their next meeting.

Nancy Larkin felt panic-stricken when her husband walked out on Labor Day weekend. But as soon as she arrived at her busy publishing office on Tuesday, she was caught up in the hurly-burly of work, and her separation anxiety quite disappeared; it didn't come back until the evening. The pattern might have been repeated on Wednesday—but by then, Nancy had decided what to do. Since she had been married for only two years, was childless, and had kept in close touch with some of her unmarried friends, the singles world didn't seem remote. In fact, during the weeks before her husband left, she had often had fantasies about the new men she might meet, the affairs she might have, as soon as she was free. Well, now she was free.

When Nancy got home from work Wednesday she called three unmarried women she often met for lunch, told them about her separation, and candidly said that she needed a start. They all promised to introduce her to a man or two.

Next, resolutely mustering her courage, Nancy called a man with whom she had had a brief affair before her marriage. He sounded glad to hear from her, and was friendly and sympathetic when she explained her situation. He said that he was going with someone now, but he and his girlfriend would be delighted to take Nancy along to a big party next Friday night; once there, she would be on her own.

She breezed through the next days waiting for Friday, thinking about what she would wear and whether to get a haircut, putting on records and practicing dancing in front of a full-length mirror. She had a notion that her life was about to change dramatically, and she was right; before a month had passed,

Nancy felt just as she had five years before, when she was fresh out of college, trying to balance her exciting new job with her giddy social life.

Nancy was fortunate. Unlike her, most newcomers feel far from any social network at all. They have become disconnected from the peer group of their married friends and are not close enough to any other group to make an easy transition to it. People who have been married for a number of years, particularly those with children, have socialized with those who have the same problems and interests as themselves, and have usually lost contact with the singles world. When they separate, they find that their friends of single days are married, and the present never-marrieds are all too young, so that the newcomer doesn't fit in with them any more. A man of twenty-nine said he felt much the same after a five-year marriage as he had when he came home from the Army:

> When I got back from Nam I felt like a dummy; I didn't know the songs, I didn't know the dances, I didn't know the slang or the new buzz words—I didn't even understand a lot of the things people were talking about. It's the same now, only more serious. I have no idea what single people are all about these days, and I don't know what goes and what doesn't.

Older FMs feel this even more keenly. In addition, they find it much harder than the very young to imagine how they will look, physically, to other unattached people. Most of them feel unattractive because in the dying phase of the marriage they saw themselves through the other's disenchanted eyes. But even if the ex-spouse found them physically desirable right to the bitter end, will anyone else? Mightn't it have been just habit? How is one to know after ten or twenty years of marriage if one is still attractive or not? How will this hand (they wonder), this face, this body look and feel to someone else? How will they ever know what to *do* with another person? They haven't even *kissed* anyone else in ages. They read diet books, buy health foods, take vitamin pills; women change their hair styles, men grow mustaches and beards—or else shave them off.

But even as they groom themselves for reentry, most newcomers wonder, "Where *is* everybody?" A woman in her thirties who had been separated for four months said to us testily, *"The world of the formerly married?* Some joke! I think you invented it; anyway, if it does exist, *I* sure haven't been able to find it."

Since the world of the formerly married is usually invisible to those who are not yet part of it, and since the newly separated are unsure of the welcome they will receive when and if they do ever find it, they tend to expect to have a difficult time "getting back into circulation"—a term that includes finding both a friendship network and suitable dating partners of the opposite sex. How much or little they worry about it varies with their sex, age, and other factors. Common sense should be able to tell us how these variables affect their expectations—but common sense isn't always right. For instance:

—*Sex:* Common sense says that if you are a woman, you will expect to have more difficulty than men in finding partners, and common sense is right—but just barely. Over half the women, but nearly half the men, feel this way. Only one woman in six, and only one man in four expects it to be easy.

—*Age:* Common sense says that the older you are, the more trouble you will expect to have getting back into circulation. Common sense is right—but only as far as women are concerned; men of forty-five or over are actually somewhat more optimistic about finding new partners than younger men.

—*Occupational level:* Common sense says that if you have a low-level job you will anticipate more difficulty than if you have a high-level job. That's true for men but not for women; the majority of women, at *all* occupational levels, anticipate reentry problems. The explanation may be that some women with good jobs fear that many men will find them formidable. Also, a woman with high occupational status is usually interested only in men with at least equally high status, and she therefore has a small field from which to choose.

—*Parental status:* Common sense tells you that if you are childless you will be more optimistic than those with children, and common sense is right: parent FMs are twice as likely as childless FMs to anticipate great difficulty. But common sense says that this is because children tie one down, and here, it is off target: FM fathers, even when they don't have custody, are nearly as pessimistic about getting into circulation as FM mothers.

Yet common sense is right enough about two other important variables: discarders are more optimistic than the discarded, and separated people who still feel strong ties of love or dependency to the former spouse tend to be more pessimistic than those who have no such fetters.

But what people expect, and what they actually experience, are, fortunately, strikingly different: as we will see, in every category they are far more pessimistic than they need be about socializing in the new world. At first, FMs can't imagine how they will ever get started, but that's only because they haven't yet thought of using most of the social mechanisms—many of them quite new—by which the formerly married meet each other. The large number of FMs, and the new social acceptability of divorce, have worked together to produce what is, in effect, a huge bazaar, a giant meeting-place where the separated and divorced can meet each other, make friends, find dates, lovers, new life-companions.

It is only after the first emotional storms have died down that most of the separated can begin to look for the bazaar. Almost none begins to look during the first month; many make no effort for several months. But from then on, increasing numbers begin to seek—and once they seek, they find.

2. *WAYS AND MEANS: TRADITIONAL*

Many a person is astonished to discover that there has been a flourishing society of unattached people right under his or her nose all along.

One woman in her early forties had regularly summered with her husband and children at an East coast island resort, one she had always thought of as a slightly stuffy family community. She was thoroughly puzzled when, on a few occasions, single friends commented that the island was reputed to be a wild place; it seemed to her that the entire population was always in bed by eleven, and the wildest things that ever happened were an evening of bridge, or Saturday night dinner in the local restaurant. And then her marriage broke up.

I had always thought there was nobody there but mommies and daddies and children and they all lived the good clean life. It was early to bed and early to rise, and most of the married couples gave the impression of being much more interested in parenting and sports than in sex. But when I returned to the island after my divorce, it didn't seem like the same place.

The first Saturday night I went back to the familiar old restaurant, but at my date's insistence we went at nine o'clock instead of my former seven. By ten or so the married crowd had drifted off, and by eleven, the bar was jammed with people I'd never seen before. That bar turned out to be the prime cruising ground for all the single and divorced islanders—and there were lots—who only came out of the woodwork when the married folks had gone to bed. I couldn't believe it! I had been there all those summers and never suspected that there were two layers of society; people belonged to one layer or the other, but not both. The next day I discovered the non-family beach, and soon, I had shifted into the other layer myself.

This woman came into contact with the non-family layer of society because she had a date—but how, novices want to know, do you get that first date? Most of the formerly married, at least initially, rely on traditional ways and means that have long been accepted in our society, and the most traditional means of all is the direct introduction by mutual friends—married friends. A meeting with a candidate hand-picked by a trusted friend or relative seems like a safe and easy way to start; good old Joe surely knows the newcomer's tastes, habits, and personality and can be counted on to choose wisely (the newcomer thinks). So when Joe, or his wife Helen, calls and says they have someone in mind, and please come to a little dinner party, the invitation is eagerly accepted. The newcomer, rusty on dating procedures, doesn't have to look for a date, the dinner party will be in a setting that is familiar and reassuring, and Joe and Helen will be there to help things along. The newcomer is excited and hopeful —but still apprehensive; asks questions and builds an instant fantasy from the answers; wonders how to talk to the other person without sounding ill-at-ease or uninteresting; dresses for the party with particular care, peers endlessly into the mirror, stands up straighter, puts on another dash of cologne, and nervously goes off—to almost certain disappointment.

And disappointment may be the least of it, for the evening can be acutely embarrassing as well: good old Joe and Helen went to a lot of trouble to arrange this, and there they are covertly, anxiously, watching every move, listening to every word—and it must be obvious to them that they made a hideous mistake.

A man enters, looks around the room twice, thinking he must have misunderstood. *Is this she? This plain, aging, heavy, aggressive woman? How could they have thought I would like her? If they did, what can they possibly think of me? And they had described her in such glowing terms! They must be out of their minds.* He is annoyed and ungrateful—and ashamed of himself for being so. He forces himself to talk, seem outgoing, friendly, and keeps wondering if his watch has stopped.

It doesn't happen only to men. A handsome blonde, blue-eyed woman of forty told us:

> I was just starting to feel good about myself: I'd been exercising, had lost ten pounds, dyed my hair, and was enjoying little jokes and flirtations with men in the office who knew about my separation.
>
> When my best friends invited me to dinner to meet a man, I was delighted; I went, took one look at him—and wanted to crawl into a hole. He was much too old, inches shorter than I am, and he had dandruff all over his shoulders. And he was so pompous— he kept lecturing me about politics like a professor talking to a student. All I could think about was what I could say to Anne and Barney. What I need—and expected, I guess—is some big, sexy, beautiful guy my own age—but how could I tell them that without sounding like an ingrate and a nitwit?

Why do married friends so often choose so poorly? In part, it's because they don't know many unattached people. But in much larger part, it's because they perceive the newcomer as like themselves in age, sexuality, emotional, and romantic potential; they don't realize that he or she is just beginning a stage of self-discovery and renewal, and wants someone with similarly wonderful new feelings of youth, vitality, attractiveness. There's a whole wide world out there, waiting to be explored (perhaps conquered), and it's a rare newcomer who is ready to settle for what may well be a sterling character concealed in a dowdy package. So disparate are the assessments of the still-married and the no-longer-married that even if Helen and Joe or Anne and Barney knew a much younger, more attractive candidate, they would undoubtedly think that person totally unsuitable for the newcomer.

So he or she quickly becomes wary of well-meant invitations and learns to avoid them—or at least suggests to the married friends that it would be easier to meet someone new at a large party where they won't be on display, where they won't be mercilessly thrust at each other. But the problem is self-limiting: most married friends soon run out of names—and out of patience —with their old friend who, they tell each other, is going through an incredibly foolish and juvenile stage these days.

Another traditional and acceptable meeting-place for FMs is some in-group—the office, the school in which one is a teacher, the church one attends. Such a milieu is safe from some of the discomfitures of the small dinner party—the newcomer is the one who makes the choice of partner, and since she and he are both in the same place for some other reason, it is easy to talk without embarrassment. But how does one break through the barrier of the accustomed in-group relationship, and how does one restore the barrier if the breakthrough yields a negative result? A man asks his office assistant to have dinner with him; if she replies, "That's very sweet of you, but I'm seeing someone exclusively," he smiles gamely but feels foolish, then and for many days thereafter. Or, she accepts and they do have dinner together, but she turns out to be totally different from what he'd hoped; he says, at the end, "This has been nice—let's do it again soon," and she knows he doesn't mean it, and he knows she knows, and every day he has to work with her, and keeps wishing she would quit.

If the newcomer is a woman, the problem is compounded: in most cases she is subordinate at work to the men who interest her, and she hesitates to trespass on the business relationship. And how can she initiate anything by innuendo—or by a direct invitation to accompany her to a concert or the ballet—and then back away if it doesn't go well?

Beyond these obvious difficulties, the work milieu is an intrinsically limited marketplace: what brings people together there is employment rather than availability—and few are available. Only about a quarter of the men and women in our survey said work was an important source of new partners—no more than said so a generation ago,[1] even though today many more formerly married women work. The work milieu is probably useful chiefly to those who have no other opportunities, or who find any other milieu undignified: the professor in a small college town knows no townspeople and would regard it as infra dig for him to go to a singles bar, so he, perforce, turns to his colleagues on the faculty, or even to his students for companionship.

Far better than a college or office date, or the introduction by married friends, is the introduction that comes from an experienced FM. Most novices recognize fairly soon that it is only the old hand who can understand their feelings and who knows how vulnerable and awkward they feel.

The veteran knows enough to act not as a watchful host, but as an expediter; he or she may give a free-and-easy cocktail party, or simply call and offer the newcomer a name and description, then leave the two to meet when and as they like—or not at all. The veteran will either speak to the prospective date and prepare the way, or just supply a phone number and permission to mention his or her name.

To make such a call for the first time is difficult, for a man as well as a woman; he fears a rebuff, doesn't know how to introduce himself and get the conversation going. But often, it goes surprisingly well, especially if the other is also an FM and accustomed to the easy acceptance, within the world of the formerly married, of contacts between strangers. The voice that answers the phone is helpful; she talks first, perhaps about their mutual friend, then drops an informational hint about herself ("Wait while I turn down the record player—I'm wallowing in Verdi tonight"). It takes only one such clue to start the conversation flowing.

For a woman, calling a stranger may be even harder, at first, than for a man, yet today it is fairly common for a woman to initiate contacts. "I *can't* call a strange man," she may wail to her experienced friend who replies, "Nonsense, it's done all the time; you've been out of it too long to know. Just say that you and I are old friends and I thought you and he would like talking to each other since you're both ski buffs (cat lovers, stamp collectors, from Toledo, Ohio)."

The biggest danger in the phone call is that it is a tabula rasa on which one projects an image to fit the voice; the owner of the charming voice, when he or she appears for the blind date, may bear no resemblance to the fantasy. *Looks shouldn't matter so much*, the disappointed tyro thinks—but knows they do. At this moment in life one is like a teenager in some ways, wanting a magical immediate attraction, setting great store by the appearance of fantasy come true. If what sounded like manly self-assurance on the phone looks like blowhard egotism in the flesh, or if what sounded like enchanting femininity looks like over-aged and inappropriate girlishness, the date is a calamity.

After a few calamities, most new FMs become wary of blind dates, but at the same time, they are growing less fearful and more willing to take risks, and so they may turn to the method they thought they would be least likely to select—the pick-up. While pick-ups have been both common and acceptable among working-class people for generations, they have become conventional for the middle class only during the last decade. Pick-ups may be made at dances, meetings, or lectures, in museums, on the ski slopes, on the beach, in singles bars, or at large singles parties—wherever people gather.

Bars and parties, different though they may be, are alike in that they offer the largest selections, for everyone there has come to cruise and be cruised. In one crowded room the newcomer can see ten, twenty, fifty times as many possible partners as at a friend's dinner party. Everyone is approachable, even though many will not prove receptive; one commits no *gaffe* by starting a conversation with anyone at all. The newcomer is neither in the limelight nor under the watchful eye of a friend; it is easy to hang back and do nothing, or to talk to many briefly, and move on if they prove uninteresting.

But the very virtues of the cruising singles scene are also responsible for some of its most unpleasant features. It is about as amiable as the floor of the Stock Exchange—a buy-and-sell, competitive melee in which the bidders and askers are ruthless, coldblooded, and rude in the pursuit of their goal. After a few minutes of conversation, the blunt statement, "Excuse me, there's someone I have to see" (or "I have to freshen my drink," or "I'll see you around"), is an obvious dismissal; it means, "I want to get away from you so I can look elsewhere." All this, and worse, is startling and repellent to the newcomer accustomed to conventional courteous social behavior.

> [Woman, forty-five] My very first shock was that people actually *admitted* they were looking. I was still fresh from the school of treating men as if they were Galahads, and thought I would meet a man and then one day accidentally discover a wondrous love and passion slowly blossoming forth between us. I never expected to hear a stranger say to me, "Hi. Ya got any kids? Got a pad? A job? Alimony? Any competition? Wanna ball?"

> [Man, thirty-one] My first couple of parties, God, how I hated being there! The worst part was the eyes. You're talking to some woman and trying to be really charming, and her eyes keep wandering off over your shoulder, and you know she's checking around to see if there's anything better than you. But I have to admit that now I do the same thing myself—because, let's face it, that's what you're there for.

Disagreeable or unpleasant as a singles party may seem to the initiate, it does have some familiar—and therefore reassuring—elements. The pick-up in a bar or other public place is, by contrast, a complete departure from any aspect of married life; yet, singles bars are in far wider use today than ever before, and are used by middle-class, generally conventional FMs to an increasing degree.[2] The bars appear in every city and most suburbs, and as soon as the word spreads that a new one is a meeting place for singles, a cruising crowd gathers nightly and may create long waiting lines on weekends.

While some places attract only the never-marrieds, others draw a somewhat older crowd, almost all separated or divorced (or pretending to be). At first glance, a singles bar looks like a lively enough place; the hubbub of voices, the faces eagerly turned toward each other, the clinking glasses, the merry laughter—all connote amiable socializing. But the crowd is not a group; it is only a mob of strangers, not bound to each other by ordinary rules of good manners or consideration. The cruising is straightforward, crude, sometimes cruel. The opening questions—by women as well as men—are often remarkably blunt ("You married? Live alone? Where? What do you do?"), for there is little time to waste. Opening gambits are critical, for they may result in a curt, "I'm waiting for someone," or, sometimes (at the opposite extreme but equally crude), after five or ten minutes of good conversation, "Let's get out of here and go to my place," or even, "Want to have dinner first or afterwards?"

It is hardly a comfortable atmosphere for anyone, especially for one beyond the bloom of youth who has been away from the dating and mating game for some years. Most accounts of singles bars agree that practically no one likes them; yet, they are so useful, in a limited way, that from a minor phenomenon fifteen or twenty years ago, they have become a large and thriving industry. In our sample, about one FM in six said that pickups, mostly in singles bars, were one of the principal methods by which they met new partners; a number of others said they visited the bars only now and then but did consider them a minor source of contacts. Young FMs are the most likely to frequent singles bars, but a fair number of middle-aged persons do so, too.

Novices learn about singles bars from experienced friends or from singles or general publications. But no matter what they've heard ahead of time, the first visits are apt to be both anxiety-producing and startling. Here are a few reactions:

[Woman, thirty-three]   The thing that shocked me most was the aggressiveness of both men and women, especially about sex. It seemed to me that people wanted to get to know each other in bed first.

[Man, thirty-nine]   I was appalled at the brazenness of many women. One woman I met sat at a table in bars, and if she saw a guy that she liked, she called the waiter over and told him that she'd like to buy the guy a drink. A lot of people I mentioned it to didn't think it was unusual.

[Woman, forty-five]   I've begun to visit the singles bars three times a week. I've never enjoyed drinking, but I drink to be sociable. I want to find out if the love of my life will materialize on the next bar stool. He hasn't yet. And having escaped with my "honor" from a few would-be strong-arm types, I may just give up the game and take up fossil collecting or scuba diving instead.

[Man, thirty-one] I go to singles bars from time to time, and I'm dismayed that so many of the women are interested only in one-night stands. I'm a man and I guess I'm supposed to like that, but it dismays me anyway. It's as if they refuse to have a relationship—as if they've envied men, and now they're feeling their oats and acting like us.

With so many complaints, why do FMs keep going to singles bars? Many do it because having been so recently wounded, they are afraid of anything but the most brittle, impersonal contacts. But others go because, whatever the drawbacks, the bars are functional:

[Woman, forty-one] This is a small town I live in and there isn't much social life for singles—so my motto is, get out and get around, find it wherever you can. There's no telling where or when you'll meet someone. Sometimes I get lazy—the idea of getting all duded up and ending up with nothing for the night's effort is depressing, and I wonder why I keep trying. But the very next time, I meet someone neat, and it gives me great hope and makes me keep trying.

[Woman, thirty-six] I think I was most surprised that I could meet desirable dates in bars! They were always considered off limits for "good" girls, but now they're not for anyone; I've met some of my nicest dates in this manner.

3. WAYS AND MEANS: NEW STYLE

But the traditional methods of socializing and mate-shopping, even the best of them, have been too slow, too special, or too limited to fill the needs of the swiftly growing ranks of the formerly married. And so, even though the bars have not yet attracted the majority, there are already a number of much more recent innovations. These, too, have been utilized by only a minority of FMs so far—but they *have* enormously expanded the marketplace.

Some of the new mechanisms are radical modifications of old ones, others are genuinely original. Like the singles bars, they all create a social milieu that is not dependent on social linkage or on intermediary acquaintances: you need not wait to be invited but only to pay the admission price. The new non-traditional devices are more structured than bars, however, and are designed to cater to a large variety of tastes. Many have some special prerequisite such as a college education or a particular religious affiliation, and this provides a degree of respectability and homogeneity that bars lack.

The market is run—that is to say, strangers are brought together—by go-betweens with whom they have no social connection; these are business people pursuing profit, do-gooders performing a social service, or amateurs practicing a hobby for their own gratification.[3]

The new methods vary greatly in a number of ways. Along the dimension of ambience, for instance, they range from the coarse to the refined.

At one end of the spectrum there is the "hotel dance," which is usually operated by a business person. Typically, it is held in a motel, a hall of some kind (Elks, V.F.W.), or a small hotel; anyone may attend for a modest entrance fee ($2.00 to $3.00) and there is a pay bar. The smaller dances feature recorded music, but at the larger ones, a "live band" of two or three bored musicians blasts amplified sound at ear-splitting level—or else plays in the dreamy "nostalgia" style that takes the patrons back to their high-school days. The patrons are, in the main, middle-aged, lower-middle-class and working-class people—and while some of them do dance, many more stand or sit around edgily watching, studying, starting brief conversations, then breaking away and moving off to try elsewhere.

At the other end of the spectrum are events that draw the "more discriminating" singles, as they are called in at least one singles newsletter: tennis parties, wine-tasting, late afternoon poetry readings, lectures and discussions about the theater. They all feature ad lib "mingling" or "socializing"—the real business of the occasion—before and after the ostensibly main event. These affairs, which also are usually run by entrepreneurs in the singles business, tend to cost more than the dances, are attended by better-dressed, better-educated, and more well-to-do people, and have a considerably more sophisticated atmosphere.

Along another dimension—the basis of the approach by one stranger to another—the new methods range from the candidly commercial to the indirect and intellectual.

At one extreme, you can pay a video-dating service to see and hear possible partners on a television set (fees range from $35.00 to $125.00); you, in turn, are then taped so that you can be judged by opposite-sex clients. When the bureau has a "fit" —you and another person who are mutually interested in each other—it either furnishes names and telephone numbers to both of you, or actually arranges the initial contact.

At the other extreme, seekers can attend discussion groups run by a local church, where they are asked only for a small donation. The free-wheeling sessions, often conducted by trained leaders, deal with such topics as "The Meaning of Self-Actualization," "How Can I Find Someone Who Will Meet My Needs?," and "Why Can't My Partner Be Perfect?" Much may be learned from such discussions—especially about the people taking part in them. When the formal discussion is over, those who want to can comfortably continue the debate on a one-to-one basis, proceeding from intellectual matters to personal ones.

Along yet a third dimension, the new mechanisms range from heavily capitalized businesses with elaborate physical plants to those that consist only of a box of stationery, a roll of stamps, and space that is rented for an evening at a time.

In the realm of big business there are large resorts that feature singles weekends; private singles clubs with their own city or country facilities; and, one of the latest developments, scores of singles apartment complexes springing up all over the country. (Some of these are virtual cities of singles: Woodway Square Apartments in Houston houses 2,500 and features daily poolside, clubroom, and cocktail lounge socializing; Marina del Mar, near Los Angeles, is twice as large and even more socially frenetic.)

At the small-business level there are hundreds of social clubs across the nation—New York City alone has well over fifty— most of which consist, as one expert in the field put it, of "nothing but a letterhead and a mailing list."[4] These clubs are owned by various private individuals (themselves usually single) who advertise for dues-paying members, then rent public halls in which to run dances or other events to justify their fees.

All these and other new-style ways and means of meeting and greeting have become so numerous in the past several years that many large metropolitan newspapers now carry special calendars of singles activities. In a few areas there are regional newsletters and magazines which list, in the manner of the tourist guides one finds in hotel rooms, all the singles events in the local area. And they may be confusingly abundant: for the Greater New York City area (which includes various communities in New Jersey, Connecticut, and Long Island), the magazine *Singles World* listed about 200 events per month in late 1976.

But neither *Singles World* nor any similar publication has much to say about the mood or atmosphere of its offerings. And for good reason: the truth is often unappealing. Public singles parties and dances, particularly those for "over-thirty-five" are frequently rather depressing affairs.

An attractive woman in her early forties describes her adventures at a singles dance for us:

It was the night before my daughter's college graduation and I had driven upstate right from work in order to be on hand for the morning exercises. It was close to ten o'clock when I pulled into a crowded motel parking lot. As I registered I could see that the dining room was nearly empty and I wondered where all those car owners could be. Then as the bellhop led me toward the elevator I saw the pink and white sign trimmed with silver sparkles. "SINGLES GALA" it read. "SINGLES FROM 35 TO 100 WELCOME. OUR LAST DANCE OF THE SEASON. THE LAST DANCE MAY BE YOUR BIG CHANCE." I smiled at the sign, then forgot about it.

But as I entered my room I heard the band, and the unmistakable strains of *Stardust*; I had obviously lucked into a room close to the "grand ballroom." I unpacked, tried all four TV channels, then restless, bored after the long drive, thought, "Why not? I *am* a single between 35 and 100 and—who knows? Maybe this is where they've been hiding all the good men."

So I followed the music—*Deep Purple* now—until I reached the ballroom lobby. There were several dozen men lounging around the entrance and I could feel them all looking at me as I went to the table to pay my admission fee. Five dollars! But I was entitled to a free drink, the ticket-seller assured me. She was in her fifties, twenty pounds overweight, and wore a lavender and white flowered dress, a sign that said "Hi! My name is Flo," and harlequin glasses with rhinestone frames. Her hair was the color of lemonade and it was arranged in a beehive hairdo of a kind I had believed extinct ten years before. I didn't look at the men.

Inside, the ballroom was ringed with tables, most of them occupied by one or two women. About half of them appeared to be sisters of the ticket-seller. Twenty or thirty slimmer, zippier specimens—in long skirts or slinky pants, and wearing great blobs of blue or green eye shadow—frolicked about the dance floor doing what I seemed to recall as the twist. There were only about half as many men out there, but no one seemed to mind. I noticed, with some surprise, that most of the dancers were very *good* dancers. They all knew a great many very intricate steps and routines and had a full repertory of arm, hand, and hip movements. But they were all in such deadly earnest, like marathon dancers doing it for money instead of for fun.

I made my way to the bar and surrendered my free drink ticket, then, glass in hand, found an empty table. Now I looked at the men. In addition to the few on the floor, fifteen or twenty others circled the room, in both directions, like a Latin *paseo*. Hawaiian-print shirts were clearly the height of chic here, and so were hairpieces, and paunches, and those Western string ties with sliders. I was far and away the baby of the crowd. If that "35 to 100" sign was supposed to be funny, it was the "35" that was the big joke.

I sipped my warm drink and watched the scene while the *paseo* crowd watched me—in fact, studied me from every angle. I had just decided to make my escape when someone pulled out the other chair at my table and sat down.

"Mind?" he said, although he was already comfortably settled. "New here, aren't you? Never saw you before. Care to dance?"

He reminded me of my father's oldest brother, a gentle man and my favorite uncle, so I said, "Sure. Why not?"

As we reached the floor the band, without warning, launched into a tango. Uncle seized me with a grip of iron and proceeded to walk me first this way, then that, sometimes pushing me down so that my knees bent; every time I thought I had the direction right, he swooped me the other way. "Just relax," he advised. "Nothing to a tango. Just keep your head turned the way you're going (if only I knew!) and think 'slow, slow, quick quick, slow.' Good! Real good! I was asking you before. You new in town? Just tonight? Here? In the motel? Hey, that's great! Whaddaya say we cut out of here and have a little nightcap up in your room, huh? I've got a pint in the car."

I mumbled something about making the opening speech at commencement at the crack of dawn, broke the iron grip, and did a broken-field run across the floor. As I made my way through the lobby, three or four of the loungers came to life and asked me if I wanted a lift.

I ducked into my room like a thief, glancing behind to make sure I hadn't been followed. The room looked infinitely better than it had before and I was just in time for the eleven o'clock news. I hadn't met my dream man but I *had* had an adventure. All it cost me was five bucks, a slightly sprained knee, a shoeful of somebody's drink, and one very small cigarette burn on the end of my scarf. Maybe it could have been worse—but I couldn't think how.

One of the most unpleasant aspects of many singles events— true of all cruising situations—is the suspicion with which strangers regard each other; each fears being rejected or em- barrassed, getting stranded with a bore, being exploited sexually or financially—or having his or her own exploitive intentions detected. It is probably no accident that one of the largest and most active New York clubs is named "Le Jungle."

In addition, the atmosphere of many of the functions, espe- cially those sponsored by social clubs, is often soured by the low self-esteem of those present. Sam Blum, a writer who often reports on the American social scene, said in a *New York Times Magazine* article on social clubs for the middle-aged, that a divorced person who shows up at such a club is generally assumed to be the rejected one (the ex-spouse, the assumption goes, had someone waiting). Accordingly, patrons of social clubs regard each other—and themselves—as losers, and the clubs as their last resort. When Blum asked one woman why she came to the club despite its obvious drawbacks, she replied simply, "It's better than suicide."

Not all singles clubs are dismal, however, and not all club members are rejects and losers. One New Jersey club for profes- sional people only, specializes in group attendance at cultural events: they buy blocks of seats for the theater, concerts, or the ballet, charter buses to carry members to museums or on weekend trips of various sorts, go to weekly Dutch-treat dinner parties in restaurants. While some pairing off inevitably takes place, the group generally operates as a unit so that no one feels rejected, excluded, or exploited. A divorced woman in her forties described the club as "the warmest, most caring, best bunch of friends I've had since high school—and you wouldn't believe the fun we have!" The club is both exclusive and expensive and gets its new members only by recommendation from those who are already members.

The Barnard/Columbia Alumni Social Committee, also middle class, is not a committee at all but a singles club made up of several hundred never-marrieds and FMs ranging from twenty-five to the early forties and all graduates of Columbia University. It holds its meetings in handsome hotel suites and lecture rooms, and invites such distinguished speakers as Margaret Mead and Eli Ginzberg to address its members. *The New York Times* called the Barnard/Columbia A.S.C. "the city's most intellectual singles club," a good observation, for behind the serious façade, the main purpose of the meetings is none other than partner-shopping, which is done during the social periods (with pay-as-you-drink bar) before and after the lecture. The members, who tend to be better-dressed, slimmer, and more poised than most social club members, are also more talkative and outgoing—perhaps because of the common bond of their Columbia alumnihood. The club is successful because even if one meets no possible partner during the evening, at least he or she has heard a worthwhile lecture—and hasn't had to dance either with some stumblefoot or an exhibitionistic graduate of a Fred Astaire dance course.

Most singles clubs lie somewhere in between the extremes. Their advertisements and directory listings suggest the atmospheres one can expect to encounter:

> SINGLE, widowed, divorce
> in process (lonely?)
> Christian Singles Fellowship Club
> El Monte, Ca. 91732

> TUESDAY NIGHT PUB PARTY
> Miramar Hotel, Ocean Ave. and Wilshire
> Blvd., Santa Monica, Ca. sponsored by
> Malibu Singles. 5:30 P.M.

FIFTH AVENUE SINGLES Dinner & Show. Stouffers, 666 Fifth Ave., [N.Y.] Pershing Rm. Dinner at 6 for $4.50. Return to church at 7:30 to see "Shakespearean Scenes in Opera," performed by the Community Opera. Voluntary contribution.

> South Shore Widows and Widowers—a dance at the
> Elks Club, Veterans Blvd., Massapequa, L.I., from
> 9:00 P.M. to 1:00 A.M. There'll be over 100 people dancing
> to taped music. You don't have to be widowed,
> but you should be over 35 to feel comfortable.
> An open bar and snacks are included in the $6 admission.

Le Jungle—"Old Country Hoe Down" at La Pace, Continental Plaza, Hackensack [N.J.] at 8:00 P.M. An informal evening (wear your casual or country clothes) of all kinds of dancing—Latin, disco, and square. Free to members and trial members, $3 for non-members.

Such offerings hold out promise to a great many who have found the traditional ways of partner-shopping inadequate. But for most of them, the promise is not made good: there is a high rate of turnover in the social clubs, and many who pay a year's membership fee (usually $50 to $100) drop out after only a few visits. Yet some who come on a trial basis do discover enough of value to join and attend regularly; they find comfort in having a place to go and people to meet. A few do make friends, begin to date, and sometimes even develop lasting relationships.

But it is the higher-status, special-purpose clubs that have multiplied most rapidly to serve the great influx of new FMs into the singles population, for their members don't feel like losers and are not ashamed to belong or attend. Like the professionals and the alumni, many singles band together under some bond of fellowship and with some avowed purpose other than partner-shopping. Dances, discussion groups, cheese- and wine-tastings, picnics, and theater parties are held by charities, church groups, Parents Without Partners and similar organizations. And there are singles opera clubs, theater clubs, and tennis clubs, and a vast variety of Human Potential activities; the latter include encounter groups, sensitivity groups, EST, awareness seminars, and Transactional Analysis workshops. Even the supposedly therapeutic groups implicitly offer social contacts as well as growth experiences, and some are quite explicit about it; a recent ad in *New York* Magazine read:

I'm OK—You're OK. Workshops in Transactional Analysis.
Growth, Change, Fun, New Friends!

While all special-purpose events are considered "OK," a legitimate means of solving the legitimate problem of meeting peers, this is not true of all singles activities. Although many FMs use whatever means they can to meet partners, they all agree that some means are more acceptable than others. There is an onus that hangs over those clubs that are open to the public, and that have no activity other than dancing and drinking. The same is true of "open parties" held in the house or apartment of an amateur or semi-professional entrepreneur; they are advertised in newspapers and anyone with the price of admission (a few dollars) is invited. People who frequent such events often do so furtively and keep their activities secret from their friends.

And so do many who use dating services—even the latest video-tape kind—since paying a stranger to find possible partners is still suspect. It not only smacks of Old World matchmaking (and is, in fact, its lineal descendant), but violates the romantic tradition by which we are supposed to choose mates for ourselves on the basis of felt or intuited rightness—the "elective affinity" of the late-eighteenth-century romantics.

Even more widespread is the strong disapproval of the use of "personals"—those plaintive appeals to the fantasized ideal that appear in so many magazines:

> Divorced male, brown-haired, blue-eyed, 6' tall, college grad with well-established professional career; avocationally interested in music and the great outdoors; attracted to patient, common-sense, true-grit high-school teacher or R.N. types who value family ties and home life.

> Attractive woman, Jewish, 5'6", 105 lbs., psychology student, professional model, divorced, two children, sensual, charismatic, perceptive, dynamic, viable, real. You're 35–45, tall, attractive, professional, financially and emotionally secure, a 100% real American man. I prefer monogamy. Dislike: Plastic people, obesity, toupees. I'm vulnerable!

Was the poet, writing his love-lyric to that not-impossible she, where'er she be, any more unrealistic, any more surely doomed to disappointment?

And we did hear, among the formerly married, plenty of disgruntled and embittered comment about the new ways and means. Most of those who admitted to advertising via personals said that nearly all the replies are from "kooks" and "freaks" of one sort or another, and that those who place ads rarely look anything like their self-descriptions. Many who have tried dating services have found them equally disappointing. One woman's faith in computer technology was badly shaken when a man showed up to take her to dinner and proved to be four inches shorter than she (although she had specified her desire for a tall man), pedantic (she had said that she liked unpretentious people)—and in addition, he had double earlobes, which she couldn't help staring at in helpless fascination throughout the whole evening.

Unfortunately, there seem to be problems with all the mechanisms. In many of the clubs and organizations (including Parents Without Partners), women outnumber men by a large margin; moreover, the average social status of the men is often lower than that of the women. The explanation is, in part, that men have long been freer to hunt for new partners through unconventional methods (such as cruising), and therefore have not needed to turn to organizations as much as women have. Probably, too, many men still have a traditional feeling that the man is the hunter and stalker—a single predator, so to speak—and that to join an organization in the search for partners is to admit weakness, or inability to live up to the classic image.

The social clubs, as we have heard, may seem to some preferable only to suicide; as for the hotel dances and open parties, they were described as "meat racks," "discard heaps," and "creepsville" by three disillusioned people we interviewed.

The unabashed and voracious questing of the cruising scene in general is disconcerting and even repellent to many. One college-educated woman in a medium-sized southwestern city reported her initial alarm at this aspect of the new marketplace:

I had been married at sixteen years of age and I entered the world of seeking a partner for the first time at thirty-eight.... Man, was that a trip! I was astounded by the singles bars, the singles clubs, the open parties, the singles organizations,... at the common goal of single men and women searching for one another.

It's a whole new ball game at thirty-eight—but not really a game; it's played in dead earnest.

Nevertheless, she admits that after she got over her shock and learned to handle the new situation, she found the uninhibited partner-shopping "useful." And this is rapidly becoming the norm. Although it remains true that the majority of separated and divorced people meet new partners primarily through two of the traditional methods—introductions by friends (especially FM friends), or parties given by other FMs—a large minority now find themselves turning to non-traditional ways and means, and finding them productive. Six out of every ten men in our survey said that since the early days of their postmarital lives, they had become more daring and more willing to take chances in their efforts to meet new women. A surprising 5 per cent of the men and 3 per cent of the women have used dating bureaus and introduction services—surprising because even these small percentages suggest that perhaps three times as many FMs are using such services today as in the early 1960's.[5] And far larger minorities named one or more of the new ways and means as a principal source of dates: for instance, one man in six and one woman in five named public events, including all the many kinds we have mentioned above, and fully half of the men and women named singles organizations. Since so many of our questionnaire respondents were members of Parents Without Partners, it may seem that this last datum proves little about FMs who are *not* PWP members; however, it does prove that an organization with stated purposes other than partner-shopping—and millions of FMs do belong to such organizations—can also be an effective source of new-partner contacts.

And that is certainly true of PWP, despite its imbalance in numbers and social level between the male and female members. Its officers publicly maintain that its purpose is not that of serving as a dating bureau, an identity that has far less prestige than that of a service organization offering support, advice, and parent-child activities. But some of them admit the truth from time to time—and even occasionally publish that truth. PWP's national journal, *The Single Parent*, recently reprinted a comment written by Dave Sherk, an officer of the Huntsville, Alabama, chapter.[6] Whatever the official position about PWP, Sherk said, in truth it is primarily a social organization—but

> one with a vital difference. And that difference is this: we have class. The bounder, the artist-on-the-make, the gold-digger, the cad—they are all found out and . . . [eventually] shunted to one side. We are, inexorably, a dating outfit . . . but we are like the genuine aristocracy of old, in that we do have some very exacting standards.

Like him, a number of our survey respondents seem pleased— and a few wildly enthusiastic—about the results that can be obtained by using the new ways and means of getting back into circulation. An unusual tribute to them was paid by a thirty-eight-year-old woman who is a school counselor in a Midwestern town. She had begun to fill out our questionnaire two years after her marriage had broken up. She rated herself as very attractive and had expected it to be easy to get back into circulation but had, in fact, found it very difficult. She completed only a small part of the questionnaire, then scribbled a dated note in the margin: "Have recently gone to both dating bureaus and computer service—don't know how it will work out." Months later we received the questionnaire with the following letter:

> This questionnaire is not complete, but I am sending it along anyway because I will never finish it. The reason is that my situation is rapidly changing and many of my answers are no longer valid. I went to a computer dating agency, I took out a subscription to and placed an ad in (as well as answered a couple of ads in) the *Singles News Register*. I got a different job and moved into ——— [a large city]—all of which increased my social life astronomically, plus bringing me into realistic proximity to educational opportunities, plus increasing my income 50%. My cup runneth over.

4. SWIM OR SINK

Within the first six months of post-marital life roughly three-quarters of the men and half of the women in our survey had begun going to parties, public events, or organization meetings. The same proportion also had their first dates within that period, and by the end of the first full year, five-sixths of the men and nearly three-quarters of the women had done so.

Whether they found a rich social life or a meager one, highly desirable partners or mostly unacceptable ones, by virtue of their early reconnaissance most are adapting. Those who didn't reconnoitre at all are failing to adapt. A few of them remain withdrawn or cling to relatives and married friends; most of them will enter the world of the formerly married but either fail to attract any friends of the opposite sex or even deliberately avoid them for emotional or sexual reasons. Those who make the adaptation preserve their original vision of themselves as social and *partnerable* persons; the others abandon the vision and see themselves as solitaries.

Newcomers are often disheartened when they see how many of the formerly married remain alone, and they fear that this is the all-too-common outcome of the failure of marriage. But the first impression is misleading: non-adapters seem numerous because they accumulate in FM society, while adapters either marry or establish quasi-marital relationships and disappear from the scene.

Very few men and only a tiny minority of women whose marriages terminate when they are in their twenties and thirties remain alone. Those who are in their forties at the time of marital breakup are more apt to do so, particularly if they are women—chiefly because it is harder for them to find and attract partners.*[7]

Although the great majority of FMs do try, not all of them have an easy time getting into circulation. Nearly a third of the men, and half of the women in our survey sample said that they had found it difficult, or even almost impossible to meet partners. Still, two-thirds of the men and half of the women *did* find it easy, or, at worst, only moderately difficult.

And not only did the majority find it easy, or fairly easy, many found it less difficult than they had expected it would be. Nearly a third of those who had anticipated great difficulty found it not so hard after all. Only a quarter of the men and a sixth of the women expected that it would be easy to find partners, but twice as many found that it *was* easy. Apparently,

* The chances of remarriage will be discussed in more detail in Chapter IX.

many newcomers based their expectations on the obsolescent image of the FM as failure, dropout, or castaway; this is hardly the present-day reality.

The relative degree of ease or difficulty of achieving reentry runs pretty much as you would expect: obviously, if you are young, good-looking, interesting, financially solid, and self-confident, you will have an easier time of it than someone who is none of those things. But self-confidence may be the most important factor, since success in adjusting to post-marital life generally depends more on psychological factors than on physical or material ones. Middle-aged men make their social adjustment as easily, or even a bit more easily, than younger men, undoubtedly due to their greater self-confidence—the product of experience, status, and higher earning power. Discarders begin dating somewhat sooner than those who were discarded. The highly educated are quicker to date than the less educated. And so on.

But even though these and other data indicate that class, education, and other externals better one's chances of getting into circulation rapidly, it remains reassuringly true that each newcomer can exercise a great influence over his or her own destiny. Quick and easy resumption of social life depends in large part on participation in the marketplace, and one can speed up one's own adjustment by consciously pursuing all kinds of social opportunities, taking chances on new and unconventional methods of meeting possible partners, and deliberately becoming involved with groups of other unattached people. Any experienced FM knows that it's worthwhile to drop in at the Big Bore's party just to see who might be there.

The new permissiveness and the new ways and means of partner-shopping go far to democratize divorce by offsetting economic and other special advantages. The wide-open bazaar now permits almost all to enter and participate—if they will. Like most bazaars, the ambience is hectic, untidy, and often anxiety-producing—one may be tricked, sold shoddy goods, or robbed. For all that, FMs who adapt and who are willing to take chances tend to find, sometimes in unlikely places, the things they need: new friends, new relationships, healing and enlarging experiences, a new sense of oneself as partnerable. Those who cannot—or will not—adapt are defeated more by themselves than by circumstances.

Nancy Larkin, as we have already seen, swiftly made contact with the singles world, and within weeks was caught up in a round of social activities and dates.

Linda Grey was slower about it. It had taken her two months to realize she had to get out and look for her peers, and several more passed before she had any real success. The first two men she met were both dinner partners at the homes of married friends (after she called to say she would like to meet any unattached men they knew). She disliked one of the men on sight and found the other pleasant enough, but unexciting, even dull. Her lack of enthusiasm must have been evident in both cases for neither man ever called her although both had seemed attracted to her initially.

But those two contacts made Linda realize that there *were* men out there; it was just a question of finding the right ones. She realized that with a little effort, she could now slip rather easily into conversations about postmarital life with divorced colleagues at the university, and as a result, a woman on the administrative staff invited her to a Wednesday-night discussion session of a divorced-persons' group in a downtown church. Linda, a non-joiner, went with misgivings—which proved to be well-founded since she loathed everything about the evening. She found the meeting room depressingly dreary, and the people too old, too loud, too pushy, too blue-collar. She thanked the woman who had invited her, then said that she was going to be tied up for the next few Wednesdays.

But several weeks later Linda took a chance on something else far outside her usual purview: a singles cocktail party given by a woman in her department. She was surprised at how much she enjoyed herself —but she knew exactly *why* she did; two attractive and interesting men, a lawyer and an antique dealer, quietly competed for her company, and before she left both had asked for her telephone number. The lawyer called the next day to ask her to a buffet dinner party he was giving a week later, and the antique dealer called a day later to invite her to a Thanksgiving dinner a divorced woman he knew was giving exclusively for her divorced friends. Linda accepted both invitations and was filled with delight and pride. She had begun; she had set out to do it, and she had done it.

Bill Novak had no such luck. He saw his divorce counselor and tried to discuss his fears about trying to get into the singles world, but the discussion backfired. The counselor, ineptly, to be sure, kept asking Bill why he was so frightened of women and why he had such a low opinion of himself. Bill was so upset that he never went back.

He did, though, make some effort to break out of his solitude. He forced himself to attend a dance at a social club that he saw advertised in the paper, and while there, he signed up for a singles weekend at a mountain resort. The dance was a wretched ordeal. He felt utterly silly, standing around with a glass in his hand and trying to look nonchalant. Several women came over and spoke to him, but he found himself at a loss to respond to their bright chatter or to make small talk of any kind. He danced with two of the women—because they asked him to—and perspired profusely, more from embarrassment than from exertion. When one of the women asked if he could give her a lift home, Bill was seized by panic and stammered some idiotic and unconvincing excuse about a babysitter.

At the resort, Bill escaped to the nature trails immediately upon arrival and put off all problems until the evening. At dinner he looked around the dining room and spotted several attractive women, but he couldn't think of any way to approach one of them and start a conversation. One of the women did seem to be looking at him in a friendly and encouraging way— but what if he was wrong and she brushed him off, or was scornful, or amused?

So he did nothing. But later, during the floor show, a woman who had been at his table (and at whom he had not dared to look because she was so close) started to chat with him. By this time Bill had had two drinks and was feeling relaxed enough to get into a lively conversation. He ordered another round for both of them, began to feel mildly daring, and after a while found himself—at the woman's suggestion—walking her back to her room. There he did all the appropriate things until they reached the critical moment; then, to his horror, his body would not obey him. He apologized and said he must have had too much to drink; the woman made light of it and was very reassuring, so in a little while, Bill tried again—and failed again. He dressed, shaking, and rushed back to his own room. Too wide awake even to close his eyes, he waited for the first light of dawn to appear, then packed his bag and fled.

That was nearly a year ago. Bill has made no further effort to become part of the singles world. He has attended a few parties given by married friends, and although he met a total of three unattached women on these occasions, he felt that one of them found him boring, and the others were too aggressive for his taste. Bill tries to combat his sense of failure by telling himself that at fifty-two sex just isn't important any more (hadn't he read that Freud himself gave it up even earlier?). Besides, he tells himself, life is so much more peaceful without a woman around. For companionship and something to do after work, he has become active in the local Republican Club and this brings him into contact with other people and gives him a pleasant sense of accomplishing something worthwhile and being respected. He doesn't need anything more, he tells himself.

IV

Dating–Old Game, New Rules

1. BEGINNER'S NERVES

Unaccountably, his mind slips him back to the house he grew up in. His older sister is pounding on the bathroom door yelling, "For Pete's sake! Will you please, please, *please* come out of there? I have to *go!*" Why? Why this particular image, so sharp now, after so many years? But then, feeling the cold edge of the washbasin against the tops of his thighs as he leans forward to study himself in the mirror, he makes the connection, and he knows why.

Who would have thought that a mature man of forty, married and separated, would act and feel exactly like a teenager getting ready for a first date? Would stand before the mirror again examining hair, pores, teeth? Rehearsing smiles, frowns, gestures? How disconcerting, how *annoying*, to feel like a jittery and inexperienced adolescent again after having made such an enormous investment in becoming an experienced and mature human being! But so much time has passed since his premarital dating, so much change has recently taken place in the ways that unmarried men and women behave with each other, that he rightly fears to be a kind of Rip Van Winkle, quaintly dressed, using obsolete expressions, wandering lost and alien in what used to be familiar territory.

Most second-time beginners feel much like adolescents—and in some ways, worse. All the hours of broiling in the sun, the days spent in work and play, the nights without sleep, the countless shufflings and breakages in the molecules of DNA in the cells, have made innumerable alterations in the skin and in the flesh beneath it. How will this somewhat used and time-worn body appear to another who looks at it with the appraising eyes of a date? And what of the equally time-worn personality, scarred and shaky from the breakup of a marriage? How will the other person react to one's history, with its record of past successes and failures—so unlike the blank pages of teenage years, upon which an ideal history might yet be written?

Still, the other-person-of-the-first-date has done some living, too, and *might* understand and sympathize. What if, from the moment he and she meet, they feel a current of attraction between them? What if they discover that they have had similar experiences and share the same enthusiasms? What if they look at each other in surprise and say, "You too?" What if . . . the daydreaming mind enters the theater of fantasy, sinks down comfortably in the dark, enraptured by the scenes magically unfolding on the screen, and only breaks away to rush into the fresh air of reality when reminded by the clock that it's time to get ready, for the actual date is at hand.

There are so many things to worry about, so many questions for which the second-time beginner has no answers.

Fred Gustafson, a Chicago real-estate agent, has been mulling about some of them ever since he made a date with an attractive middle-aged woman who came to his office apartment-hunting last week. Fred, whose thirty-two-year-long marriage fell apart half a year ago, is a silver-haired, slightly paunchy, and rather dignified man of fifty-seven, but today, with his first date imminent (the word "date" makes him squirm, but he can't think of another), he is acting like a boy. His partner has asked him twice this morning whether there's anything wrong; both times Fred had been staring out the window and sighing heavily. What his partner didn't even know was that he had also dialed three wrong numbers, forgotten to return an important call, been an hour late for an appointment, and was uncharacteristically testy with his secretary when she interrupted his train of thought to ask him a question.

As soon as she closed his door (a little harder than necessary) the thoughts began again. How should he act on a date? He has read so much about the new manners of equality; will the woman think him sexist if he helps her on with her coat or strikes a match for her cigarette? (Does she smoke? He doesn't know. If not, will she find it disgusting if he smokes? Or consider him stupid, or weak?) Will she think he's a male chauvinist for having picked out a restaurant without consulting her? If they cross the street from the parking lot to the restaurant, should he change sides to walk near the curb, or will that strike her as silly and demeaning?

His thoughts drift back to the restaurant again. At first, he had made a 7:30 reservation at a showy, popular place—then canceled it in favor of a small, quiet French restaurant. Now it occurs to him that if they got there at 7:30, they'd probably be finished by 9 or 9:30—and then what? A night club? Fred hates them. Dancing? He loves it, but doesn't know how people dance these days, thinks she would find his graceful ballroom style too old-fashioned. After-dinner drinks at some bar? Almost as bad as a night club—and perhaps she (like Fred) doesn't care to drink after dinner. So now Fred changes the reservation to 8:30 and decides to take her to a skytop lounge for a drink first. That way, by the time dinner is over, it will be late enough to call it an evening if it isn't going well and he (or both of them) wants to escape. He gets up from his desk to study his reflection in the glass door of the bookcase.

For days Fred has been fretting about his looks; he has bought a new velvet jacket, had his hair styled, and gone to the health club regularly. Now he leaves the office early, takes a workout at the club, then sits in the steam room wishing the steam would instantly, miraculously, melt him down to a slimmer shape. He looks at his belly, tries to suck it in, and is filled with misgivings. He should have lost fifteen pounds before going on a date, before taking a chance that he might have to reveal this body. He isn't ready; perhaps he can call her and say there's an emergency. No, it won't do; he has to go through with it. Fred sighs, heads for the shower. A man of fifty-seven, he tells himself, shouldn't act like a scared kid.

Jennifer Hays finds the day remarkable because it seems to drag on so slowly—and because, at the same time, she hates seeing the hour of her date draw closer. Jennifer, thirty, is at home with her three-year-old son in a suburb of Atlanta (she used to teach, and hopes to find a job when Sam is in the first grade). All morning she cleaned and polished the house, mentally grumbling: he probably won't even notice—and what if he does? Who wants to be a *House Beautiful* woman, anyway? That's her mother's act, not hers. Little Sam tugs at her skirt, wants her to help him build a Lego car. Jennifer wishes he'd leave her alone, but though she begs off Lego, she agrees to read to him for a while. She does, and her thoughts are elsewhere the whole time.

After lunch, during Sam's nap, she showers and washes her hair, studies her body in the mirror, finds it firm and slim—but flat-chested; she is immediately irritated with herself for her self-critical attitude. Next, she drags out several outfits, lays them on the bed, then tries them on, one after the other, but still can't decide what to wear.

When Sam wakes up they leave for the supermarket. Absent-minded, she drives through a red light which is called to her attention rudely by a furious truck driver; the incident leaves her shaken and jittery. She tries to focus on driving but instead wonders how much to tell her date if he asks why her marriage broke up. (It's humiliating to say that her husband fell in love with her best friend.)

Back from the market, she tries to imagine what her date will turn out to be like. She met him briefly at a party, found him attractive and interesting—but a trifle too young, perhaps? And maybe a bit overbearing, too sure of himself? He's taking her to a cocktail party and then to dinner. What will happen afterward? Surely he won't expect—not on a first date—yet what if he *does*? Jennifer wouldn't want to (she had slept with only three men before her marriage, knew them all well, and cared for them in varying degrees), and even if she did, she had stopped taking the Pill when her husband left.

But suppose he does try? Will she be flustered or graceful in her refusal? Will he take it pleasantly or be hurt or angry? Or if—just for the sake of argument—she did want to (there's always her old diaphragm, put away somewhere), where would they do it? She has never locked her bedroom door; what if Sam woke up with a bad dream, came running and found the door locked?

The clock strikes five. Good Lord!—only an hour to go, and she still has to feed and bathe Sam, straighten up the living room once again, and then get dressed. Her finger tips feel strangely cold, and she suppresses a shiver, although the house is warm. She wonders if she should take a hot shower to warm up, but there's no time. Damn!

Nor is this all that worries the FM who begins to date again.

How does a woman explain to the children why a man is coming to the house? If they're very young, she can just say he's a friend of Mommy's, but this makes her feel as if she's being less than honest—and children always sense evasions anyway. If the children are older, they may be hostile—or worse, they may giggle and smirk when she tells them, even act incredulous: "*You're* going on a *date*? Why?" She could, of course, meet the man elsewhere and simply hide him from her children, but it goes against the grain, makes it seem as if her having a date is shameful or wrong. (In fact, fewer than one out of ten women ever hide from their children the fact that they are dating.) But explain as she will, she can't help worrying about how the children will behave when he arrives.

If the man is new at dating again, he worries, too, for he has no idea how to act with a date's children. If he seems fatherly and interested, she might think he's being phony, trying to win her approval. But if he seems uninterested, she might be offended, find him cold and unfriendly. He certainly never worried about any of these things before, when he met his married friends' children—but this feels distinctly different.

And so does the question of how much to spend for dinner. If he spends too much, she might think him vulgar, ostentatious. If it's a fine night and the restaurant is only five or six blocks away, might she find it pleasant, as he would, to walk there—or might she think him cheap for not taking a cab? For that matter, is he expected to pay for everything? Ten years ago or twenty (whenever he last dated), men were expected to pay, but today, he hears, some women prefer to preserve their independence by splitting costs. Besides, if he pays alimony, and his date *gets* alimony and also works, she may be better off than he. If she offers to pay her share, can he refuse? Should he accept? Will it make him uncomfortable? Will she think less of him, one way or the other?

And if they get along well during dinner and there seems to be some rapport between them, what then? What is expected or permissible between formerly married people on a first date? Would it seem only natural to her, or would it seem gross, if he were to embrace her, hold her close, and perhaps, by word or deed, suggest that they make love? Or if he doesn't, if he merely offers his hand goodbye, or kisses her on the cheek, will she think he doesn't care for her, or that he has a problem about sex? One hears so many things—but what do people really do?

With so much to worry about, it may be that the formerly married man or woman about to go on a first date feels even more stress than the teenager. And certainly, the mature person has more to lose—more self-esteem, a slowly acquired dignity, a sense of self, all subject to damage if not outright destruction. There is less time to experiment, to make mistakes, correct them, try again. There are more impediments and complications. There is a greater need for restorative, reassuring experiences. Above all, there is a much stronger sense of the strangeness of it all.

Who can blame any FM getting ready for a first date for having an attack of nerves?

2. RESEARCH AND DEVELOPMENT

After all the worry and anxiety, how does the first date work out?

Sometimes badly, sometimes well, most of the time passably. But however it works out, it is almost always full of surprises and revelations—unexpected behavior by the other person and discoveries about oneself. And the surprises, agreeable or not, are all valuable, for the first dates serve latent purposes; more than a recreation or a way of filling a gap, early dating performs two important functions that ease the transition to postmarital life.

First, it is a means of *socialization,* a form of training in the customs and values of the world of the formerly married, particularly that area concerned with dating and pursuit, with sexual needs, satisfaction, testing, and exploitation, and with emotional needs and involvement.

Area?—*arena* is more like it, for the games played in it are far faster, tougher, more intricate, and bloodier than any that the unmarried young play. Not only are one's partners—who sometimes seem more like opponents—more socially skilled than the unmarried young, they are also much more complex as personalities, more in conflict with themselves, more cautious in many ways, and yet more driven to take chances. And they are a more diversified and hence a more bewildering lot: the young tend to date within their own immediate peer groups based on school, neighborhood, and church associations; but the formerly married, using less orthodox and selective mechanisms, meet and date people whose life experience, habits, and expectations are often radically different from their own. In addition, one's date may be in any of the various stages of postmarital adjustment and so have feelings, needs, and aspirations different from one's own.

The second important function of dating is *self-reappraisal*—important because it leads to self-development. Dating provides a series of learning and growth experiences (in hit or miss fashion, to be sure) through which one reappraises his or her personality, tries out new ways of behaving that are appropriate to the new way of life, and begins to expand certain facets of the inner self which have had little or no exposure or growth in the past. The person who takes shape and emerges is not merely restored, but often significantly altered and greatly enlarged.

The process begins with the first dates. Sometimes they yield dismaying revelations of awkwardness, fearfulness, or hostility to the other sex, and such revelations, depressing though they often are, usually impel the person to start taking corrective action. But more frequently, the first dates yield discoveries of quite a different sort: the FM, it appears, is generally a far more appealing and desirable human being than she or he had thought, quite unlike the image so recently reflected in the distorted and discolored mirror of the failing marriage.

A few brief accounts will suggest how widely first postmarital dates can vary and yet, despite their differences, can all administer a first dose of socialization and self-reappraisal.

To begin, here is feminist author Susan Braudy's description of her first postmarital date at age twenty-nine, five weeks after the breakup of her six-year marriage:[1]

> Last night I went on my first postmarriage date. Harrowing. George...called me to initiate me into "the dating culture." ...When [he] came through the front door, I found myself nervously stumbling through a conversation. At the restaurant he insisted on ordering for me, making me feel self-conscious and a little helpless. By the time we were having a demitasse, I felt as though I had completed only two full sentences, while he had spun out several anecdotes proving that he was the best and most sensitive of journalists. I found myself concentrating on keeping my lips smiling. I noticed we weren't making any eye contact at all. At the evening's end he asked me back to his apartment. I was bewildered and almost said yes. When I declined, explaining I had to go to work the next day, George yawned and hailed me a cab. "You must be shattered by your marriage breakup," he said testily, slamming the cab door.

A thirty-two-year-old man, a department manager in a large store in an Eastern city, told us that as a new FM he believed that six years of marriage "had turned me into an utter bore." Worried about supporting his wife and two children, he had worked slavishly, with little time out for recreation. A passive and willing martyr, he spent many evenings babysitting while his wife went out—which she did more and more often, since she had a lover for whom she eventually divorced her husband.

In addition to feeling like a bore, he said, "I guess primarily because of my wife's continual unfaithfulness I concluded that I was a sexual dud." As a result, when he started dating, his sexual ability was uppermost in his mind and he was eager to test it, but he didn't know how to make a graceful or effective approach. He reports what happened:

> The third time we dated, even though I had been too shy to kiss her goodnight the first two times, I just plain asked her to go

to bed with me. She was shocked, but she did somehow say yes. I wasn't too surprised when I turned out to be impotent, but I didn't much like it. The very next night I went out with someone else and tried again and the same thing happened. I got so depressed then that I decided to see a psychiatrist, and when I told him my troubles he said that both the impotence and the depression were expressions of rage with myself for being such a dope with my wife, and letting her use me the way she did. Within three weeks of beginning treatment I began to think maybe I wasn't such a bore after all, and by now, my sex life is pretty good.

By way of contrast to these two dismal (but educational) early experiences, here is a thoroughly joyous (and even more constructive) one. The narrator is a strikingly attractive woman whose fourteen-year marriage was so stormy, and ended in so brutal and ugly a fashion, that she did not date for nearly two years after the divorce. Then, when she was thirty-eight:

A friend fixed me up with a blind date. I accepted to please her and my mother, who wanted me to start going out. My sons were excited and delighted for me. And I—I cried! I could hardly bear the thought of being untrue to my ex, even though there was no reason to feel that way.

The man turned out to be a lovable cuss. He drank like a whale and smoked all through dinner, and came on very strong. At first it scared me. I realized how completely vulnerable I was to a male —especially this one. I made up my mind early on that he was definitely not my type and that I just hated him and wouldn't ever go out with him again—if I even got home in one piece the first time.

But, you know what? There was something so charismatic about that character that by the end of the evening I forgot all about being scared and I was enjoying him like I have never enjoyed anyone. Of course I went out with him again and again, and he eventually came to play an important part in my life.

An account of another successful first date comes from an engineer in the public works department of a Southern city:

I was thirty-three when I left my wife after being in a really empty marriage for nine and a half years. I felt like a cork that had been hooked on an underwater log and had just worked loose and shot up to the surface; I bobbed up and down on a high. I still refer to it as "the day I broke out." I expected to find it difficult to get started again, and having been intimate with no one but my wife for ten years, I was unsure of myself and felt unprepared. But I broke into single activities almost at once, almost two weeks to the day after I split. I went to a PWP meeting, and as luck would have it, I met a woman who needed a ride home. On the way, I suggested (nervously) that we stop at a lounge for a drink, discovered (honestly!) that I didn't have enough funds for a second drink, so suggested (*very* nervously) that we have the second at my apartment. She agreed, we did, I put on some music, we danced, I hinted that we go to bed—and nearly fainted when she accepted.

It was an evening of discoveries, of lots of *Ah-hah's* about myself as a person and as a lover that filled me with pride.

A thirty-five-year-old West coast teacher gave us the following account of her early dating:

On my first date I was amazed to be considered an attractive, appealing female. And I was humbled and shocked by how desperately I wanted to feel cared for and (gulp) taken care of. I kept wondering what had happened to the self-sufficient, independent wife I had been, the one who believed in open marriage?

The man I was with was very attractive and it made me uneasy to realize that his looks, physical condition, and height were so very important to me—again, this was contrary to what I thought I knew about myself.

As if that weren't enough, I was frightened by how inept I was at male/female approach maneuvers, and I was/am concerned about how incompletely I've dealt with the task of becoming an autonomous person. In that respect I'm a thirty-five-year-old adolescent—ripe with undeveloped potential.

Good, bad, or indifferent, the early dates of the formerly married are a virtual laboratory, an environment in which to observe behavior, perform tests, and make a number of discoveries about others and about themselves.

At the outset, one is most aware of testing and practicing new role behavior. After having talked to, walked beside, and sat across the table from one husband or wife for a number of years, it is distinctly strange to do those things with a stranger, and in the role of that person's date. The kind of smile you smile, exactly how long you look into the other's eyes, are only some of the hundreds of subtleties of behavior that express the role of date and the relationship of date-to-date. At first, you feel as if you are participating in a complex religious ceremony in an exotic culture, desperately afraid of making some grievous error.

And beyond the details of body language, one wonders what overall persona one should present. Every FM, whatever the truth of his or her feelings, has available for use the roles of the lonely sufferer, the courageous escapee, the late-blooming hedonist, the earnest seeker of a more meaningful life, or any one of a number of others that are both possible and plausible for a recently separated person. Which one fits best? Each FM tries them on, tests them, selects a role.

Simultaneously, he or she is busy trying to learn new customs, for the dating practices of the formerly married derive from their own special circumstances and are different in some respects from those of young singles. Women with children may prefer to meet their dates rather than be called for, in order to avoid presenting too many new faces to their children, to avoid tears at departure time, or to withhold from the man (for the first date or two, anyway) the homey but unglamorous sight of diapers, playpens, and toys on the floor.

Then too, many forms of traditional chivalry are on the decline or have even gone out of style now and this has some special meaning for the formerly married. Men who are heavily burdened with alimony and/or child support are fairly often happy to let a woman pay her own way, or even, sometimes, pay for both of them; women, aware of the financial burdens of many men, invite them to their homes to dinner, or buy a pair of tickets for the theater or a concert; men who go to work early, or who have custody and leave babysitters with the children, may prefer to let their dates go home unescorted.

But these are all minor matters. The most startling change that one has to get used to is that FMs are too pressed for time, too desperately in search of the "right" person, to waste many hours on a first date that might not go well. The experienced FM commonly makes the first date just for a drink, apologetically mentioning some meeting or other that is to take place later the same evening. At some point he or she goes to a telephone, fakes a call, and—depending on the success or failure of the date so far —says ruefully, "I checked, and they're there ahead of time, waiting for me, so I'll have to leave," or, announces gleefully, "Hey, they've canceled, so I'm free for dinner if you are!" There are other techniques, all fairly transparent but all more or less face-saving, and sparing of the time and energy of the FM who feels like the impatient Andrew Marvell:

> But at my back I always hear
> Time's wingèd chariot hurrying near.

As the new FM soon discovers, one of the striking differences between the dating of young singles and the formerly married is the speed with which the latter learn about each other on the first date. Most beginners are made quite uncomfortable by the directness of the assault ("Are you divorced or just separated? How long? Do you have children? Get along with your ex? Pay (get) alimony? What do you do? Where do you live?"), but as soon as they become accustomed to it, most of them feel that, for the first time in years, they are talking about "real" things, for as soon as the preliminary questions are out of the way, FMs move right on to discuss their own deepest longings, fears, hurts, and joys. Beginners are frequently astounded at the amount of intimate information they can exchange on a first date.

The single young are far slower to confide, not just because of a greater hesitation to reveal themselves, but because they don't yet have a great deal that they need to confide. But the formerly married have souls like old attics, stuffed to bursting with the collected memorabilia and leftovers of a lifetime, including the treasures and trash of marriage and post-marital life. A few are too reticent to engage in personal talk, but most take advantage of a first date to indulge in an intense exchange of biographies, a trading of stories, a swapping of one *apologia pro vita sua* for another. The new role is rehearsed as the pair present themselves either as they see themselves or as they wish to be seen. They are fascinated by each other's conversation—but even more by their own. "The reason lovers never weary of being together," said La Rochefoucauld, "is that they never stop talking of themselves." He could have been speaking of FMs dating new people. Even those who dislike confiding may find it not without compensation, as this man points out:

What I dislike most about dating is having to explain my divorce; the question always seems to come up on the first date. Since it was due to my wife's compulsive sleeping around, I either have to explain it in full or expect the woman to take me for a sexual incompetent. So I go into all the gory details, which are pretty boring, I guess—but it's not without its rewards: about half the time I end up going to bed on a first date since the subject of sex just seems to lead to it.

To be sure, there are hazards in talking about oneself. Those who feel mistreated or abused by their ex-spouses may sour the occasion with prolonged diatribes; those who were abandoned may do it with lengthy lamentation or with expressions of longing for the lost partner. "It really bothers me to go out with a guy whose woman has 'done him wrong,' " says one outspoken divorced woman. "It's all he can talk about. I tell friends who are trying to fix me up with poor old Ted to please spare me; I know I'd just waste an evening with another melancholy baby." The poor old Teds occasionally recognize, belatedly, that they have overshot the mark. A man admits that it was only after a number of unsuccessful dates that a brutally frank woman finally told him the truth: she said he sounded "like a first-class masochist and a number-one injustice collector." "I complained and whined too much about my divorce," one woman says, "and it really put men off, but it took me a while to realize it."

But for most, the early exchange of personal stories is highly utilitarian. A woman put it bluntly: "The likely candidates surface, the unlikely ones sink, straight off. It saves a lot of time." Another says, "It's how you know whether to bother—you look for a kind of telepathy, an instant understanding and sharing."

Beginners, listening to themselves pouring forth their own stories on a first date, are astonished and delighted by their unsuspected ability to be so open and emotionally outgoing—and to act as empathetic listeners and elicitors of confidences. One man, a thirty-seven-year-old computer programmer, says, "My wife had always complained that I was a cold, guarded kind of person and it was wonderful to find out that I could be—am —just the opposite."

Most FMs like most of what they discover about themselves through early dating. Among discoveries frequently cited by

FM men and women are that they are more interesting, more intelligent, and more physically appealing than they had realized. Here are a few typical statements:

[Man, thirty, salesman] I learned that others see me as considerate, attractive, and responsible, even if moody at times.

[Woman, thirty-six, teacher] I'm much more interesting to men than I ever imagined I was. I have a new respect for my own head and my own personality.

[Man, forty-four, liquor-store owner] I really appeal to women, both as a human being and physically. What a discovery! I had no idea about myself.

[Woman, thirty-four, nurse] It's great to feel wanted by many men. My ex-husband always wanted to change something about me—butt, bust, face, hair, etc. I didn't like my body, thought it ugly. Now I feel accepted—and self-accepting. It's not a great body, but it's me—and I generally like me.

A host of other positive self-discoveries are also reported by our survey respondents: sensitivity, enthusiasm, willingness to try new things, greater sexual capacity or intensity than formerly, a good sense of humor, intelligence, competence; the list goes on and on. Whether or not all of these self-assessments are accurate, we cannot be certain; probably some part of what people learn about themselves is an artifact of the dating relationship, in which each presents a best self and tends to act admiring or approving of the other. But in the main, the discoveries are real, for the dating relationship is corrective of many distortions of the bad marriage interaction and restorative of the valuable traits of personality that had been lost in the fray. Moreover, the marital breakup was a crisis, and crises—as is now well-established—are not usually wholly destructive; often, they disrupt habitual or rigid modes of thought and feeling and make possible an expansion of the personality that would have been impossible in a stable, undisturbed life style.[2]

Dating plays a large role in just such an overhauling of the personality—even though most of the FM's dates are far from perfect. One third of the people FMs date turn out to be so disappointing or inappropriate that the two never date again. And even among those couples who do continue to date, very few find each other so suitable as to be possible future mates. Yet most FMs benefit from these imperfect pairings—and do so even when their findings about themselves are negative. One man in six and one woman in six discovered that they suffered from personality faults, or sexual fears or inadequacy, or social ineptness, and the like—but nearly all responded with earnest efforts to improve rather than with hopelessness or retreat.

One woman recognized that she was doing poorly in her early dates because she was unduly fearful of saying or doing anything for which she might be criticized—a behavior pattern left over from her marriage—and as a result, she was acting stiff, formal, completely without spontaneity or joy. She loosened up.

A man made a thoroughly unpleasant discovery about himself but used the knowledge constructively:

> I came off as a very critical and judgmental person, very bitter, very hard on other people (so several angry women told me). I had to take a good long look at myself and begin to try to accept people who weren't as hard-working as I, or as reliable, or as moral, or whatever. It took about a year and a lot of sessions of group therapy, but eventually I began to find women liking me much more than they had before.

But by the time people can speak like that, they are no longer novices suffering from beginner's nerves; they have had time to feel at ease with the ways of their peer group, to establish themselves comfortably in their new role. They are wiser by far about themselves than formerly—not yet as wise as they will be, but all in all, very different from the people they so recently were.

3. SHE: *DO I HAVE TO?* HE: *SHOULD I TRY?*

Nothing is so anxiety-provoking for the novice as questions of sexual behavior: Should I, shouldn't I? Will he, will she? Must I? What if I do, what if I don't? These are understandably major issues of vital concern to new FMs for the simple reason that while they hear all sorts of rumors, they are completely unfamiliar with the rules; they don't know what to expect of others and don't know what others will expect of them.

They are well aware, of course, that the sexual liberation movement of recent years—quite recent, because its full impact wasn't felt until the 1970's—has greatly modified the sexual behavior of youth. But what does that have to do with the formerly married? The inexperienced have no idea whether FMs are as sexually liberated as the unmarried young, or more liberated, or less so. They wonder if the formerly married behave, sexually, as they did in their own premarital days, or in some wildly promiscuous, thoroughly alarming fashion. They have little idea what is customary, permissible, or likely to happen on a first date.

Recall, for a moment, that the typical new FM is a woman of about thirty, or a man in his early thirties, who had been married for some six years. These median people, and certainly the great majority to either side of the medians in age, are bound to feel ignorant of and apprehensive about what lies ahead sexually. Few of them experienced the major impact of sexual liberation before marriage, and in any case, they have had years of monogamous conditioning since then; even those of them who were unfaithful during marriage were, for the most part, involved in affairs rather than in swinging single society. Consequently, while some fear that what they have in store sexually will be too wild for them, and others hope it will be as wild as their fantasies, nearly all are distinctly uneasy—and many are thoroughly anxious about it—when they begin dating.

Most commonly, a woman wonders whether her date will suggest sex on the first date or make an overt physical approach without verbal warning. If he does, how should she react? Her instinct would be to refuse—but, she asks herself, would that be abnormal in this new world? Might he think her some kind of prude or neurotic? Would he act polite and understanding, or scornful and nasty? Even if it's the expected thing, *how* expected is it—does she really *have* to, in order to have dates?

Most commonly, a man wonders whether he could—and should—suggest sex or make an overt physical approach on a first date. Is it permissible? If he does, will she reject him and think he's just one more crude, insensitive male, interested only in physical gratification? If he doesn't, will she be disappointed, think he doesn't like her? Or might she suppose that he's afraid of women, impotent, neurotic, a closet gay? Should he try whether he wants to or not? *Must* he?

It comes as a distinct surprise or even a shock to about half of all new FMs to discover that the world of the formerly married is sexually even faster paced, less inhibited, and more experimental than that of the unmarried young. As for the other half, they don't find the general idea particularly surprising, but they are startled by the fine points, the everyday rules of sexual behavior. The first big surprise is that formerly married men so commonly suggest intercourse (by word or deed) to women they hardly know, women they are dating for the first or second time. The second surprise is how commonly the women expect and accept such overtures.

Nearly six out of every ten women in our survey said that most or all of the men they had dated made some kind of serious sexual approach on the first or second date. Men understated the matter; only four out of every ten said they seek sex on a first or second date.* The difference is undoubtedly due to differing perceptions of what constitutes a serious approach. Women probably include jokes and innuendos, and physical contacts that are projected as merely friendly or affectionate, because they recognize the real intent behind them.

At first, many women are upset, angered, or revolted by the swiftness of the approach; some never do get used to or learn to deal with it. "Crude," loathsome," "animalistic" are only a few of the words they use. "Even gorillas have more finesse than most formerly married men," says one bitter Midwesterner. "At least they spend a little time sniffing and saying hello." Even in cynical, hard-boiled New York—"the city without foreplay" as Bruce Jay Friedman has called it—one attractive thirty-five-year-old magazine editor spoke in equally harsh terms:

> The first thing I learned as a divorced woman was what to expect on a date with a new man. I can sum it up in three words —dinner and bed. They seem to think there is no reason to get to know me as a person, or for me to get to know them. They don't see any need for a feeling of relationship or friendship, any reason to waste time taking a walk in the moonlight together or reading

---

* These figures from our 1976 survey are virtually identical to those in Morton Hunt's smaller survey of 1965.[3] The world of the formerly married was then sexually ahead of its time, so that today its sexual customs are already traditional, but the tradition is of its own making.

poetry or any of that good old stuff we used to believe in. It's just dinner and then back to his place or my place, and get to work! Pay off! Well, I've decided the hell with it; I'd rather stay home and read a good book.

A woman in Iowa summed up the dilemma she, and a fair number of women, face: "I find 'sex first, fellowship later' is alien and unacceptable to my value system. Do I have to compromise my values? *Should* I compromise them? Or should I be true to myself and remain in a noman's—spelled 'no man's'—land?"

But a minority of women are delighted by such immediacy right from the outset (and many more are pleased after they have had some experience), taking it not as a crass and impersonal exploitation of their bodies but as a reaffirmation of their desirability. Whether or not they accept, they enjoy the offers that are made on their first dates. A young woman we interviewed in Massachusetts recalled:

> I was so afraid the man would try on my very first date—afraid mostly because I thought that turning him down might make for an ugly end to the evening—but having sex with someone I'd known for only a few hours would make me feel like a whore; I need to care, first. As it turned out, he did try, and I did turn him down—and he seemed to understand why I wouldn't, and respected my feelings. But it was obvious that he was ready, and I found myself very titillated, very turned on by his excitement. After he left I felt terribly frustrated but very happy and good, because for the first time in a long while my juices were flowing and I felt like a fully alive woman.

"On my first date," writes a middle-aged woman from a Chicago suburb, "the gentleman gave me a rush act, which did wonders for my ego! It had been a year and half since I'd been intimate with my husband, so I welcomed it, and it seemed only natural for me to be intimate with this man."

Predictably, men are more often delighted than distressed by their discovery that sexual approaches on a first or second date are more or less the norm, and are acceptable even though they are not always accepted. They may learn about it through word of mouth from a veteran FM or from direct experience, either by trying it out spontaneously or getting hints from their dates;

these range from relatively subtle non-verbal signals of interest, to forthright prodding ("Aren't you going to ask me to sleep over?").

"I couldn't believe how easy it all was, how simple and natural," one forty-year-old Midwesterner said. "I learned that my old courting techniques aren't necessary any more, so I can cast them all aside and get right down to basics."

"It's so much more honest," says a middle-aged man, "so liberated; men and women are really equal, nobody's playing hide and seek."

A forty-five-year-old high school teacher in a large Eastern city writes, "Was astounded by the freedom of sexual expression among formerly marrieds. Great!"

4. "DATING AROUND"—A BALANCE SHEET

Safely beyond the first dates, and thereby graduated from earliest beginner status, most of the formerly married "date around" for months or, in rare cases, for years before getting deeply involved with one partner.

While dating a variety of people has great significance for a time, it occupies an ambiguous position in the value system of the formerly married. It is generally seen as enjoyable and exciting as well as an important and necessary stage in the process of postmarital adjustment and development. But at the same time, there is something a little sophomoric about the spectacle of adults dating around (the term itself lacks dignity), and most FMs consider it to be far less prestigious than having an exclusive, intimate relationship.

However, dating around is a self-liquidating activity; it meets certain emotional and social needs for a time, but in doing so, it brings about healing and growth which, eventually, make a single, loving relationship desirable and further dating both unnecessary and unwanted.

Thus, the limits of the dating period are governed largely by each individual's internal needs. Two cases serve as illustration that each individual's behavior is a result of internal much more than external factors.

Margaret Dogherty, a secretary in a Connecticut high school, loves dating around. Her married friends would be surprised if they knew, for they all assume she's just waiting for the right man to come along so she can settle down. Margaret *looks* (to them) like a settled type: neither a great beauty nor a femme fatale, she is a working mother of two teenage children, forty-four, short and a bit chunky, and going grey; she has the bright, chipper, friendly look and manner of a chickadee, and a generally wholesome, no-nonsense air about her.

A submissive and passive wife throughout her marriage—the "classic clinging vine" she says—Margaret left her husband three years ago, moved to another city, found an apartment and a job. It was the first time in her life that she had done anything of importance on her own, and it gave her a totally new view of herself and her capabilities. Eventually, she found the courage to make her way into FM society and that made an even greater change in her self-image. "I gloried in it right from the start," she says. "I loved being part of it all, I loved dating, dancing again, exchanging views with different men, having them pay attention to me. I learned that I was still young at heart, attractive to men, and capable of having fun." The best part, she adds, was the vibrant excitement of each new relationship, the marvelous diversity of experiences she could have—as long as she stayed free, disentangled herself quickly from any situation that threatened to become serious and exclusive.

> I enjoy this life more than being part of a couple. I don't like the imposed social life that a couple gets into, or the emotional drain that it involves if things aren't going well. I've been burned once—and I suppose I'll get over that stumbling block one of these days, but I haven't yet.

Richard Hartman is a telephone repairman in a city in the Northwest. Although he was married for ten years and has been an FM for two, he is still only thirty. Richard is a tall, rawboned man with a crewcut, bespectacled, earnest of manner, and curiously without humor. He is non-sectarian but deeply religious ("I pray every day to be a channel of God's Good"). He has strict ideas about sexual morality: although his ex-wife refused to have sex with him for the last three years of their marriage, he never sought it elsewhere, and even after they separated he remained celibate for another year, until the divorce was final; to distract himself from desire, he sought overtime work and spent many hours each week working out in a gym.

Then he joined a church-sponsored support group for the divorced and began what, for him, constituted dating around: he went out with three women during an eight-month period and saw two of them only one time. He comments on this phase of his life:

> My early dating experiences were somewhat invigorating and exciting. But since my convictions were and are quite conservative, I could never become an active part of the swinging single scene. Dating around is okay for those who enjoy it, but basically I felt that too many of the people I met were wearing a false face. Such tactics have been labelled "the games people play" but I never wanted to play such games. I desired an honest relationship, a meaningful relationship, in which I could really be myself, especially with a woman who would appreciate the loving good I had to offer, and who would create a family with me, in work, love, and cooperation, one in which I could raise my two children (my ex-wife will give over custody when I remarry). I prayed very hard that I might find such a woman, and God has blessed me with her—my fiancée, Verna, whom I met through the support group, and with whom I will be united two months from now.

Neither of these people, different as they are, represents an extreme. We encountered a few who never dated around at all either because they began an exclusive relationship with the first person they met or because they continued one that had started while they were still married; we also found a few—perhaps one man in twenty, one woman in fifty—who had dated a hundred or more different people over a period of years without having any major relationships at all. But the great majority of FMs fit somewhere between these extremes: within the first two to three years, the average FM man dates fifteen to twenty different women, the average woman dates seven to ten different men. Along the way, they may have two or three fairly intense affairs, but for most of them, it takes this much experience to ready them for a really enduring relationship.

Much of what FMs like about dating—and even those who

dislike it generally, do like it at times—is obvious: they themselves spell it out in such trite but nonetheless accurate terms as *fun, freedom, novelty, new world, pursuit, conquest, variety*. Of this cluster of words, *variety* is the focal one: dating provides a variety of faces, places, conversations, ideas, activities, emotions, sexual experiences. After all the years of limitation to a single partner and to a more or less fixed way of life, dating fulfills the opposite and long-stifled desire to have access to many partners, to taste and to sample, to try everything, to indulge one's whims, to live out one's fantasies.

In traditional terms, this is a typically masculine point of view, and, in fact, more men than women do enjoy dating. But a large minority of today's women have the same outlook as men, and the same reasons for enjoying a variety of dates; in part this is so because women have become increasingly independent and liberated, and in part because the FM woman needs time (just as the man does) to rediscover herself and to experience different kinds of partners in a safely uninvolved context.

And dating around *is* a way of avoiding involvement, for as long as one keeps moving, there is no danger of getting emotionally entangled. One woman who has two or three men on her active list (this is more or less the norm) feels that the list is her emotional insurance. She says, "Safety in numbers is what keeps me from making a mistake, getting into anything that can hurt me."

Another woman, a secretary in her mid-thirties, told us:

> I know a helluva lot more about men than women, so I ask the men I know about the women *they* know, in order to have a basis of comparison for my own characteristics and to establish some norms for my own behavior. I also "use" my dates to improve my social performance. Many of them have been important to me only as teachers and sounding boards for testing behavior, but this has been vital to me in making the transition to FM life.

Although few express themselves so clearly and candidly, many FMs are sharply aware that dating is a valuable learning experience. They consciously use it to acquire new social skills, and to test out new ways of acting and interacting. It also helps them to like themselves again—not just because they see themselves as restored, but because so often they see themselves as enlarged, liberated, and bettered.

Perhaps equally important is that FMs learn from dating what kind of person they feel most comfortable with, what kind of partner fits them best. They probably discovered in the failing marriage that their own ideas of their needs, formulated in adolescence, were either long out of date or wrong to begin with. Now they are fearful of making another mistake, and are eager to try out various other kinds of persons to ensure a right choice next time.

Dating provides the opportunity to interact with people who are different from each other, and who are also different from the ex-spouse in important ways. A woman whose spouse was domineering knows that she doesn't want another one like him, but she needs to find out whether she feels best in an egalitarian relationship or one in which she herself is dominant. A man whose wife was kittenish and rattle-brained may think he wants a womanly, intellectual partner—but until he tries various shades of womanliness and intellectuality, he doesn't know how much of it makes him feel good, how much becomes threatening. A man or woman whose ex-spouse was charming but selfish may need to experience a variety of other, less charming but more giving, partners before knowing his or her real needs.

Among other things the FM learns about potential partners is that, for the most part, other FMs are more congenial and easier to relate to than either the never-married or those who have been widowed. Of those we asked, only one man in thirteen and one woman in fifteen say they prefer dating never-married partners, and to a somewhat lesser extent, the preference is shared by even very young and childless FMs. FMs feel that they have less in common with never-marrieds than with other FMs; a thousand intimate, everyday experiences of marriages set them apart and cause them to find each other incompatible, alien.

The formerly married have equally negative feelings about widows and widowers. Only one man in fifteen, one woman in seventeen, prefers to date widowed persons; they are deeply fearful of the lingering loyalty to the dead mate—who often looks far better in memory than he or she ever did in the flesh, far better, indeed, than any living competitor. "I'm terrified of the glamorized departed," says one woman. "Widows have placed their departed on a pedestal," says a man, "and I'm beaten before I begin." "I can't talk about my marriage to widows," says another man, "because they have this superior, condescending, or even resentful attitude. If you're divorced it's because you fucked up, but in their case, it was *Fate* that did them dirt."

Not surprisingly, the majority of widows and widowers also prefer their own kind; while the bias isn't as strong as that of FMs, it does exist. "I can't relate to divorced people and their grievances against their former spouses," says one widow. Says a widower, "Divorced women will practically rape you and then start putting on the pressure to get married, ready or not. Widows aren't in all that much of a hurry."

More than seven out of ten FMs—men and women alike—definitely prefer dating other FMs, and among people in their thirties and forties the proportion is even higher. The predominant feeling, as one man succinctly put it, is "They have more in common with me." Other men and women say virtually the same thing, but in different words:

> [Man, forty-two] They tend to realize what's important in life—i.e., to agree with me about what *I* think is important.
> [Man, forty-five] They know the pain of failure, as I do.
> [Woman, fifty-one] We speak the same language.
> [Woman, thirty-eight] Never-married men haven't learned all those things you learn from living with another person, and widowers look down on a woman who has been divorced. With another FM I find that the fact of divorce gives us a common bond; we often discuss our respective cases with understanding and sympathy.

Despite all the advantages of dating around, a large minority of men and a majority of women dislike it. Many of these liked it at first and came to dislike it as they outgrew the need for it, but others disliked it from the start. Their reasons fall into three general categories.

The first group of reasons center around the machinery of dating—the business of inviting, planning, dressing, going, paying. These burdens still fall mostly on men, and it is from them that we hear most complaints of this type. A thirty-four-year-old dentist writes, "Marriage spoiled me. My wife and I liked to do things on the spur of the moment, which was good; I don't like having to plan things a week ahead of time, or to have to invent an activity just to have something to do on a date." Many other men similarly object to the trappings of traditional dating after having been married.

But few women echo these objections; in fact, many of them seem to like some of the very aspects of dating that men deplore. Yet, many women (as well as men) are troubled by artificiality and wasted effort. After the relative honesty of a marriage relationship—even a poor one—they distinctly object to phoniness, and women particularly dislike the obligation to be unfailingly charming to the man just because he has gone to some trouble and expense. "It's a chore to be witty and vivacious every time," says one woman, "especially with men who don't deserve it." "What drags me," says another, "is the high percentage of wasted time—evenings spent with men who turn out to be stupid, or boring, or heavy-handed and juvenile about pitching for sex. One guy reached across the table ten minutes after we'd sat down and pushed up my sleeves. 'What's that for?' I asked 'Just checking,' he said. 'Women with slender wrists are terrific in bed.' And I had to smile even though I felt like throwing my drink in his face. What a creep!"

And men, too, complain of the high proportion of disappointing experiences. One, a divorce counselor in his forties, writes, "I have to date so many to filter out the few who are compatible. . . . The ratio is about 10 to 1; that means that I waste nine evenings for every one that's worthwhile."

But whether they have enjoyed dating around or not, most FMs finally come to dislike it for the simple reason that its time has passed. It can be compared to the old German *Wanderjahr*, a year during which an apprentice traveled and improved his skills before settling down to the serious practice of his trade. So, for the formerly married, the dating period is a *Wanderjahr*, a time to travel from date to date, improving the skills that will enable them, once again, to practice the trade of loving, this time with unerring skill. When the *Wanderjahr* is over, they are eager to go home.

V

Sexual Behavior In The New World

1. GROUP PORTRAIT

Every known human society has had two sets of sexual customs and rules: one for the unmarried, another for the married. Our own society may be the first to have established yet a third set, generated by a population of separated and divorced people so large and so specialized as to require its own sexual mores and folkways.

Divorce has been common at certain other times and places (though never so common as today[1]) but the divorced person has generally reverted to the status and behavior of the unmarried person, often even returning to the parental home. Now, however, in our own society, this system no longer prevails. The formerly married are drawn together into a semi-separate social order and within it have created the pattern of sexual behavior that meets their special needs.

It is unlike the patterns of either their premarital or married years, but that is not to say that the sexual behavior of the formerly married is homogeneous; on the contrary, it is bewilderingly diverse—and for good reason. FMs come from all parts of the country and all social strata of society, and so bring with them into FM society widely varying sexual attitudes and customs. Moreover, FMs are not members of a stable order, but rather one of transition—a reconstructive and adjustive milieu; due to the very nature of that milieu, each individual's needs and behavior undergo constant change.

Nonetheless, sexual behavior in the world of the formerly married is characterized by widely known and accepted standards of behavior so that in order to understand the sexual behavior of individual FMs, we must look at the background against which it occurs—the sexual behavior of FMs en masse.

Casual Sex

As we have seen in the section on dating, casual sex is commonly acceptable among the formerly married; indeed, more so than among the unmarried young. A 1974 study by Morton Hunt, based on a major national survey of sexual attitudes and behavior, shows that even though young unmarried people are very favorably disposed toward sex before marriage, most of their own experience—particularly that of the women—is limited to partners with whom they have strong emotional relationships.[2] A small number of young women and a fairly large number of young men had some experience with casual (or "recreational") sex, but for most of them it consisted largely of occasional and brief experiments. Despite all the talk about sexual revolution, the majority of unmarried Americans under twenty-five still believe in what sociologist Ira L. Reiss calls "permissiveness with affection."[3]

But what about the formerly married? You might expect older people—and 90 per cent of FMs are over twenty-five—to be more conservative. You might also expect those who had been married, and are therefore "the marrying kind," to have a strong bias against sex without love. You would be wrong on both counts. Nearly three-quarters of the men and nearly two-thirds of the women in our sample have had at least some casual sex since becoming FMs; six men out of ten and five women out of ten have had nothing more than friendly feelings (or, at best, moderately affectionate ones) for most or all of their sex partners; and more than one man in four and about one woman in five have had purely physical relationships with most or all of their partners. A majority of women and a slightly larger majority of men have been in love with none or few of the people they have had sex with as FMs.

Egalitarianism

While men are still far more apt to be the sexual aggressors, most FM women are no longer timid about making their sexual desires known. Two-thirds of the men we asked said that at least some of the time, women were the ones to suggest sex first. Women confirm this: one out of five says that at least sometimes, she suggests sex before a man does.

Some men welcome such initiative but others wish the "good old days" were back and complain that they feel required to perform even when they don't want to. Some say that they are repelled by sexually aggressive women:

> I was amazed at the aggressiveness of women I met—women who made it plain after a dance or two that they would like me to take them out and wanted me to know that they weren't hampered by any outmoded conventions, etc. Many women I meet think no more of hopping into bed than they do of blowing their noses.

Many men would take a more positive view than this man's, but would agree that he has the facts correct. Four-fifths of the men in our sample say that when they make sexual advances on the first or second date they are accepted most of the time. Only one man in twenty-five says that he is rarely successful in such efforts.

But women see it quite differently. Only one in five says that she always or often accepts sexual advances on a first or second date, and another one in four says she does so fairly often. But more than half the women say they never accept first- or second-date proffers.

The difference in male-female estimates is probably due, once again, to differing perceptions. Since men like to think they are rarely turned down, they tend not to count their more feeble efforts or don't make a serious approach unless they feel fairly certain of success. Many traditional women get an ego boost from considering minimal overtures as serious efforts, and from seeing themselves as highly selective.

While the traditional woman is still in the majority, that majority is fast waning. This thirty-six-year-old copywriter, the mother of two children, speaks in the authentic voice of the new FM woman:

Lots of sex is exciting and appeals to my ego needs. I seek the conquest and the challenge, and don't ever feel "used" even in a "one-night-stand." I meet men as my equals and expect to gain as much as they do from recreational sex.

Openness about Sexual Behavior

Only a dozen or so years ago, FMs who slept together went to great pains to conceal it. The man left the woman's house with the rest of the guests, then doubled back a few minutes later. If the housekeeper was due the next day, they were careful not to leave two sets of breakfast dishes in the sink. A man and woman going off together for a weekend worried inordinately about whether to register falsely at the hotel as man and wife or to pay for separate rooms in case they ran into anyone they knew. If they visited friends overnight, they were shown to separate rooms—and suffered the separation silently. And in a suburban area where a car in the driveway is a public announcement, the man either parked far away and walked back, or else dragged himself out before dawn.

Today, except in the more conservative areas of the country, FMs act much as the married do: if they mean to spend the night together, they make no effort to conceal it. For example, they would not hesitate to mention to friends they met at a resort that "their" room was large, or faced the beach. A couple sharing a cab with others after dinner would, without embarrassment, ask to be let out together at the man's address.

But they are no more likely than the married to freely discuss their sexual activities with others. If they do so at all, it is not likely to be with friends who have never been divorced:

[Man, thirty-nine] They're like I was—uptight, conformist, afraid of actions that are off the norm. So if I want to talk about my sex life, I talk to other FMs or to married people who were once FMs.

[Woman, forty-five] Knowing how limited and moralistic my conceptions were when I was married, and knowing my married friends aren't much better, I don't discuss sex with them. I don't think they can relate to my problems and my needs. But I *can* talk to married people who have been through it; they're different.

Similarly, many FMs no longer lie to their children more than married parents do. Some, especially women, are less than truthful with very young children, but with children who are old enough to understand, well over half the men and a third of the women in our sample say that, if asked, they give honest (if incomplete) answers. Most of the FMs we queried have not actually had to discuss the matter, but fairly often the children —especially those approaching or beyond puberty—are simply aware of the truth because the parent, while discreet, has made no particular effort at concealment. (By contrast, in 1966 Morton Hunt reported that the great majority of both men and women went to great length to hide their activities from their children.)[4]

Nearly 20 per cent of the men and women in our survey say their children do know about their sexual behavior, and almost none of the children seem upset by it; a few show definite approval and the great majority appear to be simply accepting. The parents whose children accept or approve are probably those who have become comfortable with the FM sexual ethic and so transmit little anxiety or guilt. An avant-garde few explain that adults need sex and have a right to it, but most rely on the justification of love: they say to their children that they sleep only with persons they care about enough to think of as possible marriage partners. This statement from a thirty-seven-year-old businesswoman in the New York area is probably typical of much parent-child communication on the matter:

I fail in many areas as a parent, I suppose, but I want them to trust me and to know me as a real person who makes mistakes, has needs, and so on. So I decided to tell them that I was sleeping with someone I cared for—someone they also knew and liked. I told them that sex was just another human need and shouldn't be shrouded in mystery or made to seem evil. Three of the children were very matter-of-fact about it, but my oldest daughter reacted strongly, and still seems somewhat uncomfortable with the knowledge. I try to minimize the impact for all of them by not kissing or embracing the man in front of them; also, only two men have ever slept at my house, both of them only after the children knew and liked them. I don't let them see a parade of different men spending the night—and what I do away from home I don't share with them.

Incidence

How many FMs actually take advantage of the new freedom? Nearly all. Newcomers may be celibate for months or, rarely, years, but of those who have been FMs for a year or more only one man in twenty and one woman in fourteen has had no intercourse. (Two other recent studies show close agreement with these figures.[5]) In contrast, in Kinsey's time, things were dramatically different. In the 1940's, a tenth of all the younger men and a fifth of the middle-aged ones, and a third of the younger women and a majority of the middle-aged ones, had no postmarital coitus at all.[6]

Today, once they begin, the great majority of FMs remain sexually active. In our survey, only one man in six and one woman in three said they had ever had a year or more of celibacy since the end of the marriage. A majority of men had never been celibate for longer than three months, a majority of women never longer than a year—and most of this inactivity came in the early stage of postmarital life and was due to emotional unreadiness, the unavailability of partners, or the lack of desire for those immediately available. But the more traditional reasons for abstinence—morals, fear of sex, and fear of disgrace —were only rarely cited as factors.

Numbers of Partners

Since new FMs find that casual sex is more acceptable than they knew, most of them have sex with more partners than they ever expected they would. The young are often surprised, and the middle-aged astonished, at their own behavior. Their reactions range from guilt and alarm to delight and pride.

Even though most FMs do not begin to have intercourse for some months, the typical man in our sample had coitus with four different women during the first year, the typical woman with two different men. (Once again, by "typical," we mean median.) The typical man, after several years as an FM, has had nearly ten partners, the typical woman five; some have had scores and a few have had a hundred or more.

These are overall medians, but there are some interesting differences between the medians for various groups within the FM population. Women under forty-five tend to have more partners than those over forty-five, but among men age has little influence on the number of partners until after fifty-five. Discarders have more sex partners than the discarded—probably because they adjust sooner and start dating sooner. Those who feel indifferent toward their ex-spouses have more partners than those who are still bound by either anger or warm feelings. Upper- and middle-class men and women have more partners than working-class men and women; perhaps they are making up for their relatively circumscribed behavior before marriage, or perhaps they simply have enough money to get around more freely. Finally—and surprisingly—those who live in small cities, suburbs, or villages have as many partners as those who live in big cities; since there is less anonymity outside of urban areas, this points up, once again, how open and unashamed FMs have become about their sexual behavior.

Frequency

The frequency of intercourse varies for FMs, as for all people, with age and certain other factors. There is nothing particularly noteworthy about the variations, but what *is* noteworthy is the contrast between the overall frequency today and that of a generation ago, the era of the Kinsey studies. The 1974 study by Morton Hunt, cited above, found that FM men have coitus more than twice as often as their 1940's counterparts, and FM women four times as often as those of the 1940's.[7] For FM men of all ages taken together, the median frequency is more than twice a week, for women nearly twice a week. Age for age, FMs are now at least as sexually active as married people, whereas in Kinsey's time, they were distinctly less active.[8] And although G.B. Shaw once said that marriage combines a maximum of temptation with a maximum of opportunity, two-thirds of the men and over half the women in our sample said that they were at least as sexually active as they had been in marriage; in fact, most of these people said they were more active now.

Pleasure and Satisfaction

Most FMs find that their postmarital sexual experiences are more pleasurable and satisfying than their marital ones had been, though naturally, they tend to remember most clearly the latter part of the marriage, when sexual pleasure was likely to have deteriorated.

A large majority use more variations in sexual technique as FMs than they did as married persons. Seven men and women out of ten say that postmarital intercourse is more intense, in general, than their marital intercourse was. An even larger majority find it more expressive or communicative as well. Almost as many say it has been more satisfying, overall, and—despite the incidence of casual intercourse—emotionally warmer.

Yet this is not self-contradictory, for these FMs are not comparing postmarital sex with marital sex, per se, but with their *own* marital sex, which may have been defective all along and was almost surely impoverished toward the end of the marriage. In a recent study, Dr. Paul Gebhard, director of the Institute for Sex Research, has shown that separated and divorced women reach orgasm in a higher percentage of their coital experiences than they did when married—or even than married women do in general.[9] Dr. Gebhard attributes this partly to novelty, partly to variety (and the chance to learn from a number of partners), and partly to what he calls the "rebound" effect—the release from unhappy marriage and the discovery of more satisfying sexual expression in new and happier relationships.

The last item doesn't seem to have much to do with casual sex, and in fact, the majority, who say that postmarital sex is warmer and more satisfying than married sex was, are telling us something basic about FM sexual behavior: casual sex, for all its high incidence, is not dominant; emotion-connected sex is. Most of an FM's partners may be casual but most of his or her sex *acts* are not casual. Although a man or woman may go to bed once or twice with half a dozen partners and have no special feelings for any of them, the *next* partner may be one with whom an important emotional relationship develops, and who then becomes the exclusive sex partner for a number of months or years. Most of the sexual acts of the formerly married probably do not take place between partners who are casual or merely friendly with each other, but between partners who care about each other.

The great majority of FMs use sex first to restore their belief in themselves, then to discover their own potentialities, and eventually to reassemble sexuality and feelings of deep affection and love. But although this is the dominant pattern of sexual behavior in the world of the formerly married, it is not the only one. Two other patterns, far less common (and each generally disapproved) coexist with the first: one of them is chronic exploitation, promiscuity, and compulsive conquest; the other is chronic abstinence. Let us look now, in reverse order, at each pattern, and at some of the people who exemplify them.

2. REFUSERS

The refusers, though they make up only about 5 per cent of FM men and 7 or 8 per cent of FM women, are intriguing: where formerly it was the "gay divorcée" and the divorced "man about town" who were the social deviants, today the man or woman who abstains from sexual intercourse in postmarital life, refusing to seek it or accept it, is the deviant, the one who differs from the norm.

As we have seen, many men and women are celibate for some months after separation but the desire for social and sexual activity usually reemerges within the first year. A tiny minority, however, remain chronic celibates; either they never have intercourse at all after the marriage, or they abstain from it for years at a time, following a few troubling experiences.

Less than a generation ago a certain number of FMs—mostly women—were abstinent because of strong religious convictions about the sinfulness of sex outside of marriage. Others lived by similar values embodied in the partly moral and partly aesthetic doctrine that sex outside of marriage (or at the very least, a committed love relationship) was wrong, debasing, or ugly. Twenty centuries of Judeo-Christian tradition lay behind these attitudes. Man and woman had been innocent in Eden until they broke the Lord's injunction against knowledge; then they knew the truth —that they were naked—and they were ashamed. Sex was inextricably involved in the Fall and therefore inherently sinful; yet, to propagate the race, it was necessary to condone it in marriage, where, said the early Fathers, it was sinless—as long as one did not enjoy it overly much. Down the centuries the schizoid tradition descended: sex within marriage is necessary, decent, even potentially beautiful; outside of marriage sex is sinful, vile, and inescapably loathsome.

Today, however, both the religious and the moral-aesthetic condemnations of sex outside of marriage have lost most of their force. In a society that has become increasingly tolerant of premarital sex, and in an FM subculture that is thoroughly tolerant of postmarital sex, those FMs who abstain on the grounds of belief usually have some underlying emotional or sexual problem that makes them shun sexual activity. In this, they are one with most of the others who abstain.

Consider, for instance, Dr. Daniel Tompkins, a fifty-three-year-old minister in a large Southern city. Dr. Tompkins was married for twenty-five years and sired four children; then his wife, bitter because her husband's professional activities left her so little of his time and attention (so his story goes), demanded and got a divorce four years ago. After a period of despondency, Dr. Tompkins began to adjust to his new situation. He joined Parents Without Partners and attended meetings of other groups of divorced people as well. But while he took part in group discussions, he totally avoided any interactions of a personal nature, and he has not dated a woman or had any sexual activity since his marriage broke up. In explaining his abstinence, he first attributes it to his religious beliefs and his law-abiding nature: "When the marriage terminated, the need for sex also terminated. Since sex was no longer permitted within the framework of religion or law, I was able to control the desires until they were eliminated."

But as he goes on with his explanation, it becomes quite clear that what accounts for his moral purity is a pathological mistrust of women and a neurotic fear of entrapment through sex:

> I found, in efforts to meet females, that I was increasingly aware of their shallowness and their being tied to a materialistic world. When I learned that they equated love with money or things, I realized I did not need their kind of affection or attention. I

noticed for the first time that women use sex as a means of getting their personal desires, whether security or whatever. If I felt I needed sex, it would only involve me with women, but the price of sexual activity is too high in terms of venereal disease and emotional involvement. Nor is it worth remarriage: my commitment to God, country, and profession is more important than a wife.

Admittedly, Dr. Tompkins is an extreme example. But even a celibate who outwardly seems much more normal shows signs of sexual-emotional malfunction behind the façade of religious morality.

Rosalie Oberst is a case in point. Blue-eyed and pink-cheeked like her German forebears, thirty-four-year-old Rosalie is a dental hygienist in a Midwestern city. Strictly reared as a devout Lutheran, she was a virgin when she married at twenty-six. The marriage lasted only two years and it is now six years since her husband left her. She was even more depressed and withdrawn than most rejected wives and lived in virtual seclusion for two years; then she joined a divorced persons' club and attended meetings and social functions, but refused to date, although she was frequently asked. Her reason, she says, was that she regarded the sexual aspects of FM dating as "immoral" and "terrible." Sex outside of marriage is "nothing but fornication" to her and, sounding like an old-time preacher, she labels it a sin and the source of personal and social disaster: "Fornication habituates one to loveless sex. It ruins the individual and civilization. Sex and gluttony caused the fall of the Roman Empire. Put *that* in your book and it might not sell!"

But after a couple of years of mingling with other FMs in the club, she finally conquered her repugnance enough to start dating—and actually enjoyed it. During the past two years she has gone out with eight different men but if any of them made sexual overtures she "gave them the cold shoulder" and didn't see them again. She became somewhat involved twice, but neither man gave her any trouble, since both of them had "respect for her feelings." She actually had some hope of marrying one of them, but unconsciously, she had chosen a man who would never cause her any problems:

He was fifteen years older than I—forty-five when we met— and had always lived with his mother. He is very shy—in fact, perhaps a little weird—he has never in his life kissed a woman! He's a real mama's boy, a *very* devoted son—he takes his mother everywhere. There was a lot of jealousy between the mother and myself; I think she was the one who made him break it off. It was too bad, because it had real possibilities, and he has money.

Most, though not all, of the others who ascribe their celibacy to moral convictions seem to have similarly pathological inhibitions for which their beliefs serve as a disguise. One young man says that he will never have sex with a woman unless he and she are sincerely in love with each other. "I would find it too sordid otherwise, so until that time, I prefer to masturbate."

A woman of forty-three says proudly, "I come from the old school and I feel that sexual relations should be had only with a person you love." But much later in the discussion she reveals her real attitude: "Frankly, I don't believe that indulging in the sex act can ever improve any relationship, even a marriage."

Unlike these self-deluded people, a certain number of those who abstain recognize that they are inhibited not by ideals alone but by some internal disorder. A twenty-seven-year-old accountant began dating several months after he was separated; now, a half year later, he has still not made even a feeble attempt to have a sexual relationship with anyone. He explains, frankly and convincingly:

> My wife ran around on me and used to brag to me about how great her sex life was outside our marriage—she'd tell me about it in great detail. She cut me apart inside and I think it will take some time for me to get myself back together. There have been some women I wanted to make love to, but I always hold back from it. I'd like to do it but I find it very threatening.

A much older man, nearing sixty, has not had intercourse for six years and hasn't sought to for four or five. He, too, knows why he hasn't:

> Fear of failure, part of my whole new picture of myself as a failure. I was impotent a number of times and it was awful, so I just quit trying. I settle for an off-and-on relationship with one woman who doesn't allow intercourse—but sometimes we sleep together and touch each other, and once in a while I have an orgasm.

Women voice a variety of fears: fear of sexual inadequacy and frigidity ("It's better to do without than to try and fail"); fear of male domination; fear of entrapment in a physical relationship that would put them at the mercy of the man; fear of the sexual act itself.

A New England schoolteacher exemplifies those who avoid sex out of fear:

> A girlfriend talked me into going to bars with her, and I did it a few times, but I felt absolute panic and loathing whenever a man approached me. I realized that I felt totally incapable in the sexual area, and very much afraid of men in general. After I admitted it, I felt better, because then I just contented myself with my children, my job, and my own growth, and I began to feel really independent and secure.

Others who have no such fears or inhibitions avoid sex and even dating because they remain so closely bound up with their ex-spouses that they are incapable of playing the single role in post-marital life. As we will see in a later chapter, this is a fairly common syndrome but one which rarely is permanent.

Finally, there are some FMs who abstain from postmarital sex for reasons that have nothing to do with psychosexual problems, fear of male-female relationships, or ties to the ex-spouse. These problems include certain physiological conditions (advanced diabetes, for instance, may make men impotent, infection or severe estrogen-deprivation may make intercourse painful for women); disfigurement of the body due to obesity, arthritis, or trauma; or advanced age which diminishes—and finally extinguishes—sexual desire.

3. ABUSERS

To say that certain FMs abuse sex—use it wrongly or improperly —is not a moral judgment; we mean it in a purely functional sense, for instead of using sex to satisfy healthy psychological and social needs, they use it in ways that perpetuate their internal problems and keep them alienated from others, no matter how many physical contacts they may have. Such sexual behavior is maladaptive in that it is harmful both to the abusers and to those they have relations with; it is for this reason that we call it abuse or misuse.

To the observer, however, most of those who misuse sex appear to be enjoying themselves thoroughly and making the most of their freedom. They are not only sexually very active, but tend to be free of any traditional restriction that would limit them to partners they care for. They are the truly promiscuous, delighting in endless variety and an ever-higher score; sex for them is best—or perhaps possible—when it is free from emotion, uncontaminated by intimacy or love.

Many of the formerly married go through a period of this kind of behavior (as we shall shortly see), but for most of them it is only a transitional stage. Just as early dating prepared FMs for more serious relationships, so too does early sexual experimentation become part of a learning and developmental process that makes meaningful sex possible; promiscuity soon outlives its usefulness and is replaced by behavior of a different order that is far more gratifying.

But some fail to make the transition: instead of developing as a result of their experiences, they learn to use sex to placate and maintain their neurotic or sociopathic disorders. Some of them, for instance, use sex as an analgesic or intoxicant: it becomes either a pain-killer that gives temporary relief from a sense of failure or personal undesirability, or a mood-elevator that counteracts chronically low self-esteem. Those who abuse sex this way often claim to "need" so much sex that they require numerous partners and constant variety for satisfaction. But the claim is based on a psychic need, for which they get no lasting satisfaction after all; they feel good about themselves, reassured, for a short time after each "fix," but within a day or two, or even within hours, the buoyant mood dissipates and anxiety, despair, and self-contempt creep back in.

You might not be aware of any interior problems the first time you met a sex addict. You might see only the seductive exterior —particularly if you were a potential partner. If you are a woman, you would possibly be fooled by Roger Weiner—for a very short time.

Roger strikes most women not only as attractive but as dynamic and exciting because he seems so strongly sexual. An automobile salesman in a medium-sized Midwestern city, he is forty-six but looks younger; tanned and trim, he wears expensive and tasteful clothing, and has an air of total assurance that intrigues many women.

The self-assurance stems from the fact that, in his own terms, Roger is very successful. He has been an FM for ten years and has had at least 150 to 200 different sex partners in that period of time. With 90 per cent of them the relationship has been purely physical; with the rest, companionable or moderately affectionate. He has never been in love. When he explained this to us, Roger laid aside the façade he presents to women and spoke candidly and without apology:

> There was no real love or caring in my marriage from the beginning, and the sex in it was always unsatisfactory. When we broke up we had a terrible struggle in court—and I lost. It was a financial disaster for me, and still is, and she's as hostile and as vengeful now as she was ten years ago. I learned from her, and from my life since then, that women need emotional and financial stability, but my own need is strictly for a companion and a lover on a part-time basis, with no ties of any kind.
>
> And one person doesn't do it for me; I find sexual variety important for my ego—although I do think that over the years it has corrupted me to some extent and made me rather cynical. I've dated hundreds of women and had sex with most of them, and now, after ten years of it, I seem to need a new one every week. Actually, I dislike real dating, it's so full of game-playing and pretending. Lately, I often prefer to go to an all-night laundromat or supermarket to pick up women—it's much more honest.
>
> I've been slightly involved with a few women, but could never see where it would benefit me to marry them. I've been leading this life for ten years and don't really want anything else.

Although compulsive promiscuity used to be associated chiefly with men, it has become somewhat more common in women than formerly. In our sample, one woman in twenty has had more than twenty postmarital sex partners, and one in a hundred has had more than fifty. Some of them habitually use sex as an analgesic or intoxicant, but unlike Roger Weiner, they generally seem dissatisfied with their own behavior. One young woman says she is frightened by how desperately she wants to feel wanted—a need that impels her to accept every sexual invitation that is offered even though, she admits, "I know that the joy it generates will be fleeting."

An even more poignant statement by a woman sex addict comes from an extremely articulate forty-three-year-old waitress in a city in the Southwest:

> In twenty-three years I had slept with only one man. Now there have been—I don't know, 50? 100? More?—two or three different ones a week, most weeks. One can't keep track of something of no consequence. (I guess I'm still trying to prove to myself that just because my husband didn't want me, it didn't mean that no one else does.) They're nameless, faceless men and I never hear from them again. They're mostly wealthy, married, and staying at the hotel where I work. I have three drinks, I dance with them, then sleep with them and go home. I'm not happy then but sometimes I'm tired enough to sleep, and I feel semiloved for the moment.
>
> I'm lucky to be young-looking and still pretty, so they want me; also, I have a super-happy personality that makes men laugh as I entertain them. But I don't like the pawing and grabbing they do, and I tell them to be more gentle. Then I submit and it's over. No strings, no regrets, no memories. After I take my bath, all is forgotten.
>
> I'm lucky that I'm like the guys—love them and leave them. Variety is the spice of life. Nothing is forever. Tomorrow is a better day.
>
> I never have a day without crying and wishing my husband were back and that he loved me. My loneliness is overwhelming. Sex is not love.

A second form of the abuse of sexuality is exploitiveness—conquest of the opposite sex for the sake of conquest and the power the conqueror feels. An effort to get something while giving little in return, it does not express sexual desire so much as hostility and a desire for revenge. The exploiter resembles the sex addict in promiscuity, but his or her pleasure derives not so much from feeling desired and desirable as from success in maneuvering the other person into having sexual intercourse.

For such people, the high point may be the moment of ruthless abandonment of the other after a brief relationship—perhaps minutes after orgasm. An FM man of thirty-two had had intercourse with scores of women in the past two years and has never spent the night with one of them. Immediately after making "love" he feels the need to escape; if he is in the woman's bed, he leaves, if she is in his, he sends her home. He has an ample supply of tested excuses for the purpose: he suddenly remembers that he must be at work very early, he thinks he's coming down with a cold, his young son is dropping by for breakfast before he goes to school, and so forth.

Some exploitive men are dismayingly crass in their solicitations. Such a man may approach a woman at a bar or a party and ask her bluntly whether she will go to bed with him if he takes her out to dinner. If the answer is negative, or even equivocal, he turns away and tries elsewhere. Exploiters of this kind are proud that they never pretend any emotion. "No bullshit about love," one man brags. "They all know what I am right from the start, and some of them find it a big turn-on." And that's where the exploitation begins: the naked sexual approach may make a susceptible woman think that she has a superb sexual experience in store, but instead, this kind of practitioner is apt to rush her into bed, enjoy himself without paying any heed to her wishes or needs, and be ready to get rid of her a few minutes later.

In contrast, another kind of exploiter may make an irresistibly poetic, romantic approach to a woman who is reluctant to go to bed with him, and if she agrees, he slowly and patiently devotes himself to being a spectacular lover. His aim is to make her experience the most intense sexual pleasure "so that by the time I'm finished with her she's really hooked, can't wait until the next time"—but there is no next time because he never contacts her again. If she calls him, he barely remembers who she is.

His female counterpart is the seductive woman, Eve the temptress luring Adam to do her bidding. Her sexuality is both bait and hook, and no fish attracts her more than the unwilling one. She feels irresistibly compelled to arouse a timid man and persuade him to engage in some sexual variation he has never tried before, or to seduce the faithful husband and lead him to make the first secret phone call. In an earlier era she would have been content to have men pursue her; today she dares to be the pursuer, and wants to be the possessor in a physical sense; abandoning her lovers while they still want her is as gratifying as conquering them in the first place.

Nowadays, some women even exhibit the whole syndrome of traits classically associated with the male seducer: the choice of socially inferior partners, predatory or domineering treatment of them, the absence of any tender feelings toward them, and so on. This remarkable confession comes from a thirty-five-year-old buyer in a New Mexico department store:

> Sex is the greatest possible pleasure for me, and a variety of partners makes it most stimulating. I don't like "romance" per se; I find it artificial, boring, unnatural, and in the way. I don't want a man to write me poetry—I want him to make love to me.
>
> I've learned a lot from my lovers and am frequently complimented on my talents. I date only Mexicans and Mexican-Americans; they're darkly handsome and *very* sexual—but also contemptuous of a sexually free woman like myself. I select men smaller in stature and lower in social status than I am, and definitely prefer younger men because they're easier to control. Almost unconsciously I always seek out men temperamentally weaker than I, men I can control without acting aggressive.

Finally, the third common misuse of sexuality among FMs is defensive: a concentration on one's own performance and on the accumulation of varied experiences acts as a barrier against intimacy or loving commitment. Some psychologists and psychiatrists believe that the contemporary emphasis on self-realization, the "egocentric greed for experience" as psychoanalyst Herbert Hendin calls it, is to blame; it leads to fascination with oneself and one's experience, rather than with relationships—in short, to narcissism.[10] Others, in classical Freudian fashion, attribute the defensive use of promiscuity and sexual performance to the unresolved oedipal conflict which forbids us to feel sexual desire for those we love.[11] But whether the underlying neurosis is narcissistic or oedipal in nature, the trauma of divorce surely exacerbates it and makes the individual even more fearful of loving; the collector's approach to sexual experiences provides an excellent defense against doing so.

A fifty-year-old stockbroker says that in his five years as an FM he has had at least sixty-five sexual partners and "loved most of them to some degree, but none of them very much." He has always contrived to keep three or four relationships going at once, a central one and two or three satellite associations. He claims to like this kind of life, admits that he is afraid he would be trapped by a deep or exclusive relationship, and says that the sexual freedom of the world of the formerly married "has saved my sanity."

The same kind of defensiveness is shown by some FM women, although women, by and large, are more likely than men to forge a firm link between sex and love. A thirty-four-year-old Berkeley woman has been an FM for nearly three years, during the last two of which she has had more than fifty sex partners. She has liked some of them but felt emotionally involved with only two; both times she broke away and threw herself back into the melee of promiscuity in order to feel safe again:

> I've experimented wildly, sexually, but I've consistently destroyed relationships for fear of becoming too intimate in any one. I find married men safer than FMs—they don't have a need to get overly involved. I like people who want to have a fun time with me, without strings. Actually, I'm tired of one-night pick-up sex, but I have no prospects for anything more permanent because I find it impossible to find the kind of man who really interests me and will deal with me on many levels. Most men try to trap me in one level of interacting.

It seems that what this woman fears is not being trapped in one level of interacting (whatever that means), but of being trapped by one man. As long as she can change partners and keep experimenting, she can escape entrapment—except by her own internal problems. And therein lies an irony: FMs who misuse sex may know that they do their partners a disservice, but only a few of them know that they do an even greater disservice to themselves.

4. USERS

It is common for those who have not begun to socialize to think that most of the formerly married are sexual revolutionaries ready to engage in recreational sex—intercourse without emotional content—at a moment's notice. Depending on the novice's own attitudes and needs, he or she may see this as destructive and immoral licentiousness, or as a breakthrough to healthy and natural behavior.

In either case, the newcomer's perception is wrong, for the great majority of FMs are not the revolutionaries they appear to be. Their actions are easily misunderstood, because while one part of postmarital sexual behavior does have physical pleasure without emotional encumbrance as its goal, pleasure-seeking is only its *manifest* function, the part that is both observable and consciously intended. Much more important are its *latent* functions which are hidden, unstated, and *not* consciously intended:[12] what appears to be mere self-indulgence is actually a means to the essential ends of ego-repair, the discovery (or rediscovery) of one's mature sexual self, and its integration with the FM's emergent, changing personality. Postmarital sex is far more reconstructive than the purely social aspects of dating, for it reaches all the way down to the primitive sources of masculine and feminine identity, and to the core of the symbiotic relationship between woman and man. Just as play, for children, is the foundation for adult work, so sexual play, for the formerly married, is the foundation for self-love and thereby for love of another.

While the reconstructive process is a continuous one, it can, in theory, be broken down into three major phases. Some people can skip over one phase, or even two, but many FMs have to go through all three phases in sequence.

Phase One is the stage of *ego-repair*. It begins with the FM's initial test to find out if he or she is desirable to others, can function sexually, and if he or she can successfully give and receive pleasure. In most cases the test results are positive, and this is not only reassuring but positively transforming: those who feel "dead below the waist," "unmanly," "unwomanly," or "utterly worthless," are suddenly alive, proud, confident, able to *like* themselves again. While restoration of self-esteem begins with social dating, it remains cerebral and tentative until sexual affirmation makes it fleshly and sure.

Since good feelings about one's self are a prerequisite to good feelings about others, it matters little that there are few deep emotional ties to one's sex partners during Phase One; in truth, the main business is with oneself, and the surges of warmth that are felt for the partner are mostly due to gratitude for help in learning to love again—not the other, but the self.

A twenty-eight-year-old automobile mechanic told us what his early sex experiences as an FM meant to him:

> My ex was so cool that a blowtorch wouldn't have warmed her up. She always told me it was my fault. She said I didn't turn her on, I just didn't have it. She said it and I believed her. Well, after we split I started going out with these divorced women and doing exactly the same things. And they got turned on plenty; they liked me, they really took to me. It was terrific for my morale. I liked myself better than I ever did in my life. I don't think a person who hasn't been through this can understand what it means.

Another young man, a schoolteacher with strong fundamentalist leanings, dated actively, but for a long time remained chaste. When he finally gave in and began to have sex relations, he says, "It was only then that I began to feel like a whole person again, a desirable human being, an open and vital person. It made me feel as if I had finally found my lost manhood."

Although most men say similar things about their early postmarital sex experiences, not all react so positively. Some feel guilty or ashamed after purely casual sex, and others find it so sordid or troubling that they are unable to perform at all. About one out of four of the men we queried say they have avoided casual sex in FM life.

Women, of course, are supposed to be far more antipathetic to casual sex than men; traditionally the great majority of them have been unaroused or actually repelled by either the prospect or the reality of sex with a man for whom they had no profound feelings. This is said by some authorities to have a physiological basis: woman is weaker and needs to trust her partner, she is the one who can become pregnant and so needs security, and so forth. But others say it must be a matter of cultural conditioning, since in at least some societies women have been as fond of casual sex as men.[13] Both explanations may have merit, but our own evidence lends support to the cultural conditioning theory since, as we have seen, today's FM women are rather like men in their sexual attitudes and behavior. There are differences, but they aren't great. About a third of our female sample (as against a quarter of the men) have never experienced sex on a purely physical level, and a number of others have tried it and found it unrewarding or psychologically damaging. But a clear majority of FM women have had at least some casual sex experiences, a sizable minority have had many, and a surprising number sound very much like the woman we met earlier who said, "I meet men as my equals and expect to gain as much as they do from recreational sex." The enthusiasm for sex on a primarily physical level is typical Phase One behavior. It is expressed by a thirty-three-year-old schoolteacher with a degree of pride and satisfaction that one could have formerly heard only from a man:

> I've had relations with five men in the last year, four of them "casual," if that's what you want to call it; my own word would be "friendly." For the first time I feel that the old myth that sex and love must be joined is really a myth—false. Sex can and should be fun, and you can enjoy it with a friend as well as a lover. It's been good for my ego and a great learning experience as well. I was a virgin when I married, and faithful to one man for fourteen years, even though he was a selfish lover and for the most part I found sex in marriage unpleasant. I thought of it as a necessary nuisance, and I probably hold a world's record for late-night headaches. But because of my recent sexual experimentation I'm enjoying sex for the first time, and not just enjoying it, I think it's *great!* I'm much happier, more self-confident, and more responsive in all sorts of other ways, too.

A forty-three-year-old mother of two, a church-going Episcopalian, and outwardly a conventional suburban matron, has had a number of strictly physical relationships in the past year and speaks of them with a certain amount of braggadocio:

> I'm amazed at my sex drive. I'd been frigid in my marriage and didn't think I'd ever enjoy sex or miss it, but I was really surprised! I have to watch myself because I'm just like a kid with a new toy. I've turned out to be very aggressive. I'll ask a man for a date, or a dance, and openly tell him I'm attracted to him physically. I've tickled some men to death and scared the hell out of others. An aggressive woman really separates the men from the boys!

Even women who have had good sexual relationships in mar-

riage often develop sexual anesthesia prior to divorce, when conflict is at a peak. Along with those who have never functioned
well, they enter the world of the formerly married with grave
doubts about their sexual responsiveness, but early postmarital
experimentation usually helps them discover that there is nothing
wrong with them after all; the discovery floods them with such
relief that a first orgasm may produce uncontrollable sobbing and
tears of joy. Many a man has been mightily puzzled trying to
figure out what magic, good or bad, he has unwittingly wrought.

Relief that the physical apparatus works is a great reward for
both women and men. Equally important is the reassurance to
the battered ego that one not only still desires, but is desirable,
and even when loss of sexual function has not been a problem,
early post-marital adventures are often a boon to self-respect.
A man told us, "The very things about me that were so physically distasteful to my wife are just the things other women seem
to like the most." And a woman said, "My husband used to tell
me that nobody would ever want me because I was too fat, too
sick. It did me a world of good to find out it isn't true. In fact,
fellows seem to find me pretty attractive."

Phase Two consists of *exploration* of one's sexuality and that
of others. For people who married long ago or had little premarital experience, it provides a needed sexual education; for
those who have had some experience in the era of sexual liberation, it is a refresher course, valuable in such swift-moving times
even for the relatively recently married. In either case, while
FMs may look to others like libertines or profligates, they are
actually taking advantage of the sexual permissiveness of their
milieu in order to educate themselves in ways that will make
them more adequately partnerable in the future.

Among the discoveries yielded by such exploration is that
there is a great variety of *styles* of sexual response; the newcomer may never have known, or may have long since forgotten,
how different other sexual partners can be from the spouse, and
how different they are from each other. A woman may be
amazed to learn that one man can be so rough, another so tender;
how hasty and self-absorbed is one, how patient, caring, and
communicative another. A man might find one woman slow to
respond, another astonishingly swift, one tepid and restrained,

another lusty and unfettered. Users are alternately entranced and repelled by the variations in their partners' bodies—their many sizes and shapes, textures, odors, tastes—and the idiosyncracies of their sounds, the words they use, their facial expressions, their diverse moods that range from gluttonous to poetic, combative to loving, serious to playful.

Such comprehensive experience gives one a clear notion of which styles of sexuality do or do not suit his or her needs. Some men are surprised and delighted to find that there are women who are far more outgoing, passionate, and earthy than their wives; other men discover that they dislike such women and are far happier with those who are more passive, whose style is gentle and tender. Similarly, some women discover that they respond remarkably to longer, more loving foreplay than they were used to; others are astounded to find that they are intensely excited by impassioned ravishment.

Another area of exploration involves *technique* rather than style. In most marriages, even those that are sexually satisfying, spouses tend to develop their own limited sexual repertoire. In postmarital life, the FM is made sharply aware of the range of other possibilities; every sex partner has a somewhat different modus operandi, for even if the techniques are the same, no two people use them identically—and no two people call forth identical responses from the partner. And some techniques are truly new to the initiate; even if he or she has encountered them in sex manuals, encountering them in life is a very different matter.

It suits the needs of FMs to take full advantage of their freedom to experiment, to discover, to learn. And so they do. According to the 1974 survey cited earlier in this chapter, ninetenths of FM men and over eight-tenths of FM women use oral-genital practices anywhere from occasionally to frequently —a considerably higher proportion than among young singles or among the married. Larger percentages of the formerly married than the married make occasional to frequent use of every non-standard coital position.

Every FM who has had at least a few partners—especially if one of them is a veteran—is certain to encounter these variations, and likely to be introduced to a few techniques he or she never tried before—and never expected to try. These may range from the use of mirrors and vibrators to mock-bondage, from pretended (or real) resistance and overpowering to anal play and intercourse or multi-partner sex. Some FMs are insatiably curious and ever-willing to take advantage of any horizon-expanding activity. Some are fascinated but quickly sated, aware that the curiosities hold no satisfaction for them. Still others are fearful and inhibited, or repelled by and resistant to anything that seems like a novelty to them.

What most FMs come away with, eventually, is not a vastly enlarged repertoire of techniques, but one that is modestly and selectively enlarged beyond that of the marriage. And more important, an enhanced sexual identity, and an expanded conception of their own capacity for response and for calling forth response in a partner. "I never knew what I was capable of doing and feeling," one thirty-nine-year-old man says, "and if I had stayed married I would have died without knowing." Another, age thirty-two, says, "I'm far more sensual than I would have believed. Sexual experimenting has taught me that sex can be a knockout, not just a relief. And it has taught me how to bring pleasure to a woman through a variety of techniques. I doubt I'll ever feel jaded again."

Women talk in comparable terms; many say they had no idea how passionate they were, or how totally enveloping and satisfying sex can be. Like men, they speak of the techniques they have learned and their pride in having become accomplished lovers.

From such testimony, you might easily get the idea that the great majority of the formerly married had had sexually inadequate spouses; it takes only a moment's reflection, however, to realize that many of them must be the very same people whose spouses complained about *them*. In fact, when we have interviewed both ex-spouses and heard each one's story, often each blamed their poor marital sex on the other and each claimed to have blossomed into a far better lover postmaritally.

And no doubt they all told the truth, for there is no actual contradiction in these seeming discrepancies. Each narrator *did* experience the ex-spouse as a poor sexual partner, for such was the nature of their interaction; whatever the reason, they *were*

poor lovers—of each other. Perhaps they married too young
and were locked into a limited sexual pattern in later life. Or
perhaps as their emotional climate cooled, it chilled their sexuality with each other. Or perhaps they used sex to punish each
other. But there is no need to go on with such conjectures. Most
FMs find their postmarital sex partners generally more satisfactory than their former mates, and themselves more fully and
adeptly sexual than they were in marriage; we can believe them,
for they are reporting the reality of their subjective experiences.

Not all FMs, of course, say that their marital sex was poor.
Some think of the ex-spouse as an unrivaled lover and some look
back with longing on the relatively relaxed and secure character
of sex in marriage. The challenge and threat of sex with partners
they barely know, or whose behavior is unpredictable, may, at
times, cause men to be impotent and women to be unresponsive.
Some of those who experience such failures often, or chronically,
give up sex altogether. But most do not; they either experiment
until they find solutions to their problems, or until they have
adapted sufficiently to the newness of FM sex for the problems
to disappear—or they seek professional help from therapists.

One man, who at forty-six, thought himself "always impotent
and all washed up as a lover" managed to overcome his aversion
to cunnilingus and solved his problem. "I discovered that if I
satisfied the woman with oral sex beforehand, I wasn't nervous
any more and then I could perform as well as I ever had." One
woman had the first orgasm of her life when a lover urged her
to try the astride position for the first time.

But sooner or later the period of exploration yields its most
significant discovery: namely, that sex and affection *are* linked in
our nervous systems, that they do reinforce each other.[14] The
FM begins to hunger for something more than recreational sex,
yearns to care for his or her partner, wants to have sex only with
someone who cares in return. Some feel this way at the outset,
some after one or two episodes of experimental sex; but for the
majority, it is the result of a gradual process in which casual sex
slowly becomes less exciting and satisfying, and the need for
emotional as well as physical intimacy begins to reassert itself
bit by bit. Users speak of the transition in terms like these:

[Man, twenty-nine] I did all that stuff, and it was good for me, but now it bores me to pick up some girl in a bar and make it with her. I want to like the person I'm making love to, I want to feel fond of her.

[Man, forty-four] I've changed—I somehow don't feel *right* any more about going to bed with a woman I don't care for to some degree. I'm looking for something more than sport fucking.

[Woman, thirty-seven] After five months of casual sex, I was able to have sex with a man I actually like, and it was easy and natural. Afterwards, when I tried to have a purely physical affair with a very attractive man, it didn't work. I couldn't do it any more.

[Woman, thirty-three] I liked recreational sex at first, but I've come to need a primary relationship. I find it more rewarding than casual sex as long as it's not exclusive.

The FM, though gaining courage, is still cautious as the reintegration of sex and love gets under way. Love itself remains threatening for a time and so limits the emotions; one feels friendly or affectionate, but no more.

Still, by now, as integration continues to proceed, Phase Two soon gives way to Phase Three, *reconstruction*: the reassembly of sex with deep caring and love, with the whole personality, and with social commitment to the partner. While it may happen with a single partner, it is more often a gradual process that requires a number of trials of various sorts: a brief intense infatuation that bursts into flame and then gutters out in a month; an on-and-off affair that intermittently burns bright, then pales; a warm, constant, and intimate relationship with carefully posted limits. An acknowledged, truly loving and exclusive relationship will be possible only when Phase Three has been completed (and such relationships will be discussed in a later chapter), but at this stage the FM still exercises great care, both in behavior and terminology, to keep the union of sex and love from becoming complete and to avoid commitment to the partner. One man tells the woman he sees regularly (but studiously not on an exclusive basis) that he and she are each other's SPORTs—Supportive Persons Offering Reciprocal Trust.

By this time the FM is aware of the changes that have taken place and those anticipated in the near future. Now he or she understands the long-range process, is able to talk of casual sex as a phase, and of loving again as the ultimate goal.

A thirty-year-old magazine writer from New York is rather proud of his upward Rake's Progress:

> For about a half year I screwed anything that wasn't dead. I cruised the bars, I went to parties, I picked up girls at short-order counters. I really felt freed from having to have it mean anything except a good fuck. First time in my life I was able to feel that way. Then I began to find it sort of boring, a waste of time and effort. One night I asked myself why the hell I was screwing a girl I wouldn't even want to spend the time to have a cup of coffee with, and I cut out.
>
> After that I began to get choosier and started to look for girls I would be interested in. At one point I sort of fell in love with three at once—not really love, but very fond of them, and kind of hooked on one. Right now I have one very close relationship but we're in trouble because she wants me to stop seeing other girls, and while I really like her a lot, it makes me nervous to tie myself down. Does that mean I'm not really in love with her? But I *want* to be!

Women are often sharply aware of the reconstruction, within themselves, of the sexual-emotional synthesis. Here is a typical statement:

> [Hospital administrator, thirty-six, in a Southwestern city] I needed some experimentation with sex after a long and sexually disappointing marriage. I had several experiences with men I was attracted to, but I wasn't seriously interested in them, nor were they with me. But it gave me a chance to discover that yes, I could function, my body worked okay, that I was attractive. I needed that time to get ready for a more important relationship.
>
> Now I find casual sex less satisfactory than sex in the context of a relationship. I've had several, but only one has been serious. He and I have gone together for a year, off and on. We have love for each other but he is fearful of a committed relationship and tends to feel trapped; when things get very intensive between us he disappears for a few weeks. Then we get back together.
>
> I wonder at my own desire to continue with him; he's a poor marriage prospect. Perhaps he protects me from facing a remarriage. But even if it were to end this time, I would feel that I've

benefitted—I've learned a lot about relating sexually and emotionally, I've gained increased self-esteem as a female.

5. REFERENDUM

If the sexual behavior of the formerly married is hedonistic in intent, it is rehabilitative in effect. Through their casual and experimental sexual activity, FMs achieve more important goals than they sought. Sexual play serves the goal of adjustment, and most FMs recognize, after a while, that it has had this effect.

Only a minority fail to see it this way. One out of every eight men and one out of every five women we asked felt that experimental sex has generally bad effects on FMs: they say it destroys the sense of morality, is degrading, unfits one to love again, damages one's chance of remarriage, and so on. Another one out of every five men and women either said they had mixed feelings about it, or failed to answer the question. Disapproval or lack of approval is somewhat more common among blue-collar than middle- or upper-class FMs, among the less educated than the highly educated, and among the devout than the non-devout.

All in all, though, the overwhelming majority favor experimental sex. Six out of every ten men and nearly as many women feel that its effects are generally beneficial in terms of restoring self-respect and helping to make it possible for the FM to love again. Five times as many men and three times as many women rated the effects good as rated them bad.

And they don't change their minds later. During the two years it took to write this book, we spoke to a large number of re-married FMs and nearly all of those who had a period of sexual experimentation look back on it as having been valuable to them, while very few think it was harmful or of no value.

Furthermore, those in our sample who are sexually most free—the young, the men, the economically well off—are also, according to census data, the very persons who have the best chance of remarrying and are apt to do so soonest. This seems, therefore, to be additional evidence that a period of casual and diverse sexual experience does not hinder, and may well help, those who want to remarry to achieve their goal.

Our survey also established the fact that the variety and excitement of experimental sex do not prejudice FMs against marital sex: two-thirds of the men and women said, in answer to a direct question, that they did not expect married sex to be dull or boring as a result of their experience.

In addition, they felt that experience with a number of partners does not conflict with readiness to enter a deep and committed relationship in due time. Of those men who have had numerous partners, just about the same number would like to remarry as of those men who have had few partners. And among women, there is even a definite connection between sexual experimentation and readiness to remarry: those who have had two or fewer postmarital sex partners are less likely to want to remarry—or even to love, without remarriage—than those who have had three or more partners.

It's enough to make one wonder. Two generations ago, when the trauma of divorce was much more severe and so many of the divorced remained unmarried, was it only social disapproval and the lack of a divorce subculture that were chiefly to blame? Or could it have been, in part, the social and moral constraints against the sexual experimentation that is, for many, essential to reconstruction?

VI

Parents And Children

1. WHO WILL TAKE CARE OF ME?

Two years ago the young Bregmans and their seven-year-old son were a story-book specimen of the American family. They lived in a pleasant, impeccably neat garden apartment in a suburb of a large Midwestern city. Husky, blond Bernie had a reasonably well-paying job as an airline mechanic; Linda, plain-featured but chic, was a house-proud homemaker and a student of retailing at a nearby community college; Mark was a happy, outgoing second-grader.

Today, Bernie lives in Florida, a thousand miles away, married to the woman he'd been having an affair with when Linda found out and made him leave. He operates a fishing boat—his long-time dream of the good life—only it isn't good, because he is deeply in debt. He has always been late with Linda's child-support and alimony payments; sometimes he has sent partial payments, claiming he had no more money, and for the last four months he has sent nothing at all. He recently moved, leaving no forwarding address, and he hopes to stay a jump ahead of the lawyers and the court. "Alimony is a damned rip-off," Bernie says. "Linda can work—she did before we got married. She's so much in favor of women's lib, so let her act like a liberated woman for a change."

But how does Bernie justify not supporting his son?

I was crucified by the judge because I was mixed up with another woman; I never shoulda been stuck with two hundred a
month for just one kid plus two hundred in alimony—not a guy
in my income bracket. Anyway, why should I have to pick up
the whole tab? It's her child too, why shouldn't she split the costs?
I send what *I* think is right, and to hell with the judge. Maybe her
lawyer will catch up with me, maybe not, but I'm sure gonna
make it as tough as I can. I have to; how the hell am I supposed
to make my own life work, with a new wife and a baby on the
way? I can't do it if I have to send Linda half of everything I
make after taxes.

Linda and Mark still live in the garden apartment, but it
doesn't look the same; Linda hasn't the time or the energy to
keep it up. The only job she could find in her suburban community is in a supermarket, where the work is hard, the hours
long. Mark wears a key around his neck on a chain, and he lets
himself into the apartment after school. When Linda gets home
she makes a quick dinner, spends some time with Mark, does the
household chores, and writes letter after letter to her Florida
lawyer about the missing payments. "Sometimes, at bedtime, I
feel like swallowing all the pills and killing myself," she says,

but if I did, who would fix Mark's breakfast and get him off to
school? My husband is an A-number-one bastard. He sends Mark
a soupy birthday card and a two-buck toy, but he tries every way
he can to get out of supporting him. As for me, if I were sick and
dying of starvation, he'd probably be glad. It's still a man's world,
no matter what anybody says. The woman gives up everything
to marry, then the man cuts out and leaves her with the whole
bag—with the kid and a lifetime of taking care of him. Don't get
me wrong—I love Mark—I love him a lot—but even so, I can't
help but think, sometimes, how much better off I'd be today if I
had miscarried like the doctors thought I would—and it makes me
feel awful to even think such a thing.

Mark is getting along better now, but for months he was all
but ungovernable. He flew into blind rages, screamed, threw
things, kicked Linda when she tried to comfort him, and shouted
that he hated her because she made his Daddy go away (Mark

had heard more than one of their late-night arguments). After such tantrums he had recurrent nightmares that Linda had gone too, and left him alone in the apartment. He would awaken, crying wildly, and clinging to his mother, would ask again and again, "If you go, who will take care of me?" When she assured him that she would never go, Mark would ask, "But what if you die?"

Later, when Linda began to work, Mark would often cry in the morning, clutch his stomach, and say he was too sick to go to school. Linda stayed home with him a few times even though she knew he was malingering, but finally, fearful of losing her job, told him that he had either to go to school or stay home alone.

"But who will take care of me?" he wailed.

"You're a big boy," Linda said. "You can take care of yourself until I get home."

"But I don't want to!"

"Look, I can't help it. I can't take a chance of getting fired, so go to school or stay home—it's up to you."

Mark went to school but behaved abominably all day, and wet his bed that night. That was a long time ago. Since then, he has given up the tantrums but still wets his bed occasionally, and makes a scene if Linda gets a sitter so she can go out on a date. But he no longer accuses her of having driven his father away, and in fact, almost never mentions his father. Linda thinks this may be a sign of adjustment—but she isn't sure, and it makes her feel uneasy.

Multiply the Bregmans' story twenty or thirty million times, if you want some idea of the impact of divorce upon American parenthood and childhood today. Here are the facts:

—In 1976 about two and a half million children underwent the shock of temporary or permanent breakup of their homes through separation or divorce; by contrast, only some six hundred thousand children were similarly affected a generation earlier, in 1951.[1]

—Eight million children under eighteen—one out of every eight in the United States—now live with one formerly married parent and without the other.[2] Black children are three times as likely to live in a broken home as white children, but across the nation, two-thirds of all children in broken homes are white.*[3]

—The impact is far greater than the figures for children presently in broken homes reveal, for several times as many live in families reconstituted by remarriage or reconciliation, after having spent months or years in broken homes.[4]

—An estimated four out of every ten children born in the 1970's will live in an FM single-parent home during at least part of their childhoods.[5]

Those are the statistics—but much more than statistics; they are the bell that tolls the passing of an ancient tradition, the end of the classic meaning of childhood, the vanishing of the lifetime family.

2. AN AMERICAN DILEMMA

We Americans deem unhappy marriage to be an unnecessary evil and rate the pursuit of personal happiness morally superior to the preservation of a bad marriage "for the children's sake." But we also set great store by happy and secure childhood, and treasure the well-being of our children above all else. And with these conflicting ideals, we have created a great dilemma.

When a divorcing couple has children, how can the burden of caring for them, the costs of rearing them, ever be fairly allocated? How can the divorced parents pursue the goal of a new life while burdened by the fruit of the old one? But above all, how can either of them, or anyone else, assure those children a secure, warm, untroubled childhood? How can the children withstand, unharmed, their untimely awakening from the dream of family?

There are many answers to these questions, but no good ones. Whoever keeps the children undertakes immense responsibilities without the help of a partner. Whoever pays for the children finds it a crushing burden—and even so, the other parent never finds the financial arrangements satisfactory. No matter how

* In addition, a small percentage of white children and a substantial percentage of black children live with mothers who were never married or who are widows; this lies outside our purview.

much money there is to start with, when there are two households to support, the money is spread thinner. The custodial
parent, usually the mother, resents having less money for the
family than she did before. The absentee parent, usually the
father, wants to live another life and resents being financially
trapped by his past. Even when the mother with custody works
—and, as we know, nearly two-thirds do[6]—her income is usually
lower than a man's for full-time work, and lower yet if she can
work only part-time. No matter which one is the single parent
(the one who has custody) and which one is the outside parent
(the absentee), no matter whether one or both pay the bills,
the children are left with an incomplete home, a lowered standard of living, and a deep sense of insecurity, both emotional
and financial.

But it used to be worse. Our society has been making a
number of changes in its customs and its laws which, if they have
not resolved the dilemma, have at least begun to mitigate its ill
effects. Some of the most important changes have grown out of
the increase in women's rights and the growing equality of the
sexes. We used to think that woman's place was in the home and
man's in the market place; the corollary followed that in a
divorce, the mother would get custody and the father would pay
the bills. But this rigid allocation of roles often failed to fit the
family's best needs; the mother was not always the better parent,
the man was not always able to pay the bills. And what was
worse, laws deriving from the old view put into the hands of
warring spouses weapons that wounded the children as often as
their parents. A wife seeking revenge often threatened to air her
husband's misdeeds in court unless he met her exorbitant child
support and alimony demands; a judge, if the case were heard,
sometimes penalized the man by giving the woman what she
asked for. Conversely, a wronged husband often threatened to
air his wife's infidelities in court unless she agreed to ask nothing
of him—and he sometimes even tried to take custody away from
her on the grounds of her moral unfitness to be a parent.[7] Under
divorce laws that looked for fault, the dilemma of what to do
about the children was not only unresolved, but worsened.

Today, a more fruitful and flexible view is emerging. There is, for one thing, a strong trend toward custody decisions based less on traditional roles and sins than on the "best interests" of the child. Judges in some jurisdictions are entitled to decide which parent is better equipped to take care of a child (or children), and child support is contingent on who has custody and who earns how much money. Not many judges are using the new provisions yet, but in New York, Illinois, and a few other states, landmark cases are already on record, and it seems likely that other states will soon be following suit.[8]

Nonetheless, the "best interests" doctrine only ameliorates the custody problems; the basic dilemma remains. For the fact is that custody is a heavy burden to the custodian, and will continue to be. Most men don't want the job, and neither offer to take it nor fight for it, so women's liberation notwithstanding, tradition still prevails and women account for over 90 per cent of single parents.[9] Despite a flood of popular articles on father custody in recent years, there is no evidence, according to Dr. Paul C. Glick, that the percentage of fathers with custody has been increasing.[10] What may have been happening is that a few more husbands are voluntarily taking custody when their wives prefer to pursue an education or a career, or simply find motherhood oppressive; however, the small increase in such single-parent fathers is offset by the decrease in the number of outraged husbands who win custody by proving their wives morally unfit.[11] Few men fight to assume the heavy burden of custody that interferes with so many other goals—success at work, a new social life, a new love and a new family life. The dilemma is immutable: the difficulties in providing proper child care after a marriage is broken deeply affect both parents, the children, and our American society.

Physical care is only one aspect of the dilemma; paying the bills is another. Leaving it to father has been an answer, never a solution, and now the public shows awareness of the need for change. In a Roper opinion poll conducted in 1974, two-thirds of the men and women queried said they felt that mothers with custody should share child-support costs if they were able to earn a reasonable income.[12] A national survey made in 1975 for the U.S. Commission on International Women's Year showed that even formerly married women feel the same way: only 24 per cent said the burden should be on the father alone, while 48 per cent said it should be shared if both parents work, and another 30 per cent said it depends on the circumstances.[13]

Judges apparently share this attitude and are less inclined than formerly to routinely order fathers alone to pay child support. According to the same national survey, fewer than half of divorced women with minor children have been granted child support by the courts.[14] There are probably a variety of reasons for this: poverty-level women whose husbands have deserted them and disappeared often do not bother to seek payments; women who can manage alone and are desperately eager for a divorce may forgo it; women who have some savings, and whose children are nearly adult, may not ask for it. But beyond all these reasons, judges have become aware of the problems of men who will probably need to support a new family, and they have tried not to saddle divorcing men—especially those at low-income levels—with child-support obligations that will make it impossible for them to meet their new commitments.[15] Increasingly, judges expect single-parent mothers to work if they possibly can, and more than that, they know that there is another alternative: society itself will support the children by means of Aid to Families with Dependent Children. AFDC is a massive and rapidly expanding multi-billion-dollar welfare program paid for largely by the Department of Health, Education, and Welfare and administered by the states according to their own guidelines. Between 1955 and 1975 the number of families on AFDC grew five-fold. There are now nearly three and a half million such families, nearly all of them headed by women without husbands present; more than half are FMs who receive no child support.[16] (The rest are chiefly unmarried women with illegitimate children, widows with children, and families in which the parents are incapacitated.) To put it another way: of the eight million children under eighteen who are currently living with one FM parent, nearly half are being supported in part or entirely by AFDC money.

It is curious that the growth of the welfare rolls has occurred during the very same years when the number of husband-wife families living in poverty has greatly decreased. But there is an explanation: more and more fathers make no voluntary contributions, more and more default on the payments they were ordered to make. According to various studies, half or more of all fathers who have been directed to support their children pay nothing at all; of the rest, the majority pay late, pay in part, or both.[17] Only about one-fifth pay in full and on time, throughout the years. The situation is worst at the lower economic levels—not because the men are totally unable to pay, but because so many rely on welfare to do it instead. The Department of HEW recently estimated that absent husbands of one and a third million FM women on welfare can actually afford to pay child support but fail to do so.[18]

Many delinquent fathers are black and most of them belong to the poverty culture; they are FMs, but not part of the subculture this book describes. As we said earlier, the folkways and mores of the world we picture here are those of the three-quarters of the formerly married who live above the poverty level—the working class and the middle class. Still, it is significant that an increasing number of the women on AFDC are working class, or even middle class and well educated. A recent Senate subcommittee report points out that in 1970, nearly one-fifth of families headed by college-educated women were below the poverty level, and that many of them, without child support and unable to earn enough, were on AFDC rolls.*[19] Recent word from the Office of Child Support Enforcement is that at present, over 10 per cent of all AFDC mothers have held white-collar jobs.

In the late sixties, toward the end of the hippie era, Lucy Anderson, a minister's daughter from Wisconsin, dropped out of college in her first year and made her way to San Francisco. She soon fell in love with a much older man who had deeply impressed her with his knowledge of the world, his idealism, and his deep devotion to God and religion. They lived together in a commune where Brian worked sporadically as a carpenter, and when Lucy was seven months pregnant they decided to marry. Three years and a second child later, Brian disappeared.

Lucy's parents sent her plane fare back to Wisconsin, and for a while she and the boys stayed in her old bedroom at the par-

---

* Even in our own survey, admittedly deficient in poverty-culture respondents, 8 per cent of the women with minor children report incomes of less than $5,000 a year.

sonage. But the house was small, the Andersons could not cope with the commune-bred children, money was in short supply, and Lucy was unable to find any kind of work in the small town. It was her father, experienced in pastoral counseling, who gently urged her to apply for AFDC. At first Lucy was terribly upset and couldn't understand how her own father could want her to be on welfare, the most degrading thing she could think of. But we recently received a letter from her, and here is part of it:

> After endless red tape, my AFDC payments finally began. I'm in Madison now, in my own apartment; it's small and a bit tacky, but it has *two bedrooms!* I was able to find a half-time job, and the best thing of all is that I'm taking some courses at the university and, one of these days, I'll actually get my degree.
>
> It's strange about the welfare money: I was so dead set against it at first but now I realize that I, the old flower child, was stuck with a lot of outmoded middle-class attitudes and it was my middle-class parents who were really liberated. No, I didn't figure it all out by myself. I'm in a women's group here and found that I'm not the only "nice girl" making it with a little help from Uncle Sam. When you need it, it sure helps.
>
> Yesterday, when the boys came home from school, the door was open and I didn't hear them come in. Craig burst into the kitchen and yelled, "Hey, Mom! You were *singing!* I never heard you singing before!"

For many women, as for Lucy initially, accepting help from AFDC is humiliating, shameful, and damaging to their self-respect. Still, if they have small children and have no day-care facilities available, or are unable to find work that pays enough to support a family, they may have no choice. Only those with some funds to spare—and ex-husbands who can pay—can afford to hire private lawyers to pursue defaulting fathers and force them to obey the court orders. The rest must rely on public prosecutors who, until recently, have had grossly inadequate budgets and staffs for the task.

But now the matter has reached such momentous proportions that the federal government has intervened. In 1974, Congress passed the Title IV-D amendment to the Social Security Act, effective in August, 1975, creating a Federal Child Support Enforcement Program. It reimburses local prosecutors to the extent of three-quarters of their costs for tracking down defaulting fathers and making them pay. (The service is free to welfare mothers.) In addition, it pays local agencies added cash incentives for doing the job. Most important of all, it makes available Social Security and other records for use in locating missing men. HEW estimates that when the enforcement program is in full operation, it will save at least a billion dollars of AFDC money each year, which means that much of the burden will have been shifted from the taxpayers back to the fathers. (The Program also helps enforce payment to families who are not on welfare, but these are a small part of its caseload; in many states, non-welfare families pay a small fee, generally $20 or less.[20])

It is a worthy attempt to check the massive abdication of responsibility by fathers and the massive reliance of mothers on governmental support. But it merely scratches the surface of the problem. Even if HEW's optimistic estimates prove correct, the program will produce only about $400 per child per year—less than one-third the cost of rearing a child in a three-person family at the low-income level (the upper boundary of poverty), and one-fifth or less of the cost at a moderate living standard.[21]

In any case, most formerly married mothers live above the poverty level and are ineligible for AFDC; the solution for them will be a piecemeal one, with costs met partly out of their own earnings, and partly by the fathers, plus government help in the form of more and better free day-care facilities.

But anyone who thinks that men escape lightly should consider the fact that most divorced fathers marry divorced women —most of whom have children. Despite some unfairness all around, a rough sort of justice does get done.

It may be that this is the only solution to the dilemma: if the benefits of divorce are to be available to everyone in the society, then everyone in the society must pay some of the penalties— the undivorced taxpayers as well as the divorced parents and those who are childless.

3. THE SINGLE PARENT

Although single-parent families are nothing new in American society, throughout most of our history they were relatively few in number and mostly the product of mischance rather than choice; illegitimate motherhood and death created the bulk of them. Today, there are nearly three and a half million single-parent families created by separation and divorce—roughly the same number as created by mischance. All told, there is now one single-parent family for every six intact father-mother-child families.*[22]

Welfare administrators, legislators, and social scientists regard broken families as a vast social problem, but many single parents regard their mode of living as a workable—and preferable—alternative to two-parent family life and defend it as a valid option.

Valid, to be sure, but punishingly difficult. For a single parent to work, care for children, and run a home is a monstrous undertaking, one that may never before have been attempted by a large number of people in any society. It is not just that the single parent has to do things she or he is not skilled at, it is that there are so *many* things to do. It is not just that many single mothers find it hard at first to change tires or mow the lawn, or that single fathers find it difficult to shorten a little girl's party dress or to prepare interesting meals until they have had some practice—it's that they have to do *everything*.

Many single parents who anticipated the doubled responsibility could not anticipate the deprivation they would feel from almost never having time to daydream, or simply to idle for a moment, to be alone with themselves and their thoughts. The bathroom is no longer a refuge when there is no one to intercept the two-year-old who bangs on the door, to intervene when the older ones fight, or howl to announce some new disaster. Little children do go to bed early, but they leave behind an endless stream of chores. Older children may clean up after themselves, even help with other household work, but they seem never to go to bed and are omnipresent; the parent has no solitude, and escape to the bedroom to read in privacy, or to talk on the phone, is almost certain to precipitate an urgent discussion about a problem that needs immediate attention. A single parent with teenagers can rarely spend a private evening at home with a date

* From this point on, we will be using the term "single-parent family" to refer only to those resulting from marital breakup.

unless the children go out—in which case, with unerring skill, they burst back in at the least appropriate moment. As one mother put it, "Being a single parent is something like exploring the moon: even though I seem to be alone, I know that the faithful monitors are on the job constantly, beaming my every move back to my fascinated public."

In other times and places the extended family solved some of the problems. Adults and their children lived with relatives, and the loss of a mate still left the single parent with help and companionship. But the extended family runs counter to deeply cherished American values concerning independence, privacy, child-rearing, and the ownership of property. Only a small minority of desperate mothers move in with their parents or other relatives, and these are mostly the very young or the very poor with infants to care for.[23] All too often, the combined family is torn by struggles for dominance, fights about money, quarrels over child-rearing. The single parent feels demeaned, incompetent, and childlike, and the children, according to a recent study, adjust less well to the marital breakup than the children of single-parent families that go it alone.[24]

Even though no generally applicable ways to ease the burdens of the single parent have been found, desperate need has generated an assortment of makeshift solutions; these are some that are being tried:

—A small number of single parents trade days or nights of babysitting, or form day-care co-ops at home, or take each other's children on alternate weekends. A few others trade or barter services: a father may perform heavy or mechanical tasks for a mother who, in return, cooks or sews for him and his children. But such arrangements are hard to come by, and harder to keep intact.

—A few single parents live in commune-like groups; most often these consist of two female-headed families. But as with most American communes, the bonding is frail, the structure of authority unclear, and the chances of conflict many; most of the groups last only a short while. (In addition to these built-in hazards, many communities have ordinances against unrelated families living together in single-family residential areas.)

—In Dallas, the Methodist Conference of North Texas built

and operates a small apartment complex for single-parent families. Called Maple Lawn Apartments, it is a self-supporting, self-contained community, complete with after-school child-care, recreation facilities, and counseling. So far it is only a pilot project, and while it seems like a good idea that ought to spread, funding problems make it unlikely that it will.

—In many communities there are day-care centers that enable parents to work. Some, largely federally funded but run by city and state agencies, are free; others are run by service organizations or private entrepreneurs, and charge fees. The free ones are available only to poor or low-income families, the others often cost more than most single parents can easily afford. In any case, many single parents have no centers in reach at any price.

—The middle-class (particularly suburban) single parent often has to rely on paid help in the home, but such assistants are hard to find, expensive, and prone to problems of their own that tend to make them unreliable.

Clearly, coping with the logistics of the single family is difficult—and yet, with effort, most single parents do cope. What is far harder to deal with by sheer effort are the emotional problems of single parenthood, in particular, guilt about the effects of the breakup on the children. According to divorce counselor Emily Brown, chairperson of the Task Force on Divorce and Divorce Reform of the National Council of Family Relations, "Probably no other aspect of divorce is more guilt-inducing than the parental role."[25] In our own survey sample, more than a quarter of all formerly married parents admit feeling guilty about their children, and well over half are worried about their children's development and their future.

Unfortunately, the burden is most grievous in the first days and months, precisely when the single parent's own emotional condition is apt to be poorest. A minority, it is true, see chiefly good effects on their children even at the outset: somewhat under a fifth of our respondents say that their children were immediately relieved, less nervous, better able to handle school work, more loving, and so on. But half say the first effects were wholly bad, and another third say they were mixed.

How children react to family breakup depends on many

things, but the chief one is age; our survey findings on this point are in general accord with the conclusions of a recent noteworthy study conducted by social worker Judith S. Wallerstein of the University of California at Berkeley, and psychiatrist Joan B. Kelly of Mt. Zion Hospital and Medical Center, San Francisco.[26]

The most painful experiences for single parents usually involve young preschool children, those of, say, two to five. (Children under two often show little awareness of what has happened.) Young children are helpless, grief-stricken, fearful, and above all, uncomprehending. The single parent tries desperately to explain, to reassure, but the children stare wide-eyed, baffled, wounded. They whine and fuss, wet their beds, become picky about food, and uninterested in their toys. Some cry, some are deathly silent, some are panic-stricken when the babysitter arrives, some run for the phone every time it rings, hoping to hear the outside parent. Part of what they do is annoying to the single parent, part is heartbreaking, all of it is guilt provoking. Some examples from our interviews and questionnaires:

A sobbing four-year-old boy clings to his mother's legs and says, "Tell Daddy if he'll come back I'll be good, I promise I'll be real good."

A three-year-old girl rummages frantically through toys and clothing in her closet looking for the old shred of blanket she used to carry around. "I *need* it," she says, "I *need* it."

A five-year-old boy asks his father repeatedly, "But *why* don't you and Mommy love each other any more? I don't get it." And later he asks the question that is really on his mind. "Do Mommies and Daddies ever stop loving their children?"

A four-year-old girl beats her favorite doll savagely. "Bad, naughty, dirty doll," she says, "I'm going to go away and leave you, you're so bad."

Children of grade-school age are somewhat more capable of understanding explanations and accepting reassurances, and they are also a little better able to use such psychological defenses as fantasy and denial to mitigate their fear and grief. Still, they exhibit many forms of regression to infantile behavior, have nightmares and stomachaches, become hyperactive, irritable, demanding. Unlike younger children, they show a great deal of anger; outbursts are sometimes directed at siblings or playmates, but most often—and most appropriately—at their parents. They blame them for their general unhappiness and for causing their painful conflicting loyalties.

When a mother tried to explain to her six-year-old son why she could no longer tolerate his father's behavior, the child turned beet-red, struck out at her, and shouted, "You stop that! He's my Dad! I don't want to hear about that!" A girl, similarly, screamed in a rage for hours—then, abruptly turning quiet and tearful, said, "Mom, I'm so unhappy." A seven-year-old boy told his mother his fantasy again and again: "Some day I'm going to get a million dollars and then I'll get you and Dad to live with me, and we'll all be together again and I'll buy you everything you want." When she tried gently to tell him that it wouldn't happen that way, he became furious, refused to listen, and ran from the room.

Adolescents and teenagers are no less grief-stricken, angry, and worried than young children, but they are rather more capable of understanding the real situation and of using more complicated processes to deal with it and with their emotions. Some argue with the parents, trying to reason them into a reconciliation; some take sides with one and express hatred of the other in order to lessen the dual pull of conflicting loyalties; some tell each parent in turn that they love him or her more than the other in an effort to placate and comfort them both. Many feel embarrassed with their peers, and lie to conceal the truth about what has happened at home. Others, to ameliorate their grief, use a variety of psychological defenses: rationalization ("It's just as well, it would have happened sooner or later anyway"), denial ("It's not a real bust-up, it's just a cooling-off period"), or isolation ("It has nothing to do with me, it's their problem, not mine").

Try as they may to defend themselves, however, not all succeed. Some are deeply shaken in their sense of self and become embittered and cynical ("If that's how Mom and Dad are, I guess I'm the same . . . I'm no good, nobody will ever love me, I'll never love anybody, and I'll never get married. . . . Anybody who trusts anybody else is a dope. . . . Love is bullshit"). Others express their poor self-opinion by their actions: they drink, use drugs, steal, cut school, become sexually promiscuous—all effective ways of saying to the parents, "See what you've done to me!"

When there are children of different ages, a parent may see a wide range of behavior. A thirty-six-year-old woman tells us:

> My fourteen-year-old son was mortified and went to elaborate lengths to try to keep anyone from knowing. My twelve-year-old daughter had seen it coming; she cried a lot, but in the main she seemed vastly relieved. The eight-year-old blamed herself for all our quarrels and threw up regularly for weeks. The seven-year-old told his father, "We'll fix it all up so you can come back, Dad," but he had tantrums, played with matches in his room, and stole money from my purse.

Yet, sometimes children change roles enough to be supportive to a parent, and even an isolated episode of such behavior can be of permanent help. A forty-two-year-old legal secretary with three children, who had been overwhelmed with guilt, describes such an event:

> It was after about two months had passed that I woke up one night at 4 A.M. with a terrible feeling of despair. Had I done right? I was keeping the children from their father. My agony lasted all day, and when I got home that night they asked what was wrong, so I told them. I was royally chewed out by all of them, and the two youngest, thirteen and ten, settled the whole issue by telling me I had done a very good thing because there was no more fighting and tension in the house. My relief was so tremendous I burst into tears. Knowing they felt we were leading a better life was all I needed to accept everything else.

In addition to their struggles with guilt, single parents often find themselves in power struggles with their children. Many a parent reports a loss of governing power when, without a supportive co-parent on hand, she or he is cajoled or worn down by determined children. Teenagers, in particular, often gain a great deal of power in the family and become more like peers of the single parent than like children. This can be a good thing when it redistributes responsibility, but it can be a very poor one when the child assumes the role of Mother's boyfriend or Dad's girlfriend. In such a situation the intrusion of bona fide opposite-sex friends in the parent's life may cause misery and upheaval. Some parents boast of being "pals" or "best friends" with their children when they would do better to be parents.

Conversely, some are overly parental and worry inordinately. If a five-year-old tells a fib, his mother fears that he will become a chronic liar. If a nine-year-old has a falling out with her best friend, her father worries that she will be unable to maintain relationships. If a twelve-year-old boy prefers books and water-colors to touch football, his mother is concerned that the absence of a male model may be inclining him toward homosexuality.

Studies made at the Center for Adults and Children of the Tavistock Institute in England have shown that lone parents, without the help of a second set of corrective eyes, often have trouble seeing their children without distortion.[27] Fortunately, there are now ways to correct this special kind of astigmatism. Many of the support groups and organizations discussed in Chapter II address themselves to the emotional problems of single parenthood, and so do divorce counselors, family therapists, child guidance centers, community mental health centers, some PTAs, family service agencies, and women's groups, among others. The proliferation of helping hands is but another indication of the extent to which the world of the formerly married is rapidly developing mechanisms to deal with its special needs.

The primary emotional problem of the single parent is guilt for having been party to the expulsion of his or her children from the Eden of childhood. But there is a second pervasive source of guilt, and this is the parent's anger with and resentment of the children because they present a serious impediment to the pursuit of happiness. The problem is a common one for the ambitious career woman: she can never work overtime because the children are waiting; she cannot take home a full brief-case because there is barely time in the evening for children and housework; she cannot go on trips for the company; she cannot even go to work when a child wakes up with a fever. This woman is invariably passed over for promotion—and she knows it and resents it.

Fathers with custody face the same conflict between pull of career and children. In some ways they are even worse off than mothers, for employers are not surprised when a woman has to devote herself to her children, but they don't expect it of men. They are often unsympathetic to the male single parent and regard him as peculiar, lacking in ambition, undependable, and possibly troublesome. A sales engineer for an automotive accessory firm tells us how he has been affected:

> I was thirty-six and on the way up when I found myself with three boys [of eight, eleven, and thirteen], a house, and a decent-paying job—but not decent enough for me to afford much help. So I've had to do almost everything myself, and it's been tough to keep house, prepare meals, do the laundry, attend school functions, and give the children all the attention they need. Something had to give and it's been my career. I have a lesser position now than I did when my wife left four years ago.

Children also impede the other great concern of postmarital life—the search for companionship, sex, and love. Not only do children absorb time directly, but every moment of escape from caretaking has to be arranged and scheduled, fitted into the time and money budgets. The spontaneous fling, the madcap adventure, the impetuous weekend, are not for the single parent. In our survey, single parents have nearly as many dating partners and sex partners as outside parents, but the frequency of their dates and sexual experiences is distinctly lower. Nearly half the single parents have less sex as FMs than they did when married, but most outside parents have more.

While some parents try to minimize the conflict by being open enough with the children to have sleep-over dates, others are completely defeated by what they see as incompatible segments of their lives, and claim to have neither opportunity nor energy for social activity. But most of these are people who use single parenthood as a convenient excuse for avoiding either the challenge of sex or the challenge of intimacy. Joseph Epstein, whose *Divorced in America* is the sourest picture of the divorce experience to appear in recent years, describes himself—a single parent—as wallowing in self-pity one evening over a sinkful of pots and pans. He tells himself that having custody of his boys has put a terrible crimp in his social life, that he is not considered much of a catch, that friends do not offer him delectable women

—but then admits to himself that he is glad, because the idea of remarriage is "terrible and terrifying."[28]

But few single parents feel glad when children interfere. It is common for a woman to lament the men who seem interested at first, only to melt away when they see what a complicated establishment is dependent on this woman. One of them, in her mid-thirties, offers testimony:

> It's happened three times now, and I'm about to give up. I meet a man through work, I like him, he likes me, a thing begins to happen between us. We meet, we go out, we get to know each other. So far, so good. Then he asks the girls and me to a Sunday outing—or I can't get a sitter and he comes over for the evening— and I can see his face change and I know it's happening. Because both girls are slobs, and the little one whines too much, and the older one has a reading problem and gets frustrated and angry over every homework page, and they fight with each other—and I can practically *hear* him thinking, "Who needs this?"

Often children interfere even more directly, for as long as they cherish the dream that the outside parent will return, they seek to oust the date, whom they perceive as a threat to the future. Teenagers may be hostile or defiant, or may change their plans and decide to "hang around" in order to be in the way. Small children use equally effective tactics: they develop earaches, stomachaches, toothaches, even finger aches, or throw temper tantrums when the parent is about to go out on a date. Young children are sometimes utterly overt about their feelings; one six-year-old stared sullenly at his mother's dinner guest for a time, then said very softly, "Why don't you go out and lie down in the street and maybe a truck will come and run over you?"

But after a while, when the divorce is final, or the outside parent has moved away or remarried, the children give up the dream of reunion, and switch to a new dream, that of a "new Daddy" or a "new Mommy." The youngest study each date with hopeful eyes, put on their most beguiling selves, lavish hugs and kisses, grow strongly attached to anyone who becomes a regular in the household, and are crushed and bewildered each time their hopes die. The parent suffers with and for the child, wanting desperately to love and be loved, to help fulfill the dream.

But when the children are older, they learn not to invest too much hope in any new arrival, or they become mature enough to understand that not every date is a mate. Parents grow mature as FMs, too, and when they make a good adjustment to postmarital life they communicate their adjustment to their children; those children are likely to become comfortable within the single-parent family and to lay aside irrational hopes or fears concerning the parent's partners.

Although the single-parent family strives for balance, it is always subject to a force that upsets the equilibrium—the outside parent. While he or she usually has no legal right to interfere in decisions concerning the child, influence can be wielded by threats to withhold money, arguments or fights with the single parent, and attempts to sway the children. In some cases, this is a form of continuing marital warfare, a kind of interaction that we will look at more closely in the next chapter. But in most cases, the interference of the outside parent is more a result of a lack of definition of the role. No one is really clear on how much or how little influence the outside parent should have, or how it should be exerted. Legally, it can be as much or as little as has been agreed upon, but morally, its scope is undefined, and there are no clear customs, no adequate guides to proper conduct. The result is that the outsider's influence is usually variable, and hence, disruptive.

The single-parent family is analagous to a mini-state that has exiled a former leader, yet lets him back on its soil for brief, formal visits, and even turns over to him the powers of government at such times. No wonder there is discontent among the populace after his departure, no wonder the government feels rumblings of rebellion after each visit. Even when the outside father has no desire to sabotage the single mother's government, he can hardly help doing so. He no longer lives by her rules; he is not concerned with discipline so much as with keeping some part of the children's loyalty through whatever blandishments and favors he can bring to bear.

Which is why women with custody, though they look forward to the outside father's taking the children off their hands for a day or a weekend, so often dread the children's return. They arrive feeling disloyal to her (and invariably distressed because of it), mutinous, truculent, and angry all over again at not having both parents under the same roof. Every single parent has heard ad nauseam, "Why can't I, Mom? You're mean. Dad *always* lets me." Or "Who says I can't go? That's not fair. I asked Dad and he *said* I could." (The foregoing remarks are always delivered in a whining voice, perhaps with a kick at the sofa leg for emphasis.) Single parents complain that it takes a day or so for children to return to normal after a weekend away.

But some things do change, and the interaction between the single-parent family and the rest of the world has certainly done so rapidly. Not so long ago, the divorced woman and her brood were deviant and worrisome to the neighbors, and the woman with a husband feared the bad influence of "those" children if they played with her own. The children of divorce, for their part, often felt ashamed to bring friends home, especially on weekends, when all families were supposed to be complete.

And discrimination wasn't limited to social stigma, but became survival-threatening when single mothers had great difficulty renting apartments, establishing credit, and finding work.[29] These difficulties have not disappeared but have diminished dramatically due to new laws that bar discrimination based on sex and marital status.

Fathers with custody do not have these particular problems, but they have another kind that might be called inverted discrimination: people view them with a blend of admiration and mistrust, sympathy and suspicion. A single-parent father said at a recent conference, "The hardest thing to deal with is the lack of social acceptance, and you hear about it mostly from your kids. Other kids say to them, 'What's wrong with your father? How come he always cooks and takes care of you and stuff?' " Another speaker added that *his* biggest problem as the father of a three-year-old girl was his neighbor's expectation that he would "screw up" the child psychologically. He was deeply resentful of their incessant smothering good-will and helpfulness, and said that if one more person brought his daughter a doll or a ruffly dress he would hurl it through a window.

But single-parent fathers are appreciated for their accomplishments, too, and are gratified. A forty-year-old school guidance counselor put it this way:

> It's true that some people think that what I do is bizarre or freakish but I find that FM women in the thirty–fifty range, with children of their own at home, really relate to my present situation. They are often quite impressed with my ability and my joy in handling my home and my two boys, and that turns me on. I'm proud of myself for handling what originally scared the hell out of me, and I appreciate it when others, who really understand, notice.

My joy? Do we hear him rightly? With all the special burdens and emotional strains single parenthood entails, can it be joyous?

Apparently, it can. Not at first, when newcomers' lives are in wild disarray, but after they have learned to cope with life, many FMs do find single parenthood rewarding. Difficult, strenuous, almost too much to bear at times—but on balance, deeply satisfying. A large number say they are closer to their children than they were before the breakup; the family has been through a lot together and, as partners in survival, they now have a special kind of bond.

Some of the particular points that single parents make are that rescuing the children from despair and rearing them successfully has become their *raison d'être*; they are proud of themselves for having been able to guide the children through the difficult transition; there is more love in the home without the tensions of a poor marriage; the children are more mature and self-reliant than others of their age. Despite their burdens, the great majority of single parents say they feel much better, in general, than they did after the separation—and the children do too; they think that the long-range effects on their children have either been good, or at worst, partly good and partly bad.

This is not to overlook those who cry out that they can't stand it, those who have actually collapsed under the strain, those who tell of runaways and delinquents, of teenagers who plunged into drugs and sex, or committed suicide. There are those who say quietly that their children have lost something they can never regain, and those who say despairingly that their own lives have been destroyed by the demands of single parenthood.

But most single parents weigh the costs against the gains, and count the outcome worthwhile. They aren't Pollyannas; they recognize their resentment and their deprivation, but are satisfied that they got the best bargain life offered them—and that they did well to buy it. A liquor-store owner of forty-four told us that caring for two children while managing a business has been a burden he resents, even though he went to court to win custody from his alcoholic wife, but, he adds:

> There's no use complaining because there was no alternative I would have found acceptable. It was rough on the boys at first, but now they seem to be in better shape than ever, if you judge from their schoolwork and other outward signs. They like the women I bring around, and always want to know when they're coming back; they like having a female figure around. I have made a nice home for the three of us—a home the oldest child, my grown daughter, comes to with her husband from time to time. It is a great joy to me that I have the love and respect of my children, that they've turned out so well. That we are, after all that has happened, a *family*.

Pride, achievement, love for one's children, satisfaction in seeing them grow up well—these are the components of every parent's joy in parenthood, but the single parent's joy is doubled, as the pain is doubled, because he or she has to do it all alone. Joy reaches a peak when, from time to time, the children themselves unwittingly reveal that the parent did the right thing, chose the right answer, and need not, after all, feel guilty. A thirty-two-year-old social worker describes such a moment for us. Divorced for about a year, she and Robert, the man she now lives with, were sitting in the living room having a drink while her two sons, Alex, seven, and Billy, five, were having dinner in the kitchen, when Billy called out, "Mommy, do you ever cry?"

I: Yes, when I'm sad.
BILLY: You used to be sad and cry all the time.
ALEX: Yes, you did, when Dad lived with us and you had fights with him.
BILLY: But now she doesn't cry.
ALEX: Because she's not sad.

BILLY: Because we live with Robert now and she's happy.

ALEX: And Daddy's happy, too.

BILLY: And Robert is happy, too.

I: Are you guys happy, too?

BILLY: Yes. We didn't like it when you were crying. It made us cry, too. We didn't like that fighting.

ALEX: We were awake. We heard it. Now we never hear fighting and me and Billy and everybody's happier.

4. THE OUTSIDE PARENT

Many a woman with custody is bitter about the behavior of the departed father, and sees it, in feminist terms, as exploitation: the man, like some wandering beast, sought her, impregnated her, then abandoned her to rear the young unaided while he roams free. But these days, the roles are sometimes reversed, and it's the liberated woman who does the roaming while the father becomes the homemaker and single parent. A thirty-two-year-old Philadelphia businessman is as bitter as any feminist:

She said she wasn't any good at being a mother—had never wanted to be one, but I talked her into it. She said I had stopped her from being an actress, she was really on the way until she got locked into marriage and children—and she wanted out. In the end, I gave in and agreed to take care of the kids. So now she lives in New York, and acts in a soap, and sees the children twice a year for a couple of days each time, and sends them birthday and Christmas gifts—and has the rotten nerve to sign the cards, "Your loving Mommy." Some loving Mommy! She doesn't love anything in the world but herself.

The charges against the outside parent are often true. But there is another side to the matter, too: the intense sorrow and deprivation that many outsiders suffer.

For not all outside parents wanted to leave; about half, in fact, did not discard their mates but were themselves discarded. Not all outside parents enjoy their freedom, and most of those who do, have to juggle the enjoyment against feelings of shame, worry, self-disapproval; powerlessness to shape or guide their children; and deprivation and alienation from one's own flesh. This is the stuff of Greek tragedy experienced by Everyman.

It is true, obviously, that the practical problems of the outside parent are not nearly as complex as those of the single parent. Outsiders have a more active social and sexual life, and after a while tend to be generally better adjusted—but in the early days, they are more deeply depressed than single parents; the latter seem to be sustained (or at least distracted) to some degree by the presence of their children.

Separation from their children causes most outsiders chronic frustration and discontent. In addition, the very role of outsider is a sham role, hollow, meaningless, with few functions, few rewards, little or no power, and no prestige. All in all, it adds up to a negative balance, and possibly the only reward lies in the negative value—there is so little responsibility that one is free to serve onself. But the freedom accounts for a pervasive guilt that many outside parents try to conceal with glib rationalizations ("It's not how *much* time you give, it's how *good* the time is"). One unusually candid thirty-seven-year-old man admitted what many others only hinted at:

> I've been doing whatever I want to do these past four years, but I often feel my kids have paid for it. I haven't given them much time or attention. When I'm with them, I enjoy it—I like the feeling that I'm doing the "right" thing—but before it's over I'm always counting the hours until I can take them home and be free again. At times, I see myself as selfish and self-centered—and I hate myself. Sometimes when I realize how much I've short-changed my kids and how I can never make it up to them, I feel like crying.

Deprivation—the loss of everyday experience of one's children—is a characteristic of the outside parent role, too. The days pass, and all the tiny miracles occur, unseen: the baby takes a first step or learns to use a spoon, the six-year-old manages to balance on a two-wheeler or on ice skates, the adolescent dresses for a first date or learns to drive—and the outsider is not there to see, to relish, to overflow with good feeling.

Even the outside parent who sees the children regularly often feels belittled and frustrated by the loss of influence over them. There was so much of yourself that you meant to pass on to your children, so many ways in which you meant to mold them and help them develop into admirable adults. But you can't do it on a once-a-week schedule, you have to *be* there, live with them; an outside parent is more like an uncle, an aunt, a friend of the family, than a parent.

The lack of authority or clearly defined value has a particularly demeaning significance for fathers. Traditionally, fathers were—and to a considerable extent still are—financial providers; in return they had authority and the major share of the control over family decisions. It has been hard enough for many men to accommodate to the recent shift toward equality between husband and wife—but it is especially hard for the outside father to be stripped of rank and command and yet be expected to provide financial support. It is humiliating and infuriating, and it exacerbates whatever problems the outsider is facing as a result of the contemporary crisis of masculinity.[30]

Many respond by struggling to define their rights, or by trying to gain little toeholds of advantages, but all find it difficult. By its very nature the outside parent role "gives rise to endless problems," according to a recent sociological study made for the Department of Health, Education, and Welfare.[31] One day the outsider's ex-wife calls him about some school problem; he goes to school and intercedes, and she is grateful to him. But a few days later they speak again, get into an argument about summer camp, and she tells him that it's none of his business which camp she selects and hangs up the phone. If the outsider took Psychology 101 he may remember the laboratory rat taught to jump at a white door that opened onto food instead of a black door that was immovable and made its nose hurt; when the rat had learned which was which, the colors were switched—and the rat became neurotic. And when the colors are switched, the outside parent withdraws and loses interest in his child.

The only time the outsider can legitimately play the parent role is during visits—a limited, make-believe period within which the interaction is shallow and artificial; it bears the same relation to real parent-child interaction that dating does to marriage. Even the frequency is similar to dating: the great majority of outside parents see their children once a week or less often, and only a minority see them more often or have custody for weeks at a time during the summer.* Whatever the pattern, the

* A few parents have *joint* custody, in which children are shuttled back and

laboratory rat syndrome is all too common: some of the time the outsider is criticized for not spending more time with the children—but other times, he finds visits interfered with and discouraged because it's not convenient for the child, or because the single parent has a regular date or someone living in the home whose presence has changed the situation. Separate agreements grant the outsider "reasonable" visitation rights, but "reasonable" is rarely defined and hence is subject to intermittent dispute.

It is actually during visits that the outside parent is apt to be most aware of the emptiness of the visiting relationship, the inclination to *pass* time rather than really spend time. There is an unfortunate tendency for outside fathers to fill the afternoon or day with amusements, diversions, and treats. One man described to us his typical Saturday with his eight-year-old son: He picks up the boy at 10 A.M., they spend an hour or so at an ice-skating rink or a pool, and then have lunch in a tearoom or a cafeteria; next, they go to a movie —but afterward it's only 3 o'clock, there is still half an afternoon to fill, and the boy is tugging at his father's sleeve and asking, "Hey, Dad, what'll we do now?" This kind of outsider often feels more like an entertainer, an M.C., than a father.

Some outsiders, especially those whose children spend whole weekends or weeks with them, do much better. Instead of putting on a show, they actually "live," do such everyday things as shop, cook, clean, read, listen to records, or watch TV, catch up on homework, and perhaps import some playmates for an hour or two. The time spent together in a real-life context is more rewarding for child and parent alike than an unvarying string of treats, but due to limitations of time, space, or motivation, it is often impossible to arrange.

While all children may find the visiting-parent routine a hard one to adjust to, it is especially difficult for the child if the outsider is the mother. A child cannot easily understand and accept the situation when, from thousands of clues all around him, he knows that it is far more strange for a mother to move away than

forth between the two homes for equal periods of time; if they live within the same school district, they may alternate weeks or months. Some parents alternate years, and at least one child we know of commutes between Europe and the United States each year. In *divided* custody, each parent has custody of one or more of the children.

for a father to do so. When mothers who have given up custody speak about their visits, the special pain of the children—and the mother—comes through even the most restrained telling, as in this brief account by a woman of thirty-one who holds a political office, and has her young son and daughter with her every weekend:

> They often take their father's side because I left, and they say he didn't want me to and they didn't want me to, either. At night, when I tuck them in, they get tearful and upset and beg me to come back. They say Daddy wants me back, they assure me that we could all make it so nice. We have long talks about the situation, but it's hard for them to understand how I, their mother, could want to live away from them and their father, in another house, in another town. Nobody else's mother has done that. After we talk it all over, they seem more accepting, and go to sleep— but they always raise the question again the next week. I never tell them why I did leave and give them up: my husband forced me to when he found out about my affairs. I do tell them that I only left *him*, I didn't leave *them*. But the truth is that, physically, I *did* leave them, and they know it.

For the first year or two, the outside parent's role is a particularly onerous one at important holidays, especially Christmas and Thanksgiving. It is a trial by loneliness for many FMs who see other families together, remember what the gathering of *their* family is like, and are sharply aware that they are excluded from it. It is hard on the children, too, and a number of ex-spouses try to deal with the problem by "playing family": they agree that the outsider will rejoin the family for Christmas morning gift-opening, or for Thanksgiving dinner, and all will be just as if.... The children love it, or seem to, but at what cost the parents find out only later, for playing family reactivates the fantasy of real reunion, reopens the wounds that had begun to heal. Nor is it easy for the adults, who may find the whole charade emotionally strenuous and, as an aftermath, feel not only fatigued, but angry or depressed.

Are there, then, no real rewards in being an outside parent? Surely none that derive from the outsideness itself, but only those vested in the fragmented parenthood that remains. That some does remain is evident since the majority of outside parents in our sample say that though they worry more about their children than while married, they love them more, too; few admit to being less interested in them or less able to handle them. And a sizable minority, particularly those who have had regular, close contact, do, after all, see their children reflect some of their own values. One interviewee, a research physicist now long remarried, told us that for years he worried about his young son who, under his mother's careless guidance, seemed to be growing up with little interest in study or intellectual pursuits. But in his teens, the boy became intrigued by his father's work and began to ask many questions about it. The father regularly took him to his lab and supplied him with non-technical reading material that sparked his imagination and made him want to know even more. Today, the boy is a junior at his father's old college, studying to be not a physicist, but a biologist—a career that will be all his own, not his father's—but close enough to make his father feel that his son is, indeed, a chip off the old block.

5. CHILDREN OF DIVORCE: SOME INCONCLUSIVE CONCLUSIONS

In the long run, after all the worry, most formerly married parents think their children have made good adjustments to the divorce. Only a few believe they have been permanently harmed, or would have been better off had the marriage remained intact.

Is the majority right, or do they view the evidence in a distorted fashion that allays their guilt? Public opinion runs in their favor, but there are a number of psychiatrists, criminologists, and social commentators who disagree, and argue that endemic divorce is creating an ever-larger pool of damaged human beings in our population. Divorced parents cannot help but ponder such opinions and each time a child fails a school course, flounders in a career choice, or fails in marriage, the parent wonders, *Did the divorce do it? Is it my fault?*

What is the evidence of research? What is the verdict? There should be one, for surely enough scientific studies of the matter have been done: in 1970 a painstaking review by Elizabeth Herzog and Cecelia E. Sudia of the Office of Child Development of HEW turned up some 400 more or less relevant works of which 60 were recent, rigorous, and dealt specifically with the effects of father-absence on children (mother-absence is rare, and has received little attention).[32] It would seem that in this mass of material there must be answers.

And there are. But they are both too many and too few. Too many because the conclusions are in disagreement; too few because many studies find no clear evidence either of harm or of lack of harm. Of the 60 studies, 24 concluded that father-absence *was* linked with undesirable traits or behavior in the child, 20 concluded that it was *not*; 16 were unable to arrive at any firm conclusion at all.

A later (1975) review of the literature made for The Urban Institute, a non-profit research organization concerned with problems of city life, sums up the situation similarly: "Clear-cut answers on the effect of father-absence on child development are not [yet] available."[33]

Yet even in the absence of clear-cut answers, those that seem to show a link between broken homes and troubled children are, surprisingly, somewhat reassuring to divorcing parents. For while many of the children do suffer ill effects, the bulk of the evidence shows that it isn't the divorce itself that's to blame so much as the conditions that precede, accompany, or follow it.

Consider delinquency, for instance. There is ample proof that boys in broken homes are more apt to be delinquent than boys in intact homes. But there is also ample evidence that there is more delinquency among boys at lower socio-economic levels—where, concomitantly, there is a high rate of marital breakup. To find out whether divorce is to blame for delinquency, one must first compare boys from broken homes and unbroken homes at the *same* socio-economic level, then compare each group to those from *different* levels. When the effects are thus sorted out, it appears that socio-economic conditions are to blame, and that father-absence at any given level contributes little extra risk of delinquency.[34]

Or consider school achievement. On the average, children with absent fathers do distinctly less well in school than others. But again, this lumps together multiple causes; poor and black children—whatever the marital status of their parents—do less well (on the average) scholastically, than middle-class and white children. When the various factors are sorted out statistically, it becomes clear that socioeconomic and minority group status are the crucial disadvantaging factors and that father-absence has no effect on school performance.[35] (Performance may decline for many, at first, but this is only a transient effect.)

Does the absence of one parent mean that the child will suffer from having no suitable "role model" to emulate? That boys will grow up unmasculine, girls unfeminine—or that either will become homosexual? Certain older studies did suggest such a connection, but they defined masculinity and femininity in ways that are now outmoded. Moreover, recent studies of homosexuality suggest that it is more strongly linked to faulty interactions between parents and their children in intact families, than it is to parent-absence.[36] Still other studies have shown that children with absent parents have enough sex-role models all around them —in school, among friends, relatives, neighbors, and in the media —to offset deprivation at home.[37]

The study by Wallerstein and Kelly, referred to earlier, tackled the matter from another view: it didn't compare children from broken and intact homes, but followed the development of children from single-parent families to see whether they were damaged and if so, whether they healed. Initially, a majority of children in every age group showed undesirable effects of various sorts, some quite severe. But a year later, most of the older children had made a full recovery, as had a majority of the younger ones. Among the youngest, more than four-tenths were still psychologically ailing, but some of these had been troubled before the separation, and were at least no worse a year later. All in all, marital dissolution did no ultimate harm to three-quarters of all the children studied—and about a fifth actually seemed to benefit from it, and made rapid spurts in development or emotional health.[38]

Both the positive and the negative aspects of this study must be viewed with some caution. It is a small sample and has no controls—that is, it makes no comparison with similar children in intact homes.* We have no way of knowing whether or not there is less, more, or as much distress among such children as

* Wallerstein and Kelly's sample consists of 131 children from 60 broken homes in Marin County, an affluent suburban area north of San Francisco.

among those in the study. But it is at least suggestive that other studies that do make such comparisons regularly fail to show any definite link between divorce and psychiatric or emotional disorders in children.[39]

Clearly, the evidence is not conclusive. There may well be, and probably is, more disturbance in children of divorce than in children of happy, intact homes. But that is irrelevant, since FMs did not *have* happy homes; the only question is, then, can an unhappy couple do less harm to their children by staying together or by getting a divorce? That, along with their personal desires, must be part of their reckoning.

Even two decades ago, before divorce was as acceptable as it is now, Dr. J. Louise Despert, a child psychiatrist and author of *Children of Divorce*, dared to say what had previously been unsayable: "Divorce is not automatically destructive to children; the marriage which divorce ends may have been more so."[40] She based her opinion primarily on her work with her own patients, but since then, a number of broader studies have been done; they compare children of broken and unbroken homes as to school performance, self-image, relationship with parents, and so forth. More than a dozen such studies have found that children in single-parent families have fewer and less severe disturbances than children in unbroken but unhappy homes.[41]

Although the evidence is inconclusive, it seems clear enough that divorce is less culpable of harming the children than other factors—factors that are, even now, losing some of their force. For as divorce becomes more common and less socially deviant, as more forms of social and economic support come into being for single parents and their families, as remarriage has become the norm and living-together arrangements grow increasingly acceptable, as divorced women grow more able to find adequate employment—as all this has happened, is happening, and will happen—the total impact of divorce on children becomes ever less severe, less alienating, less lasting.

Therefore, considering the evidence available, it is our conclusion that the effect of divorce on children, while not wholly good, is better than if there had been no divorce. Given the options, divorce is the only choice.

VII

War And Peace

1. THE DREAM OF EASY DIVORCE

In 1643, the English poet John Milton, trapped in a wretched marriage, wrote a radical tract in favor of easy divorce. At the time, rigid canon law made divorce virtually impossible, but Milton urged Parliament to allow it on the simple ground of "contrariety of mind," and thereby "with one gentle stroking to wipe away ten thousand tears out of the life of man." He was far ahead of his time; the idea was condemned as scandalous and heretical, and Parliament ignored it.

But Milton had raised what would remain the central question in an ongoing debate for the next three centuries: should divorce be made readily available or not? Although the debate crossed the Atlantic with the colonists, there was relatively little progress toward liberalizing divorce law in this country until the latter part of the nineteenth century. Even by mid-twentieth century, only a few states had anything resembling easy divorce. Change was glacially slow because of continuing strong church opposition, and because of the basic political nature of the problem: easy divorce is an extension of the rights of the individual; difficult divorce is a preservation of state power over private life.

But it was for this very reason that divorce reform gained

momentum at the same time as the civil rights movement. In an era when individual rights were greatly extended for ethnic minorities, women, accused persons, and prisoners, it was inevitable that the rights of the unhappily married would be extended too. Public opinion shifted toward easy divorce, and by 1974 a Roper poll found that a majority of Americans favored it if a husband and wife no longer loved each other—the simple equivalent of Milton's "contrariety of mind."[1] In the past dozen years, one state after the other has added to its divorce law such easy grounds as incompatibility and breakdown of the relationship, and many states have added no-fault procedures as an option, while others now make all divorces no-fault actions.

Yet, no legislation has succeeded completely in wiping away all "ten thousand tears" at a stroke, for even when the legal process is made relatively painless and reasonably fair, emotional divorce remains painful in the extreme. As in a bereavement, whether the loved one died slowly or swiftly, we grieve just the same. The divorce experience is no longer worsened by social obloquy, and the rigors of legal combat are being ameliorated. But there is no lessening of the struggle for emotional disconnection, of the need to sever innumerable bonds of habit and need, of mutual dependency, of lingering love and lingering hatred. The truth, unsuspected by many newcomers, is that the marriage relationship is not over when the spouses say it is, nor when one of them moves out, nor when a court declares the marriage ended. Many couples—especially those with children —remain partly married in an emotional (and economic) sense for years; some, for most of their lives; a few, forever. Almost none, when they decided to part, knew how difficult it would be to become fully and finally divorced.

2. ODI ET AMO: *THE SEPARATED MARRIAGE*

"*Odi et amo,*" wrote the poet Catullus to his faithless lover, Clodia, "I hate and I love. Perhaps you ask how that can be; I do not know, but I feel it and I am in torment."

It is an apt summary of how most people feel in the early weeks and months of separation, and they *are* in torment when they continue to have obsessive thoughts of the other spouse, endlessly replay the scenes of their life together, and experience intensified rather than diminished feelings of anger and hatred, or longing and love.

The discarded, the parents, and the long-married may suffer the torment more intensely than others, but all suffer it more than they expected to. For few realize until they are separated how totally bound they were by the threads of shared experience, friends, thoughts, habits, relatives, possessions. Every word, thought, and movement reminds them of what has been lost; every tug against the web of entanglement reawakens their yearning for what is gone, and inflames their anger at having been robbed of it.

For most of the newly separated, the opposing emotions are not equally powerful. Anger toward the ex-spouse is the predominant feeling, anger so overpowering in some people that they become alarmed and even worry about their sanity. Rage bursts forth like a scalding geyser every time they recall each separate hurt, each ruined hope, each promise unkept.

The totally inhibited, who cannot voice or even think their anger, get ulcers, suffer depressions, or have accidents, turning their anger back upon their hapless selves. Healthier people often use fantasy to release some part of the pressure, as did one man in his thirties who had lengthy daydreams of revenge each day while he drove to and from work, and often even while he sat at his desk:

> I would have stationery printed with her name and address and then use it to write the phone and electric companies and tell them to cut off the service. I'd call an undertaker and send him to her place with a hearse to pick up a dead body. I'd have a ton of manure dumped in her driveway. I'd hire some goon to slash her tires, break her windows at night to terrify her, maybe even beat her up. Naturally, I never did any of those things. But whenever I thought about how badly I wanted to get even with her, I'd grind my teeth together until they ached and I was afraid I'd break a tooth.

Most people aren't restricted to daydreams, for the practical details of separation necessitate many contacts during which rage can easily and spontaneously erupt. In the middle of a mundane phone call about picking up some forgotten belonging, seeing the children, or signing a joint tax return, the careful, polite conversation may be abruptly punctured by a barbed remark, some reminder of an old offense, followed by the exasperated rejoinder, "My God, you're not going to start *that* again!" or a dead silence, or the slamming down of the telephone. Or worse, an infuriated counterattack; words, words, words—the same pummeling and clawing with words as before, but now with even greater desire to wound and tear.

Many, in their frenzy, go beyond words; they commit acts of minor violence upon each other's property or person and are amazed and appalled—civilized people who thought themselves incapable of it—at their own barbarity, and at their perverse pleasure in hurting and being hurt. Some examples:

—A woman refuses to let her husband enter her apartment to retrieve two expensive tailor-made suits that were delivered to his old address by error; she tells him to wait on the sidewalk and she'll send them down. Then she opens the window and heaves the suits into the middle of a wet and filthy street where they are instantly run over by a passing truck.

—A man returning his children from an outing "accidentally" backs his car into his wife's, bashing in a door. He laughs wildly, says he's sorry—but does it again on the next two visits. When she refuses to let him take the children another time, she finds him dogging her steps through a supermarket, pushing an empty cart, saying nothing, but grinning evilly each time she nervously looks back at him.

—A woman has her door lock changed because her separated husband has been letting himself in whenever he pleases, ostensibly to look for mail or to pick up a book. When he can't open the door, he kicks it in, breaking the lock and splintering the frame. His wife rushes to the kitchen, seizes a carving knife; they glare at each other speechless and unmoving for minutes, until at last he turns and stalks out, sweeping two porcelain lamps to the floor as he goes.

Beyond violence to person or property, some willfully damage the other's most fragile possession—his or her reputation. They tell and retell the "story" to their mutual friends, enlarging upon the misdeeds of the other, confiding dreadful tales of such extraordinary intimacy that the friends will never dare to ask for confirmation of the facts—yet never forget them.

Ugly as all this is, it nevertheless has a purpose; it is the labor of birth, the wrenching free from the womb of marriage. Sometimes a concerned friend will urge the newcomer to stop dwelling in the past, to forget the wrongs, the hurt, to put anger aside and be free of it. But it is poor advice: anger expressed tends to break the bonds, anger suppressed or withheld for fear of retaliation keeps one tied to the ex-spouse in a hideous intimacy such as Dante might have envisioned for sinners.

Love is the other side of the terrible coin—love, or what has become of it: unbidden, tormenting visions of tender moments that flood back from the past; surges of longing that make one seize the phone, hesitate, then replace it; strange impulses that make one walk or drive past the other's home, to no purpose whatsoever.

For some, leftover love is never openly expressed. They remember the past, they fantasize scenes of reconciliation and love-making, they grow maudlin and tearful, write long letters they will never mail. A few talk about their love to their friends as catharsis, perhaps in the hope that the friend will pass the word along to the other—who, in their fantasies, will be so overcome by it that he or she will return, tender-eyed, forgiving, sorrowful, open-armed.

Many actually express their feelings to the spouse, directly or in disguised form. A man calls his wife to find out how she is or to exchange news, and says, "After all, we do still *care* about each other, don't we?" A woman greets her husband, when he returns the children, with a cuddly hug and a warm kiss, calls him "dear," and urges him to stay and have a drink. One woman, middle-aged, sorrowing, and rejected, regularly invites her scientist husband to dine with her and the children, prepares his favorite dishes, and listens admiringly as he talks at length about his latest projects. He lives apart from her and pursues other women, but continues to exploit her leftover love and enjoy these comfortable and comforting evenings, despite the fact that he considers the marriage dead.

Some FMs know that they are afflicted with residual love;

others are surprised each time it manifests itself, even though it happens again and again. A man's birthday comes and goes with no card or call from the wife he left three months before; he is deeply distressed at her neglect—and is depressed to find that he cares. A beautiful young graduate student, still on the same campus as her separated husband, dates one good-looking man after the other, always hoping that her husband will see how desirable she is to others, reevaluate her, and want her back. A man who broke away from his wife and thought he was glad to be free asks his young children what Mommy does in the evenings. When he learns that she dates, and that one friend sometimes stays overnight, he is suffocated by jealousy; he can think of nothing but "his Amy" in bed with another man, pays no attention to the children, is unable to eat his lunch, finally tells them that he has an upset stomach and has to take them home early.

And sometimes, both parties are so strongly drawn to each other that they easily lapse into seductive and intimate behavior when they are together. A couple in their late thirties, living apart, plan a meeting to work out separation-agreement details in a "civilized" fashion by themselves. They meet in the bar of a small, charming restaurant, have a couple of drinks, make social chit-chat, tell each other how they've been these past weeks. They go in to dinner, forget about their business, and act increasingly like two strangers on a date. Finally, he says that the children must be asleep by now; she feels herself blush a little, and replies that no doubt they are. Their eyes meet, they say no more, but leave the restaurant and hurry home, pay the sitter, and fall into bed in a frenzy of slightly drunken, slightly maudlin desire. Afterward, they laughingly remind themselves of the business they meant to transact, and begin to talk about it. Very soon they disagree, grow edgy and disagreeable; the glow of love-making has faded. They both feel deceived (but by whom?), and both tell themselves that the whole thing was a mistake. And yet they make the same mistake time after time, for months.

Such stories are remarkably common.[2] FMs are more secretive about having sex with their estranged spouses than with others, because they feel foolish about it, as if they are guilty of moral weakness and addiction to an old habit. There are some couples whose addiction continues to the very brink of legal divorce, and even beyond it. A man in his thirties ruefully notes, "We were actually late for our divorce because we had spent the night together in a hotel and had made love 'one last time' in the morning when we should have been on our way."

But for the great majority, leftover love and leftover desire wane quickly during the early months of separation, partly burned out by anger, partly worn away by the grieving process, partly undermined by the beginning of FM social life. One young woman, proud that she was holding a responsible job and taking good care of her son, was in fine spirits until each time her husband came to visit the child; then she would close herself into another room, tremble uncontrollably, cry, and feel upset for hours afterward. We interviewed her three months after her separation, a few days after her first date. She told us with great pleasure that her husband had come the day before, and for the first time she hadn't cried and was able to spend the day in a normal fashion; she realized that she was beginning to unburden herself of her unwanted love for her husband.

There is so much work to do before one can be even partly free of a spouse. Children, money, a multitude of objects have to be discussed, planned for, and properly divided—but the most difficult work of all takes place not in the home, and not in the bank, but in one's mind. Here, within the mysterious convolutions of the brain, is the intricate tracery that generates the hate and the love, the habit and the interdependence, of which the failed marriage was constructed; here the work of disconnecting and rearranging innumerable connections must be done.

Little wonder that time and again newcomers find themselves wondering if, after all, it is worth all this. Might it not be possible—and better—to go back, give the kiss of peace, forgive, forget, try again?

In our survey sample, 55 per cent of the men and 44 per cent of the women had thought about reconciliation, and about two-thirds of those men and slightly fewer of the women had actually suggested it to their spouses. Professor Weiss estimates that about half of all separations lead to reconciliations rather than divorce.[3]

But many of the reconciliations last no more than a matter of weeks or months, ending up in re-separations that do lead to divorce; they serve as the final proof that the marriage cannot work. The bulk of reconciliations occur soon after breakup, for the longer the separation lasts, the more of the work of disentanglement the partners have done. Yet, the task of disentangling is so massive that even after people have actually filed divorce petitions with the court, many—at least one couple in eight and perhaps more than twice that many—drop the action.[4]

There are no hard data on the kinds of reconciliations FMs have and how they turn out, but from our interviews and our survey responses, there seem to be three major patterns.

At one extreme, and not very common, are those couples who follow a pattern of repeated separation and reconciliation. The Karps—"the carping Karps," their friends call them—are in their early sixties now, having battled their way through forty years of marriage. Co-owners of a real estate brokerage, they worked together and fought together for ten years before their first separation. It was a minor one: Hal simply slept on a couch in the rear room of their office suite for a couple of days. Later, after several such episodes, he took a small furnished apartment in town and would stay there for a week or more whenever the relationship reached a boiling point. Sometimes he did so—and still does—at his own option, sometimes because Vera asked him to please get the hell out. But through it all, they have never seriously considered divorce because of their daughter (at first) and the successful business that needed them both. Or, at least, that's what they believe. An observer might find it more plausible to explain their marriage as a neurotic interaction in which noise, turmoil, and conflict are the chief ways of expressing intimacy.

At the other extreme, and also uncommon, are those cases in which a long, serious separation ends in a lasting reconciliation. Sal and Julia Bruno separated in their early forties because of multiple conflicts, including sexual difficulties (she was rarely interested, or even cooperative). Sal made his way, after a while, into the world of the formerly married, and came to like it, but he never pressed for actual divorce because every time he even hinted at it, Julia threatened to commit suicide and Sal was afraid she would. But at last he became seriously involved with a woman and began to think that he would like to marry her. At this point, Julia, either intuitively sensing that something was really different about Sal, or perhaps having passed through some meaningful midlife change herself, suddenly began to dress more attractively, changed her hairstyle, and became openly seductive with her husband. When he rather reluctantly went to bed with her, she showed more enthusiasm than she ever had before. Although he was surprised, Sal remained cool. Then Julia began to weep and begged him to come back to her, swearing that she needed and wanted him. Sal was half-attracted by the idea and half-resentful, but he finally looked at it from a practical point of view: at his age, he told himself, with probable lifetime alimony to pay, he could never make a really comfortable second life. Moving back with Julia would be the sensible thing to do, even though it would mean giving up a lot. Sal sighed, decided to be sensible, and moved back in. That was four years ago. It is not a wonderful marriage, but it is a reasonably comfortable one now, and both partners think there is no chance that they will ever separate again.

The typical pattern, however, is exemplified by Ted and Anita Barnes. When they were both in their late twenties, after three years of marriage, Anita became sexually involved with another man, and Ted, finding out about it, became distraught and abusive. Anita was abusive in return, blaming her affair on Ted's shortcomings, and the marriage broke up after a series of violent battles. The Barneses lived apart for a year. Ted came to see the children twice a week but Anita always tried to be out; when they did see each other, they usually remained cold and taciturn, and occasionally were openly hostile.

But Ted was basically a family man who missed home life, and wanted to come back. Anita's affair was having its ups and downs, she was feeling restless and insecure, and when Ted broached the idea of reconciliation, she decided to give the marriage another chance. She told her lover that she had to find out if the marriage could be salvaged, and that she would let him know in a few months whether or not she would see him again.

Although Ted was happy to come back, Anita was deeply ambivalent, and the relationship was strained and contentious from the first. Things worsened almost daily as tempers flared over the most trivial issues. In three months they separated again, and this time they both wanted a divorce. Even though Anita's lover was no longer available, they went ahead with it, were divorced within eight months, and have both since remarried.

3. VIOLENCE AT THE PEACE CONFERENCE

Divorce can be compared to civil war that flares up when a country becomes so divided in its ideology that it splits into two warring factions. Only after peace negotiations have been concluded and a treaty signed can the war-torn adversaries begin to settle down to reconstruction as two separate and independent nations.

Similarly, one couple, divided by dissension, does not become two separate persons until there has been a peace conference, a meeting (or series of meetings) at which separation terms are agreed upon by both factions, and that are later made part of a legal divorce by the court.

Unlike a nation torn by civil war, however, the peace conference of the divorcing is not conducted during a truce but is apt to take the form of a bloody battle, the last great offensive and counter-offensive of the war. This is so because in over two-thirds of the states, the laws make it possible for one party to harass the other by means of extortion, threats, punishments, and attrition.[5] Only the young and childless, those with little property and no child custody or support, or alimony, to fight over, often escape conflict and complete the legal process in an uneventful and non-combative fashion.*

The great majority of states have not yet adopted true no-fault divorce, but still adhere to the principle that a marriage cannot end unless an "innocent" spouse successfully sues a "guilty" one for some form of marital misconduct; this makes divorce an adversarial proceeding, one in which the spouses are opponents at law. Should the defendant have reason to contest the suit, the plaintiff must fight for the divorce by means of a court trial—a difficult, costly, and humiliating procedure with an uncertain outcome. Only if the defendant does *not* contest the

---

* Nowadays few young, childless women ask for alimony, and almost none who do seek it are granted it by the courts.[6]

charges, but actually cooperates with the plaintiff, is the court-room procedure easy and predictable.

In fact, over nine-tenths of all divorce suits *are* uncontested;[7] the judge merely asks the plaintiff a few routine questions, notes that the defendant does not deny the charges, and thereupon grants the divorce. It seems a peaceful enough ceremony—but behind the olive-branch-decked façade lies a brutal reality: it is highly likely that the lawyers for the spouses fought a savage and merciless battle beforehand to achieve a separation agreement husband and wife would both agree to—the sine qua non of peaceful cooperation in court.

It is usual, in such negotiations, for each side to bargain on the basis of what would probably happen if the case were tried before a judge, a situation fraught with opportunity for one side to punish the other, and for the other to retaliate by any means available. A spouse who is reluctant to divorce can, for instance, demand unfair and punitive financial terms as the price of coop-eration; this is, in a sense, a "seller's market," and the seller sets the price. If, however, the reluctant spouse is guilty of some gross marital misconduct—for example, infidelity—the tables may be turned, for the one who wants the divorce can threaten to go to court, expose the other's misdeeds, and depend upon a moralistic judge to grant harsh retribution. Either spouse may, under threat, fight back with endless delays, or with counter-threats, to contest and refute the charges, to offer evidence of the other's misdeeds in order to block the divorce, to renegotiate the financial settlement, and/or to fight for custody of the children. What should be a dispassionate, collaborative drafting of a peace treaty becomes instead a trial by combat, a savage struggle for revenge and victory; the two sides cooperate only when each, having done all it can do to the other, finally agrees to settle and to proceed with an uncontested divorce suit.*

But in the states that have enacted true no-fault divorce laws —California was the first in 1970, and fourteen others have

---

* Divorces obtained in a state other than one's own, and "quickie" divorces in the Caribbean, do not circumvent the need for ultimate cooperation; both require signed separation agreements and powers of attorney. They are resorted to only in the interest of speed, but because of the extra costs involved and the trend toward easier divorce laws at home they now account for only a small percentage of all American divorces.[8]

followed suit so far[9]—the process is quite different. Any man or woman can ask the court for a divorce on the ground that the marriage has suffered irremediable breakdown. The other spouse is not charged with having done any wrong, is not a defendant in the action, and cannot contest it. Neither spouse can delay the divorce in order to extort advantageous terms from the other; neither one can use the other's marital misconduct to force agreement to an unfair division of property or punitively high (or low) alimony. The issues of money and property (and custody) do have to be settled, but if the spouses and their lawyers cannot come to terms themselves, the judge will hear the facts and divide the property equitably, as the law dictates. The court fixes the amount of alimony—if any—according to the financial evidence, not on the basis of who was at fault or what caused the breakdown of the marriage; as a result, the ferocity of negotiations is dramatically diminished.

Divorce transactions can still be long, loud, and unpleasant, but they fall far short of the battles that rage when the goal is exploitation or punishment. Couples may quarrel fiercely when there is a good deal of property, or a good deal of hostility, or both, but quarrels can revolve only around such matters as what the house or business is worth on the market; what value to set on the furniture (if she is to keep it, she rates it junk while he says it's priceless, and vice versa); what the earning power of each is; what each needs to live on; and so forth. The process may exacerbate the couple's mutual anger, but rarely to the same extent as negotiations in fault states, since neither can take unfair advantage of the other. As a result, nine out of ten divorcing couples in California do reach agreement out of court on all or nearly all collateral matters. According to measurements made by sociologist Lenore Weitzman, director of the California Divorce Law Research Project at the University of California at Berkeley, judges typically hear the routine, uncontested divorce case in less than two minutes.[10]

What is truly revolutionary is that neither spouse can keep the other from freedom while financial and custody issues are in dispute, since it is possible (though not common) for either one to ask the court to grant the divorce at once and to settle the other issues later and separately. The following item appeared in

The New York Times on December 25, 1976; to any one of the many New Yorkers stalled in seemingly endless divorce negotiations, it must have seemed like a report from some remote and marvelously enlightened country—and the Christmas present they would have most loved to have:

> A judge in Superior Court in Los Angeles granted a divorce to Carol Lawrence and Robert Goulet. At the request of Mr. Goulet, who made his Broadway debut as Sir Lancelot in "Camelot," the "dissolution of marriage"* became effective immediately, and the court will decide later on custody for the couple's sons and division of communal property.

In fault states, each trial by combat is unique, but a great many proceed somewhat as in the following playlet:

Scene 1
HE: Well, then, I guess we're agreed. I'll move out tomorrow and we'll get together next week to work out the details. I think we can be perfectly civilized about it, don't you?

SHE: Oh, of course! I certainly know you're fair, and I believe you know I am.

Scene 2
HE: Naturally, I want you to keep the house and stay here with the kids.

SHE: That's very decent of you.

HE: But of course I'm sure you'll agree it's only fair to have it appraised and deduct the value of my half from your half of the savings.

SHE: Fair? *Fair?* You can't possibly be serious! You know what the house is worth and how much we have in savings! I won't have a cent left. Oh, you bastard, I should have known better than to trust you. You'd probably be delighted if we all starved to death.

HE: Now that's ridiculous. You're getting hysterical over nothing. You *know* I'll give you enough alimony and child support so that you won't have to worry.

SHE: I'm worried already. What do you mean by "enough"?

HE: Well . . . I figured five hundred a month ought to do it.

SHE: Five hundred a month? Is that what you said? Five hundred

---

* In California, the term "dissolution of marriage" has replaced "divorce" in court, though not in everyday speech.

a month? Are you kidding or something? You know I'll need at least twice that. Every time you launched one of your big economy drives you pointed out to me how much it costs to run this place. *You* know what we spend.

HE: What *I* know has nothing to do with anything. What *you'd* better know is that you're going to have to change your lifestyle. I have to live, too, in case you never thought about it, and the only way we can manage is for you to go back to work. . . . Well, say something, don't just stand there glaring at me. I didn't say you'd have to go out and hustle, I just said work. You know, *work?* Most women work.

SHE: Work? Work? What the hell do you think I do all day besides work to turn this split-level shanty *you* picked out into a decent home for the kids? But this is pointless. I don't want to talk about it any more. You can talk to my lawyer. I'll be getting one first thing in the morning.

Scene 3

SHE: It's not as if I'm out for blood. All I want is enough to keep things going until the kids are old enough to come home from school to an empty house. I can't make anything on a part-time job—he's got to admit that what I want is reasonable.

HER LAWYER: Forget it! Even if he does think it's reasonable, there's not a lawyer in this city who's going to let him pay it.

SHE: I can't believe it. He isn't *like* that.

HER LAWYER: They're all like that—and if they aren't at first, they soon wise up. I'm afraid you'll have to stop counting on his goodness of heart and get down to the real issues. He deserted you, didn't he?

SHE: Deserted me? Well, no, I told you, we agreed . . .

HER LAWYER: Look, according to the law, when one spouse moves out of the house and leaves the other, that's desertion; the court takes a dim view of that. And you told me that he sometimes shouted at you and embarrassed you in front of friends, right? And that he tried to keep you from going to your church, right? That's cruelty, you know, and the court doesn't like that, either. *You* didn't want this separation—he did— and you can make him pay for it. You tell me you need more money, but if you insist on acting like Elsie Dinsmore, you won't get a cent. Now, you must have come here for a reason —and I assume it's because you want me to help you get what you're entitled to, right?

SHE: Well, uh . . . yes, of course, but . . .

HER LAWYER: You never get as much as you ask for, you know, so you have to start out by asking for a lot more and then settle. Understand?

SHE: Yes. Well, uh, I guess that's okay. I mean, you know what's best.

Scene 4

HE: We did have good years together—and there are the kids to think about; I would really like to do the right thing.

HIS LAWYER: Naturally. It's clear you're a decent guy. But you have to think about your own life, too. You'll probably want to remarry, maybe have more children—it's part of my job to protect you against your own too-generous instincts. Now, as a matter of fact, I heard from her lawyer this morning, and I think that when you hear what they're asking for, you'll feel quite different about things. For openers, she wants the house, *all* the savings, and 50 per cent of your income for alimony and child support.

HE: What? All the savings? Half of my income? Is she crazy? Listen—oh my God, is there any chance that she can *get* all that? What'll I do? I never thought . . .

HIS LAWYER: Easy, now, don't panic. I'm here to help you, and if you'll just stop playing Boy Scout, we'll dig in our heels, counter with a *very* low offer, maybe hint that she'll have to get out of the house so it can be sold. . . . Don't worry, we'll deal with it so that you don't get wiped out. But the first thing *you* have to do is stop feeling so guilty. Remember how she nagged you, how she demanded you let the children go to her church when you were dead set against it. There's no reason why you should become a pauper so she can live out her life in grand style, is there?

HE: No. Of course not. What a bitch! You're absolutely right.

Scene 5

HE: Why are you trying to ruin my whole life? I never dreamed you'd pull anything like this. How can you be so greedy, so ruthless?

SHE: Ruthless? *You* talk about ruthless when you don't even care if your kids wind up in the street? *You*'re the one who said we'd be civilized. You're as civilized as Attila the Hun. You lousy hypocrite!

HE: *Me* a hypocrite? I thought you were the big women's libber. What happened to your phony independence?

SHE: It doesn't take a women's libber to recognize a prototype male chauvinist pig—you pig!

HE: Who the hell do you think you are to call me names? I don't need this crap. I'll—[blah, blah, blah]

SHE: Is that so? Well, [blah, blah, blah]

[Sound of two phones being slammed down hard]

Scene 6

HER LAWYER: Ridiculous!

HIS LAWYER: You know we can prove it.

HER LAWYER: And *you* know what *we* can prove.

HIS LAWYER: You can't prove a thing.

HER LAWYER: You'll find out what we can prove when we get to court, because you've heard our bottom line; my client won't settle for a penny less.

HIS LAWYER: Then we'll have to see you in court because you've heard our bottom line and *my* client won't settle for a penny more.

Scenes 7 and 8

[Exactly the same as scene 6, but with bottom lines approaching each other.]

Scene 9

[He, She, and both lawyers at conference table. Much smiling and good will by lawyers, who chat pleasantly with each other and make a date for lunch next week. He and She are white-faced and tight-lipped as they sign and initial pages; they avoid each other's eyes and leave after saying goodbye only to their lawyers.]

Scene 10

JUDGE: The defendant not having denied these charges, the divorce is granted to plaintiff, and the separation agreement is incorporated in the decree. Next case!

Whenever unfair advantage can be taken, it is likely that someone will take it—and that the one taken advantage of will seek a way to retaliate. It is often astonishing—even to people who deal professionally with those in the throes of divorce proceedings—to see the punishment spouses are willing to inflict on each other. A New York business man, although eager to be divorced, held up proceedings for a year while he gathered affidavits and depositions to force his wife to surrender an undistinguished piece of sculpture she claimed he had given her (by forgetting to take it when he left). A Boston schoolteacher hired detectives to smash their way into her husband's ski lodge in the middle of the night and photograph him in bed with a married woman in order to increase her own bargaining power. A Tennessee computer programmer picked up his son as he left school one day, and whisked him across a state border; he then notified his wife that she would never see the boy again unless she cut her alimony demand in half. In New Jersey, a community-property state, an irate man took "cutting in half" literally: since the law said that all property was to be divided equally between husband and wife, he used a chain saw to cut their $80,000 house—walls, floors, beams, and all—right down the middle.

These, of course, are only curiosa. The most common form of punishment, surely the one complained about most, is alimony; it has been used in that capacity by innumerable women who felt that their husbands had mistreated them or wanted to get rid of them. But this is a perversion of its original purpose, for alimony, when it came into being, was intended only to provide sustenance; since nearly all women were wholly dependent on their husbands at that time, alimony for divorced women was a necessity. But after a while, "wronged" women began to seek, and often to get, high alimony as retribution. Under fault law and the double standard of an earlier time, women were usually seen as "pure" and good, while men, known to be lustful and beastly, were nearly always the defendants in divorce cases—malefactors deserving of penalties. Even after it became commonplace for women to work outside the home, it seemed to many women that they were entitled to alimony regardless of their earning power, for hadn't their husbands promised to love and keep them as long as they lived—and hadn't they broken the promise?

But contemporary women, increasingly work-oriented and independent, have rethought their need for, and their right to, alimony. In two different national polls taken in 1974 and 1975, two-thirds of the women questioned opposed alimony for separated or divorced women who could earn a living—as most now can.[11] Even among those women who were already FMs, over six out of ten felt the same way.

There are two ways of assessing alimony, though, and the "independent woman" view is decried by many feminists who feel that women are entitled to "severance pay," "deferred compensation," or a "maintenance" or "transition subsidy" if they have devoted themselves to being homemakers instead of pursuing an independent career. Diane Blank, a feminist lawyer in New York, says succinctly, "If you get away from the word alimony, the concept is a fair one."[12]

One has only to think of a husband who unilaterally leaves his wife on the assumption that she can get a job and carry on; but if that woman has an infant, if she has no training, or if she has been out of the job market for a long time—or even if, because she is a woman, her pay is low—she clearly needs help until she can be self-supporting. It is for this reason that many feminists and divorce lawyers take what seems like a curiously reactionary stance on divorce reform: they prefer the feudalistic fault system to the egalitarian no-fault system because the former gives women advantages in the fight for money. Elizabeth Spalding, national coordinator of the marriage and divorce task force of the National Organization for Women, has said that no-fault divorce law, by permitting either partner to get out at will, "destroys the bargaining power of the reluctant spouse"—she meant the wife—to negotiate for alimony.[13] The California experience seems to prove the point: Professor Weitzman reports that since no-fault has gone into effect in that state, a significantly smaller percentage of women with young children are receiving alimony than formerly. Judges are slightly more willing to order support for older women who have not been working and who have little chance of supporting themselves; Professor Weitzman notes, however, that most women, old or young, are not granted alimony.[14]

However, many changes in alimony and other divorce practices are due not only to no-fault law, but rather to the *zeitgeist*. Philip F. Solomon, president of the American Academy of Matrimonial Lawyers, says that in contested cases in fault states, judges are more and more inclined to take into account the wife's age, health, ability to work, the length of the marriage, and whether the children are of school age.[15] During the last decade, average alimony awards have been dropping in both fault and no-fault states; moreover, there is a definite trend toward limited-term rather than permanent alimony. In 1975, a national survey found that only one out of every seven separated or divorced women had been awarded alimony or maintenance—half as many as in 1939.[16]

In one way, this represents progress toward equality—yet, it seems manifestly unfair to overlook the value of a woman's homemaking and child-rearing, or to ignore the difficulty many women have in finding adequate jobs or in being able to work at all while rearing small children. In an increasing number of states —including the no-fault states—the problem is being dealt with by a shift away from alimony and toward an equal division of property or an equitable distribution of assets.[17] Under such laws the wife is assured of a fair share of whatever assets there are— and in fourteen states, the reckoning of what is fair includes the value of her services as a homemaker during the years of the marriage.[18] In only about a fifth of the states there is still no provision for property division, and a wife can make no claim on anything the husband has chosen to keep in his own name;[19] not surprisingly, it is in these states that the fiercest alimony battles are currently waged.

But the overall trend is toward equality and in the direction of doing away with fault doctrines and procedures, and eliminating—or at least minimizing—the use of harassment, extortion, and all forms of unfair combat.

Public opinion has swung sufficiently toward the no-fault ethic so that nearly all states now have no-fault grounds for those couples who want to use them. And, Philip Solomon says, "We're all heading for *true* no-fault; I expect to see a splurge of such legislation during the next ten years."

In states where fault law still prevails, there are some mitigating forces now at work. Most divorce counselors, when they have clients going through the process, seek to reduce the intensity of hostile interaction between them and to keep them from using litigation to express bitterness. "The divorce counselor," writes Esther Oshiver Fisher, who is one herself as well as editor of the *Journal of Divorce*, "can play a significant role in reducing the anger and bitterness which so often lead to a wife's extravagant demands and a husband's parsimonious offers."[20]

Divorce mediation—an application of the principles used at the bargaining tables of management and labor—is another device that can be used to mitigate conflict. In 1975, Atlanta family counselors William Neville and O.J. Coogler founded the Family Mediation Center, Inc., the first such service of its kind. Divorcing couples using the center sign a contract agreeing to work out their settlement together, in the presence of a mediator, rather than through lawyers; if they reach an impasse, an arbitrator is available to make decisions on the unresolved points. The experiment has attracted wide attention, and Neville and Coogler are training other mediators in the hope that their idea will spread to other cities and states. Apparently it is catching on, for in 1976 the American Arbitration Association announced that its Family Dispute Services would offer mediation for couples seeking to work out their own separation agreements.

In several states—including three that have fault laws—couples who want to divorce without any kind of outside assistance can buy do-it-yourself divorce books and kits. The books explain how to do it, the kits contain the various forms that must be filed, along with detailed instructions for doing so.* A New York newspaper recently reported that one woman, using a paperback book, was divorced for a total cost of $59.00; she would have spent $99.00 for a kit, hundreds for a lawyer.[21] This is a single example, but in Los Angeles, Family Court officials estimate that 18 per cent of 1977 divorce agreements will be completed by the couples themselves.[22]

Professor Weitzman reports that in California most lawyers and judges have seen a very distinct decline in the contentiousness of divorcing spouses since the advent of no-fault law. Her research team will be undertaking a follow-up study to see whether the decline was due primarily to the change in the law or to changing social attitudes. In either case, since both law and attitudes are moving in the no-fault direction elsewhere, it seems

---

* The authors and purveyors of the do-it-yourself kits caution that lawyerless divorce is probably advisable only for couples without minor children and without complicated property issues.

clear that the trend throughout the nation is bound to be one of decreasing violence at the peace table.

An era is drawing to a close. Unfortunately for many of those whose stories are told in this book and for many others who will read the book, the end of the divorce war will come too late to spare them its miseries. It may be ten or twenty years before the new philosophy of divorce is fully embodied in law and custom in most parts of the nation; in the most conservative strongholds, it may even take generations. But regardless of precisely how long it takes, we seem to be approaching a future in which the divorce process will actually lessen, rather than exacerbate and perpetuate, warfare between divorcing people.

4. THE UNFINAL DIVORCE

By the time a final decree is handed down, the former husband and wife have almost severed the complex web that has attached them to each other. Almost, but usually not altogether; most of the newly divorced remain connected to each other—some by only a single strand, a few by a surprising entanglement of them —for months, for years, or even for most of their lives. Divorce puts a formal end to marriage, but often does not and cannot wholly end the marriage relationship; indeed, the divorce agreement—and the divorced themselves—may keep some of the strands of the web intact long after the judge has declared the marriage dissolved.

George Brotherton, tall, trim, and in his mid-thirties, is staring out of the window of a plane on a flight from Albany to Washington. He is thinking what a fool he is—but at the same time, he is aware of a touch of pride and deep pleasure as he ruminates about his romantic folly. For two years, ever since his divorce, he has gone to Washington one weekend a month, ostensibly to visit his children; but far more than incidentally, he also sees his former wife. She is now married to a diplomat, a man who is often away on official business, and she and George have fallen into an established pattern. On the two days he is in Washington, he picks up the children right after breakfast and keeps them out through lunch. As soon as he returns them to their home, he goes back to his hotel—where his former wife joins him an hour or so later. They spend the remainder of the day first in bed, later in parks or out-of-the-way restaurants, acting like two lovers who have just discovered each other. Every now and then George asks her to divorce her husband and come back to him, but she demurs and says marriage between them would fail for all the same reasons it failed the first time. But occasionally, whimsically, it seems like a good idea to *her*—and when she suggests it, George feels intensely anxious, and his replies are cautious and ambiguous. So she remains married, he continues a pallid relationship with a woman in Albany, and they both feel trapped —and entranced—by what they regard as their *grand amour*.

It lasts for one more year; then she does get divorced—and George, suddenly confronted with reality, finds that he doesn't love her at all. Instead, he is strongly drawn to the Albany woman and wonders why he was so blind to her endearing qualities until now.

Lillian Scheeler, a nervous wisp of a woman in her early forties, hangs up the phone and is stricken with an instant migraine; she has just had another shouting match with Andrew, the husband she divorced twelve years ago. They had wrangled all through the marriage; he was an old-fashioned domineering male, she a fledgling feminist, and by the time they separated, they were bitter enemies. They still are, and still carry on a zealous feud. He has often held back on her skimpy alimony payments, or sent her checks that bounced; she has had him summoned into court and ordered to pay up. He has systematically seduced the children with elaborate gifts in an effort to undermine her control over them. For instance, Billy carelessly left his bike unlocked time and again until it was stolen, and Lillian told him to get a paper route and earn another one; when Billy complained to his father, he was presented with a new bike the next day. Five years ago, Andrew finally induced the children to tell Lillian they preferred to live with Daddy and his new wife. Lillian was heartsick, but she let them go; now, however, she is the one who tries to undermine *his* influence, and when they quarrel, she often threatens to go to court to petition for the children's return. Even though she has a good job, she insists on her pittance of alimony and still demands that it be paid on time.

Divorced as long as they were married, Lillian and Andrew have been unable to relinquish their intense struggle with each other—but now it is beginning to wind down. The children are in college and off the scene much of the time, and soon they'll be on their own. As for the alimony, Lillian is considering remarriage; if the alimony ends, the Scheelers will have nothing to quarrel about and the last binding tie will be cut.

Dan Jersild, leaving the hospital at 9 P.M., the end of visiting hours, is annoyed with himself. He has just unwillingly spent a tedious evening trying to amuse and comfort his ex-wife, who is suffering from a bleeding ulcer. Dan and Elaine, both twenty-nine now, had been high-school sweethearts, were married for four years, and have been divorced for three. Although they had no children, they have remained in close contact—usually at Elaine's instigation. It isn't that she is still in love with Dan, but she is dependent on his friendship and his emotional support. Sometimes she calls him in the middle of the night because she is sleepless and worried about her health or her job (she is an advertising art director and works under high pressure). Dan is often with a woman friend, but Elaine manages to sound so desperate, always on the verge of tears, that he is unable to put her off. In spite of his friend's disgust, he spends as long as an hour on the phone reassuring and advising her. Today, Elaine's urgent call came in the middle of an important business meeting and when he heard her frail whispered plea, he promised to go directly from work to the hospital. He spent the entire evening there silently asking himself *What am I doing here?* And later, *Why do I always respond to her calls, even though I hardly even like her? When the hell will I have the guts to tell her to leave me alone?*

The answer is: In another couple of years. For that's when Dan will remarry—and will withdraw from the old allegiance in order to protect the new one.

As these cases suggest, the divorced may remain bound to each other by any one or a combination of several ties: the remnants of love or hate, money, co-parenthood, dependence, moral obligation, or habit.

Love for, or sexual attraction to, the former mate lingers on for some divorced people just as it did during their separation period. Roughly a quarter of the divorced FMs in our survey admit that they still feel jealous or despairing when they hear about their ex-spouse's relationships with others, and some of them still dream of reconciliation for years after the decree is granted.

Again, as with the separated, hatred or anger is still more common and more enduring among the divorced than are positive feelings. Many months after the final decree, anger is the principal emotion a third of all FMs feel about their ex-mates, and it is an important component of the feelings of many others. It tends to dwindle over the years, but for a few, anger is still strong enough to produce bitter conflict after ten or more years have passed.

A sense of moral obligation, while brought into play only infrequently, seems to exist, at least for the first year or two, for many FMs. Except for those who truly hate each other, most would come to each other's rescue in an emergency. A man or woman taken seriously ill, under arrest, or in urgent need of a loan, will often call upon the ex-spouse for help if there isn't anyone else to turn to; the call is only rarely refused. Some ex-spouses have supportive-dependent relationships that function without emergencies: one often calls the other for advice or information (*Who's your dentist these days? What do you think of this year's Mustang? Do you have any current information about tax-exempts? How do you make cheese fondue?*), while the other enjoys being consulted and leaned upon. When one of the pair remarries, the new spouse generally objects to the leftover relationship, and it ends.

Residual emotional involvements based on tangible connections—regular payments, or children, or both—may remain unchanged as long as the obligations are in force. Even a man who never sees or speaks to his former wife may feel enraged each time he has to make out a check to her, and each time she receives it, she feels grimly satisfied that he has to send it—or dissatisfied and furious because the amount is so little. Some men seek petty revenge by sending the checks late, for less than the full amount, or "forgetfully" unsigned. One man frequently sends his with a note saying that his account is almost overdrawn and the check must not be deposited for ten days; it isn't true—but his ex-wife isn't sure, and is exasperated by the delay. But when she is exasperated once too often, she gets her lawyer to threaten him with a court action to garnishee his wages.

Yet even such pernicious relationships come to an end when the alimony does, as is usually the case within a few years (either because it was limited in duration by the agreement or because the woman remarries). After a while, with the fuel gone, the fire dies down, the embers fade, and only a pale ash of hatred is left.

It is quite otherwise with that large majority of the divorced who had children together; they can never fully end their relationship. Once a child is born, says Paul Bohannan in *Divorce and After*, parents become kin to each other by virtue of the mixture of their genes within the child, a relationship divorce can never end.[23] Co-parents, they are intimately involved with each other when the child is small, less so later, but never wholly disjoined. For years there are conferences about visits, school, camp, orthodontia, summer jobs, and college applications. The parents will always meet, and socialize, first at school plays, confirmations, and graduations, later at weddings, births, grandchildren's birthday parties. For some of the time they will remain bound to each other not only by co-parenthood, but by money —child support, and possibly alimony.

This web of connection preserves some traces of the former relationship; if the couple is not particularly hostile, the quasi-familial interaction prolongs slight feelings of friendship—even, at times, affection. Here is a fairly common kind of statement:

[Woman, thirty-six] Three years ago I hated my husband; all I could think about was the pain and misery he had caused me. But I've learned a lot about myself and now I realize I don't have to be perfect, as he expected me to be; I understand him a lot better, too, and I can be quite calm when he starts one of his games. We see each other regularly because of the children—but without any pressure on either of us—and we've become rather close. Some of the time I have rather loving feelings about him, and I think he does about me. In a way, that isn't good because I find it hard, now, to accept the fact that he's remarried. But eventually, I suppose I'll be free of any emotional ties to him—except for the bond of the children. Anyway, I hope I will.

She recognizes that her loving feelings are a kind of captivity, but some divorced people fail to see that. Although they were unable to tolerate the demands and intimacy of marriage and family life, they can now enact a charade of love-and-family-life because they are at a safe distance. Often, one of the pair breaks away yet keeps an emotional hold on the other for some years; the exploited one, out of dependency or other neurotic need, is a willing Trilby. Here is an affecting story from a thirty-year-old woman, a junior executive in a Western department store:

When our second son was only a few months old, Curt told me he wanted more out of life than he was getting; he said he needed "more room." I begged him to stay, said I'd do anything at all, but he was determined to go. He claimed there was no other woman, but I guessed there was, and later on he admitted it. I felt as if I had no future without him, I cried all the time, I was so miserable. Then he began coming around to see the children more often; he told me that his affair was over, he had made a mistake, he loved me, I was his only friend, he missed us all, he needed us. We would talk for hours, feel closer than ever, and end up having sexual relations—and then he would leave. He was always talking about moving back in but he never got around to doing it; he kept saying he needed another few weeks to straighten out some things.

Finally, I got so upset I went to a psychologist, and he asked me why I was letting this grown man act like a child while I acted like an indulgent mommy to him. That did it, just like that. I filed for divorce—we have no-fault, so Curt couldn't fight it. He never thought I'd go through with it, but I did. I felt so pleased with myself at first—but after a while I realized that it hadn't changed anything. Whenever Curt feels down he still comes here and tells me the same old stories, and I still feel sorry for him, and we still make love. Then he leaves and I don't see him for a while. I guess there's no hope for us.

Sometimes we fight, and then he holds back the support money. I almost had him jailed once, but he paid up in time. He was mad

—but we never stay mad at each other, we always make up. The psychologist was right—Curt *is* another child to me, but I don't seem to be able to do anything about it. People love in different ways, and I guess this is just our way—although I admit it's pretty strange.

It is far more common for the post-divorce relationship to be antagonistic, since the bonds of co-parenthood and money may be inherently galling. When, as is usual, the man is the outside parent, he often finds it a constant irritant to have to keep paying money without any voice in the ways the money is spent, or the ways in which the children are raised. She, on the other hand, as often as not feels short-changed by the whole arrangement and resents his resentment. Over one-third of the women in our sample said that their ex-husbands used money as a means of getting even for grievances new or old. Women do it too, though less often; they sometimes make demands for money out of pique rather than need.

The other major bond —and major instrument of revenge—is the children. Virtually all FMs agree that it is wrong to use children as weapons because it is so harmful to them; but many, without even realizing (or admitting to themselves) what they are doing, do use their children to punish or put pressure on an ex-spouse. The single parent can limit or obstruct visits for flimsy reasons, make the outsider wait in the car or on the sidewalk for long periods of time, or move far away so that visits are difficult, expensive, or impossible. The outside parent can play similar nasty games. He may cancel plans at the last minute to inconvenience his ex-wife, lose his sense of time and be hours early or late on visiting days, and encourage the children to flout all the rules about homework, television, bedtime, snacking, dress, or manners.

One of the most damaging ways of all to use children in post-marital warfare is to confide in them and portray the other parent as the villain in the breakup of the marriage. One man turned his daughters into chronic rebels against their mother by telling them repeatedly, with tears in his eyes, how much he had loved her and how she had broken his heart. And a woman regularly told her twelve-year-old son about his father's ruinous business mistakes, his emotional instability, and his physical attacks upon her, until the boy finally refused to see or even speak to his father again.

Continuing anger of such an order is as much an enslavement to the broken marriage as continuing love; it preempts the emotional energy of the individual and stands in the way of normal adjustment and a new life. Happily, in today's world of the formerly married, the milieu is conducive to emancipation; new friends, new interests, new forms of help, and new loves break the hold of the past. Children grow up, time passes, and finally there comes a time when one can remember having felt wildly angry—but can no longer remember exactly why, or what it actually felt like. Only then can one say that the marriage is over, the promise of divorce—at long last—kept.

5. THE FINAL DIVORCE

Most ex-spouses need from three to five years (and some need longer) to reach the stage where they feel only indifferent, or mildly friendly, toward each other. Then, in spite of kinship that some have through children; a bank of stored memories, good and bad; the lasting influence of shared experience; and a lingering feeling of familial concern—in spite of everything, there is little or no affect left, and the divorce is final.

The divorces that reach this stage most easily are those of the childless young who parted without rancor. One interviewee, a woman of forty-two, long remarried, barely recalls her first husband or their marriage. They were college classmates and married in their senior year because they wanted to live together; to do so without being married would have scandalized their parents and society twenty years ago. College life involved the two in shared activities, but as soon as they graduated and moved on to jobs and an apartment in the city they discovered that they had nothing in common. When she fell in love with a fellow employee six months later, she told her husband, asked for a divorce, and went her way. "He never turned a hair," she told us, "and I guess he was as relieved to have it over with as I was." By now, she says, she barely remembers what he looked like and recalls almost nothing of their life together. No doubt a certain number of childless couples separating today will make similar comments some years from now.

While the great majority of the divorced never achieve such complete disconnection, what they do achieve is good enough, since it does not interfere with postmarital life or impede their pursuit of happiness. A composite portrait of the final divorce, drawn from our questionnaires and interviews, has these features:

—The story undergoes some revision: the FM lays less blame on the ex-spouse, and may even sound a note of compassion for him or her.

—When ex-mates meet, the traits in one that used to trigger hostility in the other have little or no effect. Once-infuriating stubbornness, flightiness, or grumpiness have no impact now. Neither do criticisms or snide remarks of a sort that formerly made the blood boil. "Still a backseat driver, I see," or "What's happened to you? You seem to be on time these days?" don't raise the blood's temperature by so much as a single degree. At most, such verbal tics produce a shrug or a snort. "Who cares what she thinks or says?" is a typical comment. Or, "He's like a stranger whose behavior I just don't give a damn about; it has nothing to do with me."

—Similarly, the once-attractive traits have lost their power. "I look at her and listen to what she says," a man may say, "and wonder why I ever loved her." And a woman may say the same thing. There are no more fantasies of reconciliation, no fugitive wishes to be rejoined; the great majority have come to think, in the light of what they have learned about human relations and themselves, that there was no way in which they could have made the marriage work.

—There is no longer any unconscious compulsion to call or contact the other on one pretext or another. The innumerable discussions about the children, mutual friends, or other matters that once seemed so urgent don't, any more.

—The interaction between ex-spouses, if they must be in contact, evolves into a civil routine. Many label their relationship "friendly"; it isn't real friendship, of the kind in which people seek each other out because they want to be together, but rather a passing sociable friendliness such as one has with neighbors, casual acquaintances, and business associates. "When I meet him now," a young woman writes, "there is a kind of camaraderie. We are mutually concerned about our child, we shared a lot of experiences in the past, we know each other better than most people do—but the camaraderie exists only because we *must* meet. I wouldn't choose to spend time with him socially." (A few think it chic to socialize with their ex-spouses, and a very few really become good friends after the tensions of their divorce have been relaxed.)

—Lastly, those who are finally divorced have filled in the gaps in their lives that were left by the failure of the marriage. They no longer *need* their ex-spouses as sexual partners or romantic lovers, as companions or confidants, as mentors or pupils, as leaders or followers—or as adversaries in battle. They have rebuilt their lives so as to meet their emotional and social needs through others—a few of them by becoming contented foragers in the garden of singleness, but most, by finding other people to love and becoming, once more, partners in partnerships.

VIII

In Love Again

1. FALLING IN L _ _ _

Kathy had been divorced for almost two years when she met Bill at a Manhattan cocktail party. He had arrived with a date and paused to scan the room from the doorway. He noticed Kathy even before he entered the room—and she sensed his notice, caught his glance for a small fraction of a second—but with the practiced eye of the veteran she saw at once that he was with a woman and turned her attention elsewhere. She was not at all surprised, however, when he shouldered his way through the crowd to reach her side several minutes later.

"I've always been a fool for raven-haired beauties in blue dresses," he said.

"And for red-haired ones in green dresses?" she asked.

"That's a promising sign—you noticed. Look, we're on our way to a dinner party and I have to leave soon, so tell me everything, quick."

In spite of the twinkle in his coal-black eyes and his bantering tone, she knew that he wasn't *just* bantering. He was about thirty-eight, she thought, not handsome, but with his rugged, lean face and straight, silky black hair, he was certainly the most attractive man she had seen in a long time. She liked his half-mocking seriousness and the way he looked straight at her, giving her his complete, intense attention.

"Katherine Spellman. I'm divorced, old enough to have a couple of young kids; I'm a book designer. And you?"

"Bill Mardin. Divorced. No children. Biologist."

"Really divorced? Or separated?"

He laughed, as if she had said something very funny. "Divorced. I *said* divorced. Would you like to see my legal papers? I could bring them over tomorrow night."

"Thanks," she said with a smile. "I'm willing to take your word. And besides, I'm busy tomorrow night."

"Oh. The night after, then? The first one you're free?"

"Sorry," Kathy said. "I just happen to be tied up the next few nights. I *would* like to see you, but my time is very scarce."

"I have the answer," Bill said as he pulled his wallet out of his pocket. He opened it to show Kathy a picture of a small, lovely beach house, all cedar and glass, perched atop a dune, its big open deck facing the ocean. "Like it?" he asked.

"Oh, yes. It's fantastic! Is it yours?"

"Yep. All mine. And just finished. Brand new. So. Why don't you plan on coming out to Amagansett with me next Friday night and we can have the whole weekend to get acquainted."

"You're joking," Kathy said, "I don't even know you."

"I know. That's why I said we can have the whole weekend to get acquainted."

In spite of her experience in the world of the formerly married, Kathy was surprised—and surprised at herself for being surprised. She thought she had seen enough, done enough, felt enough to be blasé, and yet she was strangely disturbed by this seemingly very secure—almost arrogant—stranger, smiling at her so expectantly, waiting for her reply to his ridiculous invitation.

"No," she said firmly. "Of course I wouldn't go off with you for a weekend. For all I know you might turn out to be Jack the Ripper."

"But you do know." He was still looking straight at her with his gentle smile. "You know I'm not, and you know I'd like you to come—and I think you'd like to. I have to go now. We'll talk about it again. Are you in the phone book?"

Kathy nodded; he nodded back at her, and left.

That night Kathy had a hard time falling asleep. Time and again she ran through her conversation with Bill. It was indicative of their experience as FMs that they had spotted each other instantly, and wasted no time at all but got right to the exchange of essential information. And she had apparently learned a few things, she mused. It was no accident that she had bluntly asked if he was divorced. Kathy had had two serious love relationships since her own marriage broke up. The first, during her separation period, was with a man who was separated, too. They had clung to each other like two drowning persons—but shortly after her divorce was final, they began to quarrel every time they were together, and before long, it occurred to Kathy that they were really terribly ill-suited to each other, intellectually and emotionally. When she tried to break it off, he became angry and abusive, and accused her of using him just to ease her entrance into postmarital life. It was true, she ruefully admitted. But it was also true that he had used her in the same way—only he wasn't ready to let go yet; he still need her as a crutch, and he continued to pursue her tenaciously for weeks, calling at all hours, weeping, embarrassing her acutely by showing up at her office a couple of times. She was (miraculously, it seemed) saved when the company he worked for transferred him to another city.

The second man came along a year later. They had cared deeply for each other, spoken of marriage as soon as he got his divorce; for a few weeks Kathy was wildly happy and believed that her life problems were solved forever. But then he decided to go back to his wife. Kathy never understood why, and she was devastated; she found it impossible to believe that this could have happened, and she became deeply depressed. It seemed to her that she was even more upset than she had been after her divorce. She had gone back into psychotherapy for a time and was fine now—but never, never again would she get involved with a man who was still married. And never would she get involved faster than the man, or to a greater extent. Self-preservation was the name of the game.

She was still asleep the next morning when the phone rang. Bill said without introduction, "I was thinking that since you're busy tonight, and it's a beautiful day, and Sunday besides, I could be at your place in about a half hour, ask you to give me a cup of coffee, then we could take a long walk in the park, watch birds, maybe hold hands, talk a lot, and have a champagne brunch at the Plaza."

"Make it forty-five minutes," Kathy said.

Kathy did keep her previously made date that night, but she broke the next one and saw Bill instead. She saw him the following night, too, and the ones after that. By Friday morning she couldn't imagine spending the weekend any place but at Bill's house in Amagansett. She called her ex-husband to make sure he would pick up the children by five-thirty.

Kathy wasn't being irresponsible or even impulsive. It was, she felt, a clear-cut case of moving swiftly to seize an opportunity, for this man was the one she had prepared for, had practiced for, had readied herself for with all her dates, her sexual experiences, her two brief but serious relationships. Now she wasn't grasping at straws, filling a void, testing herself, learning the ropes. She had done all that, with any number of men. By this time she felt secure within herself, felt that she had finally made a success of life as an FM; she had a nice apartment and a better-than-average job; the children seemed happy and were doing well in school. Her social life was good and so were her spirits—most of the time. But Kathy didn't find dating much fun any more. The glamour had worn off and she longed for an intimate, exclusive relationship with someone she didn't have to have *dates* with, a person who would simply be her other half as she would be his; two people who would turn each other from singles into partners again. She wanted what the current jargon called a "deep meaningful relationship."

Like Kathy, most of the formerly married need two or three years before they are fully ready to form a love relationship with an appropriate partner. To judge from our sample, many are not even willing to love again for a number of months, and a still larger number say they will never remarry. But as time passes, they begin to change their minds on both scores; within two to three years nearly all men and more than nine out of ten women are willing or even eager to fall in love and more than half of both men and women want to remarry. (As the census data show, most of the reluctant ones *do* eventually remarry.)[1]

During these reparative years, most FMs not only change their minds but have one or more relationships of some emotional intensity or importance. They are not all major love affairs: most, in fact, are trial runs or experiments: skyrocket infatuations that flare and burn out in a few weeks; dating relationships that gradually grow close and loving, then, unaccountably, waste away; friendships—with sexual intimacy—that are comforting and pleasing but never more than that. For most of the formerly married, such trials are an essential part of the process of self-discovery and development; the typical man or woman has three imperfect or abortive love relationships before entering one that is deep enough and "right" enough to seem like a realistic basis for remarriage.

Why should these veterans of love, who have known what it is and how it can fail, make so many false starts? In part, because being in love again is a trial-and-error process; they cannot be certain, until they have tried it, whether a new and unfamiliar kind of love relationship will suit them, and whether it has within it all that it promises to have.

But in far larger part, the false starts they make are due to their own ambivalence. They want to love and be loved even more than the unmarried young, for not only do they feel that a part of their past lives is missing, but divorce has proven them to be failures at marriage and now they have a driving need to prove themselves successful at it. Yet, they are terrified of making another mistake, of getting trapped in another failure. They so mistrust their own feelings that sometimes they are deeply troubled by—and often hostile to—the very partners they feel most drawn to.

And so for a time they try to set limits to their feelings, avoid emotional commitment, and keep love under control. They do it with the "safety-in-numbers" gambit, the "too-busy-to-see-you-this-week" maneuver, a few deftly dropped hints about the others in their lives.

And perhaps most important of all, they scrupulously avoid the word *love*. The formerly married man or woman may fall dizzyingly and passionately in love, but meticulously abstain from letting the word slip out. To do so is like keeping a hand on a chess piece: the move can still be unmade, nothing has been decided. But the word, uttered, is a move made, beyond recall. A century ago, "I love you" was tantamount to a marriage proposal; today, though it means less than that, it still creates a commitment, defines the relationship, implies its future.

So FMs are slow to say *love*. They may speak to each other, gaze at each other, and embrace each other like people in love, but they give their feelings other and safer labels. They say: "Do you have any idea how much I like you?," "It's so good to be with you," "I like the way we are together," and "You're very special to me." At first, such statements may seem to be warm and intimate, but as times passes, it becomes clear that they are ways of declaring that the relationship is a limited one, is not an obligation on either party, and is not a prelude to marriage. This comment comes from a middle-aged Connecticut woman who has been an FM for four years:

> I find it impossible to say "I love you" to him. I'm afraid to bare my soul and leave myself so vulnerable. I'm afraid that if this relationship breaks up, I'll be devastated—if I have expressed my feelings. My impression is that as long as I don't verbalize anything, I can control the situation, but once I say it, I destroy the self-built fence around me and become easy prey to emotional pain. Yes, truth to tell, we're in a trial-marriage situation. I tried to hold back, and couldn't. We were dating four or five times a week, and on the other days I often found myself calling him to say, "I'm coming over." And now I've agreed that we should live together for a while to see how it works out. But I *still* can't say, "I love you."

Similarly, FMs speak of "the man (or woman) I'm seeing," or "the person I'm going with (or involved with)"; they are never "in love" or having a "love affair" but are having a "serious involvement," or a "relationship."

In addition to all these conscious techniques, the formerly married defend themselves unconsciously, too, and in quite different ways. They make "wrong" choices again and again—choices so wrong that they are actually *right*, for they are safe; they have serious built-in defects that limit them in depth and duration and obviate any possibility of marriage. Ambivalent FMs are drawn to those who are still married, or to divorced people who announce that they are polygamous by nature or against marriage on other grounds; they select those who are too far removed in age or in cultural background to be a good fit, or who are too neurotic or emotionally unsuitable in some other way, and so on.

Such choices perfectly meet the need of the fearful FM to avoid a permanent commitment, although they often elicit the contempt of friends who wonder why so-and-so keeps making such foolish choices instead of doing some intelligent mate-shopping. Here is an uncommonly candid statement from a thirty-six-year-old woman who has been divorced for eleven years and has had a fair amount of psychotherapy; she probably speaks for a great many who are less insightful than she and have similar problems. Unfortunately, insight hasn't yet solved anything for her, but it *is* usually a prerequisite to change and successful outcome.

> I've had several deep involvements lasting from three to eighteen months; I'm still investigating the reasons they haven't worked out—that is, resulted in marriage. I know that a lot of it has to do with my own internal conflicts (wanting love and security but wanting independence), with the fact that I've chosen many men who have *not* wanted a serious involvement themselves, the fact that I become clingy and possessive of a man when we are involved so that he gets frightened and leaves, the fact that I fall in love too quickly, have unrealistic expectations, and am basically still scared to death of making myself vulnerable. I'm not altogether sure of what really goes on.

While she says she's not sure of what goes on, she does have a number of important clues and may be on the road to achieving her goals. Not so this thirty-seven-year-old law professor who thinks he wants to remarry but seems always to choose someone who is not a genuine marriage candidate.

> My first major relationship was with a student who moved in on me and stayed for two years. Although I loved her deeply, I felt from the beginning that she lacked the charm, the intelligence, or the beauty that I wanted my wife to have.
> The second one was also a student who became involved with

me just a short time before she was to marry someone else. She went ahead with the marriage anyway and was too immature to realize that she should end one or the other, so both the marriage and the affair dragged on for four years. Her husband finally threw her out—but by then it was too late for me.

The third relationship was with a twenty-one-year-old medical student who was emotionally and physically much younger than I. After an emotionally intense summer, she decided to break away from the relationship. I overreacted and I guess I scared her so thoroughly that she has never spoken to me again.

The professor, it seems, has unwittingly—and consistently—made wrong choices in order to avoid marriage. One of them involved one of the safest of all choices, and a common one, a partner who is married to someone else. While the FM who loves a married person may consciously believe that the best of all possible outcomes would be for the beloved to get a divorce, the alliance actually provides a temporary snug harbor, a place where one can be safe from the rough winds and water of loveless dating, and safe, too, from marrying too soon and making a mistake.

While they are in the midst of such involvements, many FMs do not see them as wrong or hopeless, though they usually do in retrospect. Yet, even then, they rarely regret the failed relationships but think of them as part of learning, growing, and becoming emancipated from the bondage of the past—and thereby, eventually becoming ready to fall in love without fear. Meanwhile, however, the imperfect involvements are not only a means to an end but an end in themselves. For a time, there is a partner, a companion who banishes loneliness and emptiness, and this is rewarding for as long as it lasts. A thirty-two-year-old woman says of her current affair:

> We have a life-long relationship going, but neither of us feels that we would be suitable marriage partners. We plan to have others in our lives, and it is even likely that we will eventually marry others. If so, we hope always to continue a very deep friendship. Of course we don't really know how the transition in our relationship will work out until we reach that point.
>
> But in the meantime, the children have enjoyed our association enormously. They have a father-figure who loves and attends to

them just as well as he does to me. He sees the children frequently and takes them out without me as well as with me. He has even attended some of their school conferences, and has sat with them when they were sick and I had to go to work. He practically gives them a father's care although he doesn't live in the same house.

Yet throughout most of the accounts of such involvements there sounds the undertone of yearning and hope for the right choice, the one that will have no limits, no required distances, no separateness, no avoidance of the special words that mean commitment. For FMs, after a while, do want it to be permanent, not temporary. They want the kind of relationship that will make them feel whole again, as they were before their marriage broke down and divorce left them incomplete.

2. IMPEDIMENTA (OR THE ROCKY ROAD)

But even when they are ready, and what clearly seems to be the right choice has been made, the road to happiness is rarely smooth. FMs bring with them all the burdensome baggage of their leftover responsibilities and experiences as married and formerly married persons. Their progress from the first recognition of each other to the full merging of their lives is often stumbling and uncertain, and sometimes impassably blocked, by the impedimenta of their own lives.

Kathy and Bill, however, met with no difficulties for a long while. Their first weekend at Bill's beach house went well, and much more than well; it was a weekend filled with discovery, the sense of break-through, of peak experience, an aura of the beginning of something of momentous import. Their lovemaking was passionate yet filled with tenderness; it left them exhausted, fulfilled in every possible way—and soon eager for more. In the morning they ran along the pristine November beach, breathless, glowing, finding perfect shells, holding hands, laughing, talking (*always* talking), so much to say to hear to learn to know to give— so perfect, so impossible to believe anything like this could really happen—don't think about it it might go away, say something funny instead, laughter is safe. Later, they cooked lobsters, sat before a great fire, sipped wine, talked, touched, loved (secret word), looked at each other, eyes filled with tears.

When they arrived back in the city Sunday night, Bill met Kathy's children for the first time. The little girl, Angela, seemed to love him on sight, but Marty, the boy, was uncharacteristically reserved—almost suspicious, Kathy thought: *In some uncanny way he knows already that this one's different, the one who could change our lives.*

Eight months have passed and it is July. The children have left for camp, Kathy and Bill for the beach house. All through the winter and spring they have spent almost every evening and every weekend together, and by now they can barely remember a time when they didn't have each other. Today they are joyous at the prospect of the vacation weeks that stretch ahead. The only imperfection for Kathy is the nagging thought in her mind, "He has never said 'I love you.' He says everything *but*— but he doesn't say it. And although we talk as if we mean always to be together, he skirts the topic of marriage. What's he waiting for? We'll never know each other any better than we do now. *Why doesn't he say it?*" Kathy decided that if Bill did not bring up the matter by the end of the first week, she would do so herself.

But on the second vacation day, the phone rang and Kathy picked it up. It was a woman and she asked for Bill. Bill frequently got calls from colleagues at his city apartment and Kathy assumed that one of them was vacationing in Amagansett and making a social call. But she couldn't help hearing his voice in the small house, and he didn't *sound* as if he were speaking to a colleague; he sounded the way he did with her: low-voiced, both warm and bantering—*seductive*, that was the word.

A moment later, Bill hung up and announced that an old friend, Linda McCurdy, had invited them to a cocktail party that evening.

They had only to walk into Linda's house for Kathy to get the impression that she was more than a run-of-the-mill old friend. She hugged and kissed Bill in a way that suggested intimacy beyond friendship, and she eyed Kathy steadily and coolly, then ignored her.

As soon as they left the party Kathy demanded to know about Linda. At first, Bill teased her about being jealous, and although he tried to joke and called her "Jelly-Bean," his voice was strained. By the time they reached the house, he was soberly telling her his history with Linda. He had broken off a serious relationship with her shortly before he and Kathy met because Linda was eager to marry and have children. Bill, not prepared to do either one at the time, had told her she had to look elsewhere, and she did—but she and Bill had never entirely stopped seeing each other. When pressed, Bill admitted to Kathy that on three or four occasions when he had claimed to have faculty meetings, he had taken Linda to dinner instead; on two of those occasions he had slept with her. He needed, he said, to keep a franchise on his freedom.

Kathy was incredulous. She poured out her dismay, her hurt, finally her rage, and in a fit of uncontrollable hysteria, piled her clothes into her suitcase and was about to rush out the door; then she realized that there was no car but Bill's. And he, furious (what did *he* have to be furious about?), cold, aloof, said courteously that it was just about train time and he would be glad to drive her to the station. She went.

For six days they remained out of contact. Kathy told herself that if he called she would hang up. But he didn't call, and she could hardly bear it; she never left the apartment except to get food, so afraid was she to miss his call. And then it came.

"I love you," he said the moment she answered. "I can't be without you any more. Ever. May I come and get you?"

"Yes," she breathed into the phone.

They returned to Amagansett together the next day, and from then on, the relationship assumed a different character. Bill explained (over a period of several days) that he had fallen in love with Kathy the week they met but had been frightened by the depth of his feelings and was afraid to trust them, afraid he would make another mistake. As long as he continued to see Linda, he felt, he could tell himself that he wasn't committed to "a" woman. Now he *was* committed—but some fear still persisted. He thought it was because he and Kathy had never actually lived together, and he had always felt that had he and his first wife spent a couple of months under the same roof before marriage they never would have married.

Kathy was offended by the comparison, but she admitted that, although eager to marry, she, too, felt some anxiety because of her children. Marty had never totally accepted Bill, and while Angela was boundlessly affectionate with him (too much so at times, Kathy thought), they had not tested a familial situation. She wondered what might happen the first time Bill disciplined the children, or how Angela would react to having to share her mother at breakfast time, their "special" time together.

With these considerations in mind, Kathy and Bill decided on a living-together arrangement; they both understood that if all went well, they would get married within the year.

Kathy and Bill's story is not unique; many FMs, even after they fall in love, need to keep a "franchise on their freedom" to allay their fears. Once, this was regarded as typically masculine behavior, but today it is exhibited by both sexes, and women often say things like this:

> [Woman, thirty, salesperson] I have a primary relationship now and much prefer that to dating around—I find it much more rewarding to invest my feelings and time in this one man than in casual relationships. But I have other men friends I don't want to give up—I don't see why I have to—and it's making trouble between us. Yet, as much as he means to me, I need to keep the relationship open. We may break up over this issue.

Many FM relationships do break over just that issue, for only rarely are both partners willing to have their love affair remain non-exclusive. Most people find that open involvements are intolerably threatening, provocative of jealousy and anger, and alienating from the partner.[2] When one partner has progressed to the need for exclusivity and belonging and the other has not, there is trouble ahead. Here is a rueful comment from a woman of thirty-eight:

> Last year I met a man who seemed just what I wanted—and he seemed to find me just right, too. But he was only three months out of a rotten marriage and he said he couldn't give up his freedom so soon even though he was in love with me. He asked me to wait it out, but I'd been on my own and lonely for four years, and I'd been burned twice by men who weren't ready. So even

though it nearly killed me, I told him to go his own way. I still cry when I think of how it might have been.

Even when the partners are right for each other and are both ready for exclusivity, there are many other complications of postmarital life that may interfere with the relationship. The existence of children is the most common. Over four out of ten men in our survey said that their interest in a woman would be blocked or limited if she had children young enough to live with her; similarly, nearly three out of ten women said that their interest in a man would be blocked or limited if he had dependent children—even if they did not live with him. It was not the financial burden that chilled the feelings of both men and women so much as the responsibility, the uncertainties of step-parenthood, and, to be brutally frank, the simply unwanted presence of someone else's children. Many a promising relationship is blighted in the bud by the early encounters of one partner with the other's progeny. Less often—but often enough—a love affair does flourish for a time, only to be killed off by disagreements over the children and methods of child-rearing. One man says bluntly, "I loved her but I couldn't *stand* her rowdy, undisciplined, selfish kids. I couldn't see myself living with them the way they were, and she insisted that I keep hands off."

Money is the second most commonly mentioned obstacle. A man who pays alimony, child support, or both, may not have enough money left to afford a second family, even if his wife works. And women often find their feelings growing cooler when they learn of the limits of a man's earning power and the extent of his obligations. Still, many who cite money as an obstacle seem to find a way to make a go of it after they fall in love, since many more FM men remarry than say they can afford to.

Differences in education and social background may seem more important to FMs than to the young unmarried, for they already have a network of adult friends and the new lover has to "fit in." And similarly, disparate styles of housekeeping may seem more significant to those who have had experience and who have developed a strong need for a very tidy or a very casual lifestyle.

Thus, even after having found what seems like the right person, the formerly married are still likely to stumble and trip over their own impedimenta en route to their goal—and sometimes they abandon the effort to get there. It can happen to an unlucky FM time after time:

[Man, thirty-six; marketing aide, electronics] The first important affair ended after eight months when I couldn't find employment 300 miles away, in a town where she had a business she couldn't sell. The second ended after five months when I couldn't adjust to her housekeeping habits—excessive tidiness—nor she to my sloppy ways. The third one turned out to resent all my friends, whom she found too intellectual; she called them "phonies" and "double-domes." I began to feel embarrassed by her. The fourth, a widow, loved me at first but then, one after another, began to find her late husband's good qualities missing in me, and I couldn't hack it. It's a big merry-go-round of problems. Today, I despair. Tomorrow, I'll say: Good hunting!

3. COME LIVE WITH ME AND BE MY LOVE

Yet, the great majority of the formerly married do eventually find partners they not only love but with whom they work out the problems of merging their complicated lives. Most do so while moving closer to each other, a step at a time: first, they date one or two evenings a week, then many evenings a week; later, they fall into the habit of spending weekends together; still later, if they can afford it, they take vacations together or share a summer house as a couple, or with their various children in residence. If the relationship remains static at this level, it may endure for months or years but will eventually disintegrate; if it continues to grow emotionally and no new doubts or difficulties appear, it generally will become a new marriage.

But for many of the formerly married, even a great deal of shared time and intimacy do not tell all they need to know to ease their anxiety about the problems that lie ahead. As long as they maintain separate residences and separate identities, as long as they still withdraw from couplehood into single privacy from time to time, they have not fully tested the relationship; if they marry, they feel, they will be taking a gamble.

The solution is often the one Kathy and Bill chose: living together in one home with no other residence to escape to, and merging their lives in every sense except the legal one. For several generations social reformers have advocated this procedure, calling it "trial marriage" or "companionate marriage." The latter term never caught on at all, and the former one is both out of date and displeasing; it implies that marriage is the only proper outcome of love (a doctrine many people now dispute) and it burdens the lovers with the ever-present unspoken question, *If this is a trial, when will we know the answer?* So now almost no one calls it "trial marriage." Making it sound more casual than such arrangements often are, they say merely that they are "living together." Since there are no fixed or traditional rules about who does or pays for what, each couple has to work out its own arrangement; as a result, *living-together arrangement* has become a popular term for such a quasi-marriage.

At the moment, there is no equally popular term for the partners who live together. "The man (or woman) I live with" is acceptable, but lengthy. "Roommate" is ambiguous. Other terms are brief and clear but somewhat jocular, thereby implying discomfort or embarrassment: "attaché," "co-habitor," "co-liver," and "live-in" (the last overly reminiscent of "live-in help" of late memory). The most unaffected and common terms now in general use are "live-with" and "live-together," as in: "Bill is Kathy's live-with," or "Kathy and Bill are live-togethers."

Living together is, of course, not unique to the formerly married, and may, in fact, be more common among those who have never been married. But it is particularly valuable to FMs because it offers them a way to satisfy their hunger for married life despite the ambivalence, fear of failure, and complications that make them hesitate to marry. The general increase in such living arrangements among the unmarried, the widowed, and childless FMs has made it easier for FMs with custody to follow suit, too. Until very recently, few single parents dared to have a live-with for fear of the effect on the children, but now, when every child with access to a TV set, newspaper, or magazine knows that living together is becoming socially acceptable, single parents are beginning to lose their inhibitions.

While there are no precise data on the number of separated and divorced persons in living-together arrangements, the Bureau of the Census has recently made a provisional estimate of the situation. As of March, 1976, there were 660,000 "two-person households" in which an unrelated man and woman were sharing quarters; in some 260,000 of these, one or both of the partners were FMs.[3] (The Bureau cautions us—not very convincingly— that some of these people may be employees or roomers rather than lovers.) The figure, 260,000, refers only to couples living by themselves; if one were to include those who had children in residence, the total would be distinctly higher.

The practice is sufficiently widespread to have attracted the attention of the courts, particularly in matters involving alimony or children. Although very few states still recognize common-law marriages, some courts have terminated alimony payments to women in living-together arrangements, particularly if the woman holds herself to be the spouse of the man she lives with. But in California, an avant-garde state as far as divorce legislation goes, alimony is not threatened unless the arrangement continues for thirty days. On the basis of some court decisions, it would appear that even when alimony is discontinued, it may resume if the living-together arrangement breaks up.

Moreover, some recent decisions about living together where children are present have been revolutionary. Historically, a divorced parent could almost always be certain of winning custody of the children if it could be shown that the single parent lived with a member of the opposite sex. But no longer. Several cases have recently been decided in which the court declined to change the living arrangement of the children even though the custodial parent was "living in sin."[4] In Minnesota, a judge refusing to return two boys to their mother because the father was living with another woman said:[5]

> This court does not believe it is necessary to either condemn or condone any relationship, but it is necessary that the court assess the quality of the relationship between the adults as it affects the child. Some marriages are not stable environments in which to raise children, and some informal relationships are very stable and can provide the emotional, psychological and physical security necessary to raising children.

And similarly, in a Brooklyn, New York, court where a father was trying to remove his children from their mother's custody, the court observed:[6]

> The criterion to be applied to determination of custody is not whether the court condones the mother's mode of living or considers it to be contrary to good morals, but whether the child is best located with the mother and there well-behaved and cared for.

While such decisions cannot, at this time, be counted on as a sure thing, they are certainly an indicator of the changed and changing times. The laws always lag behind customs and mores, but eventually they must conform.

Not all of the formerly married who are in living-together arrangements got there by the slow, stepwise process. Some newcomers fling themselves into a new commitment almost immediately, and a few others, who had extramarital involvements during the marriage, move in with their lovers directly. But most such instant affairs crumble away soon after the divorce is final. They serve as a bridge to divorce but lack strong enough foundations to stretch beyond it. When such a relationship does endure, the divorced person, having missed the exploratory and self-discovery processes, is never sure that the new love is the right one, or the best one he or she might have found, and in addition, the normal postmarital problems may have to be worked out in the new marriage instead of before it. A childless business executive in her thirties told us:

> I moved in with my present husband on the day my first husband moved out. Although it was a living-together arrangement, we began it with only a day-by-day commitment to one another. Since we had known each other and had worked as a professional team for almost three years, we had a strong intellectual and emotional relationship, but the sexual involvement was open for exploration. The relationship grew to be an intimate one in all areas and we married as soon as my divorce was final, but we still consider our commitment to each other as friends, lovers, and companions to be on a day-to-day basis, with each of us having the option to leave the other if we feel we can no longer grow as a human being. I wanted it this way because I wanted the freedom to experience personal growth, but I have felt, and still feel,

a great deal of fear about it. I believe I have grown in the last fourteen months, but looking back, I realize that going from one marriage directly into another one is risky.

While this woman was spared the loneliness and anxiety most FMs undergo, she lost the opportunity to test, to learn, and to try on different relationships to see which one fit her best. Even more important, she missed the chance to make it on her own— a growth experience that would surely have given her a greater feeling of security within herself.

She adds, later, that she and her husband are involved in "heavy therapy" this year, her own concerns being her sexuality, her self-identity, and a sharpened awareness of the conflicts in her new relationship. All may yet be well—and she does speak glowingly of the marriage—but her need for therapy so soon, and the nature of the concerns she mentions, make a good case for taking the long road to remarriage.

That, of course, is the usual approach. Generally, FMs who begin to live with a partner have already completed most of their postmarital adjustment and are concerned primarily with testing the relationship and working out its particular problems. For up to now, they have only been playing at love; despite their intimacy and their knowledge of each other, their interaction has been somewhat unreal, idyllic, and selective. Living together is another order of experience: it is like practicing a profession compared to training for it in school.

All that was good in the relationship may be even better now, and much that was missing may now become a part of it. The sense of belonging, the certainty, the comfort of waking up together every morning, the sharing of each day's experiences, the chance to do innumerable little things with and for each other, the ease and pleasure of lovemaking when there are no pressures of time or place—all this is good. And so are the practical benefits: the sharing of expenses and tasks, the help of a second adult in childrearing, the new and more comfortable identity among married and living-together friends. It is not a marriage, but it is very like a marriage.

However, certain aspects of the relationship may now become distinctly distressing, and some problems that did not exist before may now appear for the first time. Some are familiar enough: the struggles for power, disagreements about friends, conflicts over money, how to arrange the furniture, what to do on the weekend. Other problems are new: the assigning of parental duties, dealing with the children's reactions to the new situation, deciding whether to pool their money, or whether to name each other in wills.

Any of these aspects of living together may drive the livewiths apart again. So may wholly unexpected reactions of one of them to the experience of togetherness. Some men and women find this much intimacy unbearable, and may realize—belatedly —that this was one of the crucial factors in their divorce.

[Man, thirty-six, editor]   You can't control the amount of time spent together if you're living in the same house. I found that I needed some room for myself, some time alone, some freedom to be where I wanted to be. I got desperate, I had to break away. You demand too much of each other in a living-together situation, you become a burden to each other.

Others complain not of psychological discomforts but of gritty little unpleasantnesses that abrade and disfigure love:

[Woman, thirty-three, teacher]   It was essentially a real-estate problem, a logistics problem. My two kids, and his three kids every weekend, plus both of us—too many people, too much noise, too little space, too much coming and going, too much cooking and laundry, too many fights. It was more than I ever wanted or could manage. I saw things in a different light—and I guess he saw me in a different light.

Kathy has only good to say of her living-together experiment with Bill. Within half a year they had put to rest their remaining doubts and worked out one or two minor problems that arose over who would handle the money and how it would be spent. And after some noisy showdowns, Bill had established a warm, trusting relationship with Marty, and an easy, fatherly one with Angela, who no longer seemed infatuated but was ever eager to please. A little less than a year after they had begun living together, Kathy and Bill were married. That was three years ago and the marriage has proven to be all they had hoped it would be.

While the number of living-together arrangements that become marriages is not known, we hazard the guess—based on what we have gathered from various sources—that among FMs who live together with children, about half marry, half break up. Among childless FMs, who can move together or apart with less difficulty, far fewer—perhaps only a third—marry, and the majority break up.

4. BREAKING UP

Breaking up after living together is less complicated than divorce, but in many ways it is similar, or even identical to it. Breaking up is so disorienting and traumatic, in fact, that divorce counseling centers are beginning to offer their services to people who are living together.[7]

A minority of FMs are as gravely wounded by the breakup of a love relationship as they were by the breakup of the marriage, and a few claim to feel worse than ever; they say things like, "It's made me lose hope—I feel doomed always to fail." One woman, a thirty-six-year-old social worker exemplifies the minority:

> Over the six years, I hit bottom every time I broke up with someone. Each time, I've had very few resources to deal with it, and that's still the case. I'm very disappointed by that. I would have hoped that my experiences and my going to a shrink would have made me better able to handle it, but it's still devastating.

But the great majority tell a very different tale. Nearly all say they felt very lucky that they hadn't gotten married and didn't need to go through another divorce. And most of them say that although they may have been wretched, grief-stricken, angry, or numb when a serious love affair broke up, they were *not* devastated and wholly at a loss. They had learned that if love fails, they can rely on themselves. They knew how to make their way around in the world of the formerly married, and how to begin repairing the damage. And they say that after the hurt wore off, they realized they had benefitted in various ways: they had learned they could love again—and again, if necessary; they had learned more about their own needs; and in the end, they felt more confident, with each succeeding affair, that they would eventually reach the goal they were striving for. Here is a representative comment:

[Man, thirty-three, photographer] There have been three big ones. I felt bad when each one ended, but I'm glad I had each of them. They were good at the time, but more than that, they were important experiences. I had married too young, I never knew what kind of woman I needed. But by now, I've been through it with the very young adoring thing, with the big sex-bomb type, and with the frail one who needed to be rescued. I've learned a lot about what I do and don't need. After living with the last one for a year, I've also learned that I like that a lot more than the so-called freedom I was so glad to have after my marriage broke up.

Of the people in our survey who had important relationships that ended, only one woman in twelve and one man in sixteen found the experience mostly hurtful; another one woman in twelve and one man in eight thought it had done neither good nor harm. The great majority—81 per cent of the men and 83 per cent of the women—say their love affairs were mostly beneficial. In all age groups, at all socioeconomic levels, among parents and non-parents alike, there was this same overwhelmingly positive evaluation of the major love affairs in postmarital life that did not lead to marriage.

This, too, is part of the newly emergent view of divorce and of postmarital life: the divorce experience—and its consequences—are seen not as failure but as adaptation to changed circumstances; not as tragedy but as normal crisis; not as defeat but as transition. Instead of the sentimental consolation expressed in Tennyson's over-familiar lines, " 'Tis better to have loved and lost/Than never to have loved at all," today's formerly married men and women seem to feel that it is well to have loved and lost since each love brings one closer to the love that will *not* be lost.

IX

Happy, And Not-So-Happy, Endings

1. RETURN OF THE NATIVE

All divorced people once were—or thought they were—the marrying kind. Do they remain so—or think they do—after the divorce experience? Not at first: having gone through the agony of marital breakup, the vicious battles that often follow it, and the arduous labor of adjustment to postmarital life, most of them see marriage as a poor bargain and a bad risk, and their now-stabilized life seems preferable. Like most other expatriates, however, nearly all FMs eventually change their minds and want to return to the homeland from which they fled or were expelled.

But *eventually* is the key word. As we have seen, very few have any desire to remarry during the first few months; even after a year has passed, only about half are willing to do so; and of those men and women in our survey who have been FMs for three or more years, fully a third are still unwilling to remarry, though many say they might want to in the future.

As we know, most divorced people emerge from emotional isolation step by step, in ever-closer relationships; the desire to remarry asserts itself somewhere along the line, usually during a love affair. And while most love affairs between divorced persons do not become marriages, the desire to marry that they elicit lives on and grows after the affairs end. Following two involvements that looked promising but did not work out, a thirty-six-year-old electrical engineer told us that the experiences had left him eager to remarry and that he was diligently mate-shopping: "I realize only now how much I have missed married life. My life feels empty without someone to share it with. I'm looking forward more than ever to loving someone again and having that someone love me." An advertising woman in her forties said: "For a long while I felt I would never love or marry again, but six months ago I did fall in love. Unfortunately, I know that this particular relationship would not make a healthy marriage, but it *is* nice to know that I didn't die inside and that I am still capable of love and commitment. I would adore to be happily married."

As the desire for remarriage appears, many of the divorced examine themselves critically to be sure they have healed and changed enough to be ready for it. Some find that although they have not quite completed the repairs, they know what remains to be done:

[Man, thirty-nine, real estate assessor] I'm working very hard on my own contributions to the failure of my marriage. It's not easy to grow up, at my age—but I'm trying to, and succeeding. I'll get married again when I'm more mature and emotionally skillful. I wanted and expected too much from my wife. Now I believe that if I can take full responsibility for myself and be more realistic about what I expect another can do for me, my relationships will be healthier and happier.

Others feel that they have done the necessary work and need only to find the right person:

[Man, forty-two, chemist] My former wife and I were from two different worlds and had no mutual interests. The only time we communicated was when we were fighting. I withdrew into myself when I was angry—in order to avoid the fights—and I stupidly made things worse by working overtime and traveling a lot for the same reason. I know now that I have to pick an intellectually compatible woman next time and that I have to make a real effort to be totally open and communicative and to stay that way, no matter what.

[Woman, thirty-eight, artist] I hope I can find someone more intelligent and educated this time, someone who can share the things I care about and who reads something besides the sports pages. I hope I can find a friend who cares about my sexual satisfaction, not just his own. I've discovered that I like rough, passionate love-making at times, not just the brief gentle loving that was all my husband would ever do. In other ways, I'm aware of important changes in myself: I've become more tolerant of other people's idiosyncracies, I don't always have to feel that I'm right, I've become more patient and accepting. I've learned from every experience, even the hurting ones. I hope to find the right person soon.

For a number of women, the readiness to remarry, though real, is qualified: they are interested only in a marital relationship in which they will be emancipated from traditional female dependency and the partnership will be far more egalitarian than the one they had before:

[Woman, forty, paramedical]   I have come too far in my personal growth ever to be just "Mrs. So-and-So" again, or just "John's wife." I don't need to set the world on fire, but I have emerged as a feminist. I look forward to much more equality in another marriage; I'd not be an appendage to my husband but a partner in every sense, especially intellectually. However, I'm basically old-fashioned in the sense that the role of homemaker is second nature to me and I like caring for my guy, and cherishing him—and being cherished by him.

A few feminists go much further; they want to marry, but only if the degree of commitment and obligation is minimal:

[Woman, fifty-two, publisher's assistant]   I would expect to have a completely open and egalitarian marriage. I would keep my present seashore cottage, and it would be mine alone, a place to go to when I wanted to get away. I would expect that we would have different friends and different social activities part of the time, and have completely separate financial arrangements. I will not be a traditional wife and I will not have a traditional husband. But I realize that this might be an impossible dream.

A number of men, too, have absorbed some of the values of the women's movement, often as part of social evolution but sometimes because they had been married to traditional, dependent, and dissatisfied wives, and now want a more egalitarian marriage. "I will remarry," says a thirty-eight-year-old lawyer, "but never again another woman who is dependent on me in every way; it makes for resentment on both sides. I don't really need a housekeeper-cook—I need a friend." A thirty-three-year-old college professor says, "I can't say exactly what my next marriage will be like until I meet the right woman—but one thing I know for sure is that this time I won't marry a woman who doesn't have strong career motivations."

Such expectations of the next marriage vary widely, depending on the individual's age, previous marital relationship, and other factors. A young, childless man may look forward to parenthood and a reasonably home-oriented wife. A woman struggling to earn enough to support her children may yearn for a strong, loving man who will take care of her and be a good stepfather. Middle-aged men and women whose children are grown may hope for a marriage that is more fun-oriented than the one they had previously. A few men and women say they will settle only for a marriage that is sexually open, but a far greater number lay even more than average stress on absolute fidelity, since infidelity was part of their painful pasts.

But as diffuse and varied as these expectations and desires sound, there is strong consensus among FMs as to the main reasons they want to remarry. In response to a direct question that listed a number of possible reasons, the men and women in our sample proved to have lost none of the basically idealistic and somewhat romantic concept of marriage that most Americans hold: The chief reason for wanting to remarry is *companionship*, and it was cited by seven out of ten men and more than eight out of ten women. *Emotional needs* rank second, *sexual needs*, third.

In contrast, the utilitarian reasons that are central to the traditionalist concept of marriage ranked low: *Financial security* was cited by a little over a third of the women, and *for the children's sake* by only about a quarter; fewer than one man in ten gave either of these reasons. *To rejoin married society* drew a small minority of each sex, and *to avoid the stigma of singleness* only a few per cent of each; both reasons were important to divorced people a mere dozen years ago.

Without question, then, divorce does not make most FMs bitter or cynical, except transiently. After their first revulsion, they once more become marriage-oriented and idealistic in their attitudes toward marriage. Their experiences have neither turned them against marriage, fashioned them into radical revisionists of monogamy, nor made them neo-conservatives who value marriage chiefly for its practical benefits.

There is a solid foundation beneath these idealistic and even romantic attitudes. The married state is still pragmatically preferable, for most Americans, to the separated or divorced state, in a number of research-documented ways:

—If you are a separated or divorced woman, you are only about half as likely to be satisfied with your life, in general, as if you are married; if you are a separated or divorced man, you are likely to be a good deal less satisfied than if you are a married man.[1]

—If you are married you can expect to live several more years than if you are divorced.[2]

—As we saw in Chapter II, if you are an FM, you have a significantly higher risk of suicide, accident, physical illness, and hospitalization for mental illness than if you are married.[3]

It used to be thought, when divorce was still a deviant form of behavior, that the divorced died sooner or had higher rates of accident and mental and physical illness than the married because they were poor specimens in the first place—and that this same fact explained why they were failures in marriage. Today, when divorce is no longer deviant, the explanation does not hold; recent analysis of the data suggests that the longer life expectancy of the married is due largely to the protective nature of marriage itself, rather than to the inferior nature of the divorced.[4] Partners in marriage take care of each other, and shield each other from many of the stresses of singlehood. The benefits of marriage are genuine, and the formerly married of both sexes apparently know it. Even though some feminists like to point out that marriage benefits men more, and divorce harms them more, than women, the difference is only relative, and it is still markedly better for women, physically and mentally, to be remarried than divorced and unremarried.

It is not surprising, then, that nearly all divorced men and women do ultimately come to desire remarriage, and the great majority do ultimately find mates they consider right, and do remarry. It takes time—only half the time it took a generation ago, but time, nonetheless.[5] No more than one out of seven divorced people remarry within the first year after divorce.[6] A little over four out of ten divorced men and slightly fewer women remarry within three years after divorce.[7] But eventually, five out of six divorced men and three out of four divorced women remarry, some of them not until ten—and a few, not until twenty or more—years after divorce.

Less than half a century ago, two out of three divorced people never remarried at all; today, only one out of five never does.[8] Once, divorce was the end of married life; now, it is only an interval in it. The world of the formerly married is not an asylum for the maritally incompetent, but a school for the remarriageable. Since 1960, the very period during which the divorce rate has soared (inspiring the critics of marriage to proclaim that marriage is dying), the proportion of the divorced who remarry has been rising steadily; the rate has dropped slightly in the last few years but is still close to its all-time high.[9]

This is not to say that all who want to remarry find it easy to do so. The young have better chances than the not-so-young and the middle-aged, and this is particularly true of women. If you are a man, and divorce in your early forties, you have a three-out-of-four chance of remarrying, but if you are a woman, your chance is three out of five.[10] As your age rises, the chances continue to decline—and women, again, lose out more for many reasons; the most important one is the shorter life-span of men and the consequent surplus of available women in their fifties and sixties. Middle-aged men who do remarry take roughly twice as long, on the average, as young men, and middle-aged women take more than twice as long as young women.[11]

There are other notable impediments, too: If you are black, you have roughly 20 per cent less chance of remarrying within five years than if you are white.[12] If you are a poor man, you have only about half the chance that a middle-income or well-to-do man has.[13] (For women, it works the other way: either higher-income women are choosier, or it's difficult for them to find men they consider peers.) If you are a woman with one child under eighteen, you have just as good a chance of remarriage within five years as a childless woman; if you have two children under eighteen, your chance is slightly less, and if you have three children, it is considerably less.[14]

But most of the divorced remarry despite all the possible impediments. Although we live in a time when marriage has come under increasing attack and when "singlehood" has become increasingly respectable, the divorced don't stay divorced. If you would like to know whether or not marriage is obsolescent today, do not study the young never-marrieds, for their history is still to be written. And do not study the radical feminists, the advocates of group marriage, or the proponents of singlehood, for all of them, however vocal, are only small minorities. Study, rather, that vast number who have been married and then unmarried. They were once the marrying kind and—after experiencing unhappy marriage and then divorce, with all its difficult consequences—they still are.

2. THE PERMANENT EXPATRIATES

But remarriage is not the only goal. With singleness so much more approved and widespread than it used to be, there is a new militancy on the part of those divorced people who prefer to remain single, or to choose some other alternative to marriage and indeed, we heard this from a few indignant contributors to our survey before one word of this book was written. For instance, a forty-two-year-old woman, back in college for a new career, chided us:

> Nowhere in your questionnaire do I find any glimmering of a feminist view that would offer celibacy or permanent singleness as a real, conscious alternative to marriage or pairing. It is assumed, rather, that pairing is all there is, and that it is known to elevate the human condition! But there surely are persons who, for good reason, would elect other options. And more and more of us are doing so. I wonder if we don't load our expectations in favor of coupling when other alternatives do—or could—exist.

Agreed. There *are* alternatives to marriage or remarriage, and they have certainly become far more acceptable and workable in recent years. But a great deal of nonsense is being uttered these days about the prevalence of singleness and the avoidance of marriage and remarriage. It is said, for example, that currently, 29 per cent of all adult (over seventeen) males, and 37 per cent of all adult females—some 19 million men and 28 million women—are single.[15]

But a large chunk of that vast total consists of elderly widowed persons, mostly women; a second large chunk consists of people who are not yet of average marriage age; and a third large chunk consists of the divorced. Most of the elderly widows will not remarry, though not by choice; there simply are no partners for them. Most of the young singles *will* marry, but a bit later than their parents did; the marriage rate has been declining of late chiefly because many young women have delayed marriage in order to complete college and start careers—but Bureau of the Census analysis indicates that well over nine-tenths of today's young unmarried men and women will eventually marry, a mere 2 or 3 per cent fewer than a decade ago.[16]

As for the divorced, we have seen that only a sixth of the men and a quarter of the women will never remarry. There is no evidence in the census data that these fractions have been increasing in recent years. What has been changing, and dramatically, is the *attitude* the formerly married have toward their singleness: they are now unashamed of remaining unmarried for as long as they choose to; they regard their postmarital singleness as a valid option, a legitimate way of life, and a deliberate choice. The fact that nearly all of them later do remarry does not alter the fact that for many of them, remarriage was not the only option; they did feel free, emotionally and socially, to choose another. Still, only a small number remain single for the rest of their lives, and not all of them do so by choice.

Some have no other option: the old (particularly women), the seriously ill, the severely neurotic or the psychotic, the physically handicapped, the ones with too many children or too little income, the homosexuals, and the men and women with total sexual dysfunction.

But these are not the stridently vocal expatriates who reject marriage on principle, claim they "no longer believe in it," make the loudest cries of "never again," or advocate other options, goals, or alternatives. It is not always easy to classify the ideologically motivated non-remarryers, since some have more than one reason for their position, and others misstate their reasons in order to put a better face on their lack of a partner. But it seems to us that there are four major types:

Non-relaters. These people, whom we met earlier, seem unable to form even shallow relationships let alone meaningful ones; no wonder they never even come close to remarrying. They are the real casualties of divorce, for they are the ones who have been unable to adjust to it. The failure may stem from low self-esteem, inability to give up dependence on the ex-spouse, a deep sense of failure and incompetence in marriage, or some other psychological handicap. One woman, typical of this group says, "It has been four years since my divorce and I feel just as lost, and confused, and lonely, and almost as worthless, as the day I walked away from my marriage."

Such people are too depressed, fearful, or embittered ever to take a chance on a new person or to present themselves as potential partners. The syndrome, common in newcomers, is chronic in those who never learn to relate again. Some have a few sporadic dates, some have none at all. They socialize with old friends and relatives, or members of one-sex groups (health clubs, church societies), or neutral mixed groups (charity organizations, community or neighborhood groups). When possible, though, they try to make their way of life sound desirable; as the woman who chided us for not focusing on celibacy or singleness as alternatives said, "Being one hundred per cent alone disentangles me from so many of life's booby-traps. I prefer going it alone, or, at times, 'socializing in squadrons,' as someone has called it." She explained that term to mean participation in neutral group activities that require no one-to-one relationships. Another woman was divorced thirteen years ago at the age of thirty-two; she wasted five years encouraging her ex-husband to visit with the family in the hope of a reconciliation, and although it is eight years since she abandoned that hope, she has had very few dates, almost no sex, and no real relationships. "I seem not to encourage them," she says ruefully. "I've tried to fashion an interesting and quiet life in community and school work, and I hope to start a job soon."

Few males speak in comparable terms. A handful of elderly

and ailing men say they have no interest in sex, dating, or remarriage, but prefer to socialize in groups. A few younger men
shun any close contacts because, like Dr. Tompkins, the minister
we met in Chapter V, they have a profound postmarital mistrust
of women and an aversion to sexual activity.

Abusers. Many of the men and women we observed earlier,
who compulsively seek new partners for brief sexual encounters,
continue in that pattern for many years. Sometimes, as they grow
older and have more difficulty finding new partners, they make
an effort to settle down to a single relationship; more often, they
simply become aging, lonely, and disgruntled loners.

Independents. This is the genuinely new breed—the people
who feel that marriage has too many flaws or does not suit their
needs, who believe that other options are valid, and who prefer
limited and semi-detached relationships that do not infringe on
their freedom or independence. Some are militant feminists.
Others are women or men who have discovered that they do not
like, and cannot tolerate, a binding commitment or the enforced
intimacy of living with a partner. Of course this is a common
enough mood among FMs, but usually it is a passing one. The
true independent, however, means it to be a permanent way of
life. One young woman—she is only twenty-seven and may some
day change her mind, but she herself doubts it—gave us a list of
reasons why she will never remarry; among them were these:

> I doubt that I could live harmoniously with another individual
> for an extended period of time—extended being five to seven
> days; I need time alone, to and for myself. To live with most men
> would intrude on my solitude. . . . I am not willing to give up my
> set ways for anyone. . . . Even with my requisite privacy, I choose
> not to tolerate the exclusive companionship of one person for ex-
> tended periods of time.

A woman in her mid-fifties is less likely to change her mind
than one in her mid-twenties, and this architect, with plenty of
marital experience behind her, is much more convincing when
she declares for the independent option and says she will never
remarry:

> I've discovered that it is possible to live by oneself and love it.
> This is the first time in my life when I haven't been someone's

daughter, someone's wife, or someone's mother. I love the freedom
to do anything I want. In the last few years I have traveled abroad
extensively. I can eat when and where I want. I don't cook any
more and I rarely clean house because there is no one to dirty it.
I have so many different kinds of friends that all my needs are
met. I have no desire to get married again because no marriage
would ever satisfy me, now that I know what the outside world is
like. I'm a completely liberated woman and I love every damned
minute of it.

I don't negate marriage. I'm very happy to have been married
and to have raised my family within a marriage. But I say, "High
school is great fun—yet who wants to stay in high school for a
lifetime?" I'm at the maximum of my earning power, I feel that I
look better than ever, I have developed a new personality, I have
a wonderful lover whom I see occasionally. So what more could
I have?

Men, though they often talk like this in the first few years of
postmarital life, rarely make an ideological issue of it later on;
that is more often a female stance. Men prefer to explain their
status as independents in a spirit of *faute de mieux*, disillusionment, and making the best of an imperfect life. A fifty-two-year-
old businessman who has been divorced twice, and has been an
independent for the past seven years, says:

From youth, I never anticipated getting too much out of marriage, and I never had much sexual aggressiveness toward women.
Throughout my two marriages I failed to gain any sense of security, any self-esteem, or any personal benefits. Since my last divorce
I have been more or less involved with some of the women I've
dated and slept with, but *I'm armed to the teeth*. Being a fall guy
three times in fifty-two years would be too much. So any deep
involvements I might have fail as soon as I hear that she "can't
make it without me." My alarms go off. I don't want either a
dependent or a cannibal.

An appliance repairman, now forty-three, left his wife six
years ago and has been, in his own words, a "loner" ever since,
although he has dated "lots" of women, had sex with "very
many," and has had a few intense involvements.

I did have one live-in arrangement a while back, but I simply
felt too dominated, and so I moved on. I've been involved with

several women who thought they would be completely satisfied by me, but I didn't feel that way about them. I would need someone as active as myself, intelligent, stimulating to converse with, willing to share the physical sports I engage in, actively aggressive in loving, and completely satisfying to me. And since that's too much to expect of anyone, I'd rather stay single and enjoy each one for whatever she has to offer.

Single relaters. Unlike the majority who view love affairs and living-together arrangements as try-outs for marriage, a small but growing number of divorced people choose to have committed relationships that they regard as ends in themselves, alliances they consider preferable to marriage. Some find it better to maintain separate residences, others to live together; some have exclusive relationships, others insist on sexual and emotional freedom. The non-marrying relaters are not just pretending to be content with something less than remarriage; they have discovered certain truths about themselves, and made what they consider an intelligent adaptation. Two proponents of open relationships explain:

[Man, forty-one, business executive; an FM for five years] I have established a long-term relationship (two years now) with a very open, assertive, smart, motivated, energetic, sensual, ambitious woman who is attempting to become a lawyer. We can allow each other outside interactions (sexual, professional, social, and intimate) without being overly or destructively jealous. If we do get "married" again, we won't call it a marriage or have a marriage license, but rather a contract of some sort that reflects our unique ways of meeting our needs.

[Woman, fifty-one, teacher; an FM for six years] I became intimate with my lover five years ago, one year after my husband left, and it has been my only loving, intimate relationship. During the first year, I devoutly hoped the relationship would culminate in marriage, but he was comfortable in his singleness and had no desire to remarry. At the time I was disappointed, but now I'm very thankful that we didn't marry. At first, I *needed* a man, and I wanted a man to play the role that people traditionally expect of husbands. But my lover refused.

It was terribly frustrating—and then, in time, it became wonderful, because I learned to do things for myself, and make my own decisions, and be responsible for my own actions. As a result, my relationship with my lover has matured: I no longer *need* him, I just *want* him.

After five years, the situation is a comfortable one for both of us. Each of us has an intense need to be independent and so we lead separate lives and come together once or twice a week. We have completely separate lives in addition to our mutual friends. I feel secure and free enough in the relationship so that he can date others and so can I. I allow him to have other sexual relationships if he chooses to do so; I have never chosen to do so, but he has often said it would be okay with him if I did.

I feel that I have the best of both worlds: the complete freedom of a single woman, the best sex, and the best love of one man.

And now, an example of an alternative that comes close to monogamous marriage—and yet in some way, important to both participants, differs from it:

[Woman, thirty-six, laboratory technician; FM for two and a half years] My marriage failed because I completed college, got a job, and became more liberated. My husband couldn't stand it. I'm lucky because I've been involved in a stable, caring relationship for nearly two years, but neither of us ever wants to remarry. We're happier living together, though retaining some independence —for example, he still has his own house (even though he doesn't live in it), I still see my female friends at times—we don't do *everything* together. Also, it was too big a hassle and too emotionally tiring for me to get out of the first marriage, and I'd never want to do that again. Commitments are for *now*, anyway, with or without marriage, so we're committed now.

But it begins to appear that we have a problem in taxonomy: we have been talking about the permanent expatriates, the formerly married who never marry again, but these alternatives— especially the last one—have more in common, emotionally and socially, with marriage than they do with the rejection of marriage by the various non-relaters. And since marriage itself, these days, has more than one form, and often involves more independence than our parents or grandparents ever thought possible, perhaps we ought not draw a line between remarriage and the non-legal but long-term love relationships of those who never remarry. The line, really, should be drawn between those who remain essentially single the rest of their lives, and those who return to couplehood, with or without legal sanctions.

Clearly, then, the permanent expatriates are an even smaller contingent than the census data show, for sooner or later, the vast majority of divorced men and women either remarry or enter into a non-legalized but intimate, loving partnership—one of the newer forms of marriage in our society, whatever one chooses to call it.

3. BETTER LUCK THIS TIME

Still, the great majority of the divorced do remarry. Though we will follow them no further, concluding this diary of their sojourn abroad with their arrival back home, we will seek to answer, at least in summary form, two inevitable—and legitimate —questions:

Do they choose better the second time?

How successful are their remarriages?

Friends and acquaintances of people who are about to re-marry, especially if they have not themselves been divorced, often betray a certain lack of confidence in the outcome of the imminent wedding. They are delighted, of course, and full of good wishes, but at the same time, they can't help but wonder whether their divorced friends might be not very good marital material. "Congratulations!" they cry—but then add the doubt-ful note, "Better luck this time." Or, "How wonderful!" they say—and then say too much: "Let's hope this one lasts a long time."

But the happy couple themselves, despite their previous ambivalence and fear, are more sanguine than their well-wishers. They know how many poor or risky choices they might have made but did not. They have good reason to think they have chosen well, or certainly better than the first time, because this time love is based on realities rather than fantasies, on reassuring compatibility rather than titillating dissimilarity. The fact is, they *do* tend to marry people they understand and who understand them, people who are like them in important ways. Many studies have shown that the greater the differences between marital partners in certain characteristics, including age and general life experience, the greater the chance of conflict and of marital breakdown.[17] But most divorced people, when they remarry, choose mates who are reasonably close to their own age—and they far prefer other FMs, with their similarity in background and outlook, to the never-married and the widowed.

It is widely believed that many middle-aged divorced men marry single girls—yes, *girls*—young enough to be their daughters, and that young divorced women gravitate toward much older, well-to-do men. These are myths. In actual fact, of all the divorced men who remarry, only one in twenty-five marries a woman as much as twenty years his junior. If both partners in a remarriage have been divorced, the median age difference between them is less than four years, only a year and a half greater than the difference in first marriage. If the man was married before but the woman was not, the age difference is six years—a little more, but not a generation; if the wife was married before and the husband was not, the difference is less than a year.[18]

The penchant of the divorced for divorced mates is even more striking. Divorced men can choose their brides from a pool of single, widowed, and divorced women; the divorced segment accounts for only about one-fifth of the total group, but more than half the time, divorced men marry divorced women. The women, too, select divorced men more than half the time, although divorced men represent only one-eighth of the total pool available. In other words, FMs who remarry choose other FMs about three to four times as often as they would if marital history didn't influence their choice.[19]

Still, this leaves them plenty of room to choose poorly and repeat their mistakes. And what is to prevent it? Artists without talent do not become talented by virtue of their bad paintings; businessmen with no aptitude for business do not become successful by virtue of their bankruptcies. Why should it be any different where love and marriage are concerned? Samuel Johnson, at his most acerbic, said that second marriage was "the triumph of hope over experience."

Let us explore this dim view. The most obvious proof that

Johnson was right would be the selection of the same kind of partner the second time as the first; such a choice would virtually guarantee that the difficulties of the previous marriage would be replicated. The most extreme case of such uncorrected judgment is, of course, remarriage to the original spouse. There are no survey data on the number of such remarriages (the number is undoubtedly very small), nor on how they fare, but nearly all professional counselors believe that without intensive therapy or other impetus to change, there is no reason to think the marriage can be any better the second time than it was the first. At the 1976 Single-Parent Conference held at the University of Iowa, one psychologist offered an extraordinary example of a "treadmill" couple now married to each other for the fourth time. Three times they loved, married, had a child, became embattled, separated, fought bitterly over money and custody, and were divorced. Three times they were drawn to each other again and remarried. This time, in the fourth marriage, they have been in therapy all the way and, so far, are still together. Were it not for the therapy, they might be on the way to their fifth marriage by now.

But such situations are most uncommon, and so the important question is not how many divorced people marry the same person again, but rather how many marry the same *kind* of person again. A generation ago, most analytically oriented therapists believed that, without treatment, the divorced person would inevitably repeat his or her earlier mistake. The rationale was that any person who is divorced must be neurotic, and that divorce is a neurotic answer to neurotic problems. It is, therefore, no answer at all, since the unchanged neurosis only compels the same kind of choice and behavior next time.[20]

But this view was based only on observation of patients in treatment, and in those days, people did not lightly seek treatment. Recently, sociologists have looked at representative samples of *all* divorced people, not just those in therapy. In addition, counselors and psychologists today see a broad array of people who are not necessarily neurotic but who need situational support or practical help. As a result, the contemporary consensus of such professionals is that only a minority of divorces can be explained as a neurotic answer to a neurotic problem; most of the errors the divorced made in mate selection were due to inexperience, ignorance, immaturity, or a perfectly normal inability to foresee how time would change them or their mates. Moreover, there is excellent clinical evidence that healthy adults can and do learn from emotional experience, that character structure can and does change somewhat in maturity, and that we are not all destined to make the same mistakes throughout our lives.

Our survey data bear this out. Half the people in our sample say they are definitely not attracted to the same type as before, while another third say they are, but only some of the time. One in eight remains faithful to the old pattern and still prefers the same type, but many of this last group are newcomers to the world of the formerly married and have not yet had the kinds of experiences that might cause them to change in personality and in taste. Not only will many of them become different just by living, but others, before they remarry, will have had some kind of therapy; whether their addiction has a neurotic basis or not, the therapy may free them of it by opening their eyes to other possibilities.

In any event, the large majority of formerly married people tend to withdraw from new potential partners if, as they become intimate with them, they recognize the old familiar traits that made trouble in the first marriage. Whether they choose well or poorly, the second marriage is rarely a copy of the first. Leslie Aldridge Westoff, who interviewed marriage counselors and remarried couples for her book, *The Second Time Around*, states unequivocally:[21]

> Another of the many remarriage myths states that people always marry the same person, making the same mistake a second time because of their particular psychological needs. . . . I found absolutely no support for this. Many people pointed out that they had changed so much it would have been impossible for them to make the same mistake again. Not a single person I spoke to reported that he or she had married the same sort of person. . . . Ex-spouses expressed great surprise that they had met and liked a variety of different people and that they could actually love two completely different types of person.

Our own interviews with people in second marriages confirm this; a few did seem to have repeated their old patterns but most did not. And in our survey sample, those who had been divorced twice had thoroughly different explanations for the two break-ups.

How successful are second marriages?

The question, an all-important one, is unfortunately ambiguous. It might mean, "How *happy* are second marriages?"; that is, what per cent of people currently in second marriages are happy? Or it might mean, "How *enduring* are second marriages?," for these marriages, like the ones that preceded them, might be happy for a while but later deteriorate and dissolve.

The first question, then: how many remarriages are happy? We have interviewed a number of remarried people and talked to a number of researchers who have talked to many others; our overall impression is that only a minority of the remarried are seriously discontented or troubled, while the majority are satisfied. Many, in fact, are much more than that: they feel particularly fortunate in their second marriages, as if they have been reborn out of the ashes and have managed to snatch victory out of defeat. What was lost is restored: love, sex, home, friends. Much that is new is added: new interests, new friends, new dimensions of sharing with a different mate. The remarried also enjoy new skill and assurance in dealing with old problems, for most of them are far less disconcerted than they used to be by conflicts, and are more sharply aware of problem areas in themselves and each other; they are readier to talk and to listen, more willing to try to make adjustments and find solutions. As Ms. Westoff says of her own interviewees, "Many of the couples saw their first marriages as a kind of training school, somewhat similar to the college they had left with academic degrees but little knowledge of themselves. . . . All agreed that a second marriage was the real thing at last."[22]

Which is not to say that the remarried have no problems. Those who make the move too quickly, without having completed the work of rehabilitation, are unlikely to shed whatever psychological problems or areas of ignorance they had the first time. And even those who marry at a more leisurely pace, after considerable personal change and enlightenment, may have leftover complications from the past, the impedimenta we mentioned earlier: money problems occasioned by alimony or child-support payments that put a burden on the marriage and create tension; visitation of children, which may be either a disruption of, or an intrusion upon, the marriage, depending on whether the children have to be visited elsewhere or come to stay in the new home; contacts with former spouses that are touchy and awkward, and often become a source of contention in the new marriage.

Above all, there are the special difficulties of stepparenthood. Even the most loving parent sometimes finds his or her own children wearying, intolerably demanding, or just plain obnoxious; the most loving stepparent, inevitably bound to them less closely, is likely to find them so more often or to a greater degree. The natural parent has an established pattern of child-rearing and discipline, and the stepparent is quite likely to favor different methods—just as good, perhaps, but different. And if children perceive the stepparent as an intruder, or as a pretender to the missing parent's throne, they may be rebellious, hostile, or—worst of all—studiously indifferent.

So relationships in the families of remarriage are complex; yet, while much has been made of the hazards of stepparenting, there is now good reason to believe that in most reconstituted families the stepparent-stepchild relationship works out relatively well. Anthropologist Paul Bohannan, heading a research team at the Western Behavioral Sciences Institute in a three-year study of a large sample of stepfathers and their stepchildren, recently reported that, by and large, stepchildren are as happy as children who live with both their natural parents, do as well in school, and get along as well with their stepfathers as other children do with their natural fathers.[23] Moreover, many stepparents we have spoken to enjoy their stepparenthood, either because they have become deeply attached to the new children in their lives, or because they accept those children as an integral part of the person they love.

As for those who remarry in midlife and become stepparents of grown children, theirs is a special and pleasurable acquisition: they gain not children (and the responsibilities of rearing them), but young adult friends. While the young people may enrich the couple's life, the remarried pair is free of the demands that younger children make on parents' time, energy, and money, the restrictions they place on parents' freedom of movement, the intrusions they make on parents' privacy.

A number of surveys have shown that first-time married couples with children at home are less happy than they were when childless, and that they experience a resurgence of marital happiness after the children leave home.[24] This is not to deny the pleasure and fulfillment of raising a family; it is only to say that the rewards of parenting exact a price in marital happiness, and that when parenting is done, one no longer has to pay the price.

All this is equally true for those FMs who marry in midlife and who, in addition, have the intensity of the newness of their union, and the stimulation of their daily discoveries of each other. The middle-aged remarriage, spared most of the stresses of younger ones, and blessed by its own advantages, is often an especially happy marriage.

But in every age group, some of the people who remarry find their marriages disappointing from the beginning, while others, happy at first, cease to be so later.

Which brings us to the second question, how enduring are second marriages? This question can be answered straightforwardly, since data do exist. Not only do they tell us how many of the marriages endure, they tell us, in effect, how many are happy enough to endure for the lifetime of the partners. The true criterion of the success of second marriages is their survival rate, for those who have been divorced are less tolerant of a poor marriage than those who have had no experience as FMs. The once-divorced know the way, have the skills, are less likely than the uninitiated to cling to a bad marriage out of fear. The proof is that second divorces take place, on the average, in the fifth year of marriage—two years sooner than first divorces.[25]

Does this mean that second marriages are more likely than first marriages to end in divorce? For many years the data seemed to prove that this was distinctly the case, with the divorce rate for second marriages running about one and a half times that for first marriages.

But in 1976, Paul C. Glick and Arthur J. Norton of the Bureau of the Census obtained data that enabled them, for the first time, to apply the cohort approach—a far more sophisticated technique than had been used before—to estimate the divorce risk in remarriage. The statistician using this method follows different groups of people from youth to old age, and compares the redivorce rates for groups of various ages; this makes it possible to estimate what the young will do in the future since the history of the older people is already complete and offers a basis for comparison. By this means, Glick and Norton came to a new conclusion: The lifetime chance that a second marriage will end in divorce is only slightly higher than the chance that a first marriage will. (This applies to young adults; those of middle age or older who remarry actually have less chance of divorce than people of their age in a first marriage.)

The significant figures: [26]

—Of the people in first marriages who were between the ages of twenty-five and thirty-five in 1975, about 34 per cent will probably end those marriages by divorce.

—Of the people in the same age group who had remarried after divorce, about 38 per cent will probably end those second marriages by divorce.

—To look at the figures in a positive way, about 66 per cent of first marriages of people in the twenty-five to thirty-five age group will last a lifetime, and so will about 62 per cent of second marriages in the same age group.

Yet even though the success of second marriages is so close to that of first marriages, a truer measure of their success is seen in the comparison of the survival rates of the first and second marriages of the same people. *Zero per cent of those who were divorced the first time remained happy enough to stay in the marriage, but 62 per cent of those same people will stay married the second time.* When we compare the success of those who remarry to the success they had the first time, the result is a ringing affirmation of the divorce experience.

But what becomes of those whose remarriages do not succeed —the ones who are called the *redivorced* by the Census Bureau, and far less kindly, the *two-time losers* by some fellow FMs? They used to be so rare that most people had never met one, but in the last decade, with so many men and women divorcing and remarrying early in life, the twice-divorced have abruptly increased both in number and in proportion; they are, or soon will be, a commonplace. By 1975, there were about a million Americans who had been divorced twice (two-thirds of them women), and the number was increasing swiftly.[27] Among people in their early forties who had been divorced and remarried, 8 per cent of the men and 11 per cent of the women had been divorced a second time.[28] Ask a man or a woman of thirty in a first marriage what the chances are that he or she will be divorced twice, and you will probably get a quizzical smile or a shrug of dismissal for an answer—but the young man has about a one-in-ten chance of two divorces, and the young woman, one chance in eight.*[29]

What does a second divorce signify? Does it mean that the twice-divorced person is a hopeless case, or merely unlucky? Does it indicate an unremediable unfitness for marriage, or only a failure of the individual to have gained the experiences that would have fitted him or her for remarriage? These questions trouble those who are considering remarriage and fear failure, and those who have already remarried and are considering redivorce. Society used to adjudge anyone who had been divorced just once, peculiar, incompetent, and a failure. Today, while that attitude has largely disappeared, it has been transferred, almost intact, to those who divorce two or more times. Most of the divorced share the harsh judgment themselves; those who redivorce are generally deeply ashamed, depressed, and filled with self-contempt. While they have little of the panic of the first-timers, they often sound like this:

> [Woman, thirty-four, legal secretary]   I felt like a complete failure. I had overpowering feelings of inferiority. I kept wondering what on earth was wrong with me, and I couldn't bring myself to tell my family I was divorced. Even now, eight months after the decree, I still say I'm separated and can't admit to them that I'm divorced again.
>
> [Man, fifty, editor]   The first time, fifteen years ago, it was like being in a firestorm—totally terrifying and bewildering. The

---

* The chances are even higher for those at lower economic and educational levels, but somewhat lower for those at the upper levels.[30]

second time, three years ago, I was far less alarmed and disoriented, and there wasn't that terrible fear of the unknown. But I felt a great rage—at her, at the Fates—but mostly at myself, that I had made another mistake, wasted all that time and energy and emotional input, and made an utter ass of myself in the eyes of my friends and everyone who knew me.

To judge by our survey, many people suffer deeper depression after the second breakup than after the first, but they make their way around among the formerly married, and resume active social life more easily and sooner than most of those who divorce for the first time. And although the redivorced do not quickly regain self-esteem and hope, most of them again go through the slow process of rehabilitation and move inexorably back toward love relationships, commitment, and remarriage. A minority opt for remaining unmarried and making do with other kinds of relationships, but the large majority come around, after a while, to saying things like this:

[Man, forty-eight, insurance adjuster] After two divorces I hesitate to try marriage again—I couldn't face a third failure. But there is such a big gap in my life, I have to take the chance. And maybe it isn't all that chancy; I seem to have found a very compatible woman to grow old with. Neither of us wants the pain of another divorce, but surely we have learned from experience, and the third marriage should be the last for both of us.

How many of the twice-divorced do marry a third time is unknown; neither the Bureau of the Census nor the National Center for Health Statistics compiles such data as yet. But we know that the twice-divorced were the marrying kind in the first place—and in the second place—and most of them, when they divorce the second time, are still young enough for their chances of remarriage to be fairly good. Three quarters of redivorcing women are under forty-five, three quarters of redivorcing men are under fifty; their chances of remarriage (if that is their goal) are probably at least three out of five for women, three out of four for men.[31]

And since it seems to become the goal for most of them, we must conclude that if it is true that a fair number of today's young people will be divorced twice in their lives, then it is also true that a fair number of them will be married three times.

Thus the net result of the divorce experience in contemporary America is not one of permanent embitterment, disillusionment, or diminished capacity for commitment. Only a small per cent of the divorced repudiate or shun remarriage, and even of those who do, many enter into loving and stable relationships that lack only the name and legal status of marriage. But the great majority not only love again, but marry again, and more wisely than before.

Samuel Johnson's words are wrong for us today. Remarriage is not the triumph of hope over experience; rather, it is the triumph of experience over ravaged hope.

Epilogue

And so, for most of those who divorce, the story has a happy ending. But it seems fair to ask whether, after all, the ending was worth the getting there. Even if most of the divorced make a good adjustment to postmarital life, and even if a majority remarry successfully, is the personal gain worth the personal cost? Or is divorce a cure worse than the disease?

And what of the social gain and the social cost? Though it is undoubtedly harmful to society to have large numbers of its men and women tormented by marital unhappiness, and of its children warped by growing up in tension-wracked homes, is divorce any less harmful? Or does it create more social disorder than it remedies? Perhaps, like so many of our technological advances, it yields us present comforts at the price of the future ruination of our world; if so, then the happy ending is a fraud, and what we have seen is a tragedy.

It is chiefly the undivorced who question whether the personal gain to their divorced friends outweighs the personal cost, whether the marriage was truly so painful as to necessitate the divorce, and the life that came after it sufficiently better to justify it. But pain and pleasure can be judged only by those who feel them; what seems tolerable to the onlooker may be intolerable to the sufferer, what seems a doubtful pleasure to the observer may be intensely gratifying to the one whose pleasure it is.

The divorced themselves have little doubt about the balance of gain and cost in their lives or the necessity of their divorces. Most of them say that no amount of effort could have made their marriages work and they regret only that, not that they were divorced. While a minority long for the lost marriage and the lost mate, the majority long for a better marriage and a more suitable mate, and among those who have fallen in love or remarried, regret and longing for the past are virtually nil.

Yes, most of them say, *yes, it was well worth it.* If they could turn back time, they would not do otherwise. The divorce was necessary, they themselves are happier and more successful human beings as a result of it, their children are as well or better off than they were before. And most of those who are in love or have remarried—and many who are not—say that their divorce was the best and most important change they ever made in their lives.

They are not merely putting a good face on things, for a satisfying marriage (or quasi-marital relationship) is even more important to contemporary men and women than it was to their counterparts in earlier and, superficially, more romantic eras. In modern industrial society, we are not the connected cells of a single organism, but separate grains of sand swirling about in a windstorm, close to one another only by chance and for an instant. We need to belong somewhere, to have some powerful bond, some intimate emotional union with other human beings and, particularly, with one other human being. A loving marriage—a sharing, caring partnership—is our answer, our antidote to the mechanization, impersonality, and disconnection of our economic and social lives. It is not marriage that is no longer in favor, but the marriage that fails to give us what we now require of it. If it does not comfort, console, and warm us, if it does not give us a sense of belonging and identity, we are all but compelled by inner need to leave it in order to seek one that does. Those who divorce are applying a desperate remedy to a desperate disease, and the disease is not marriage but *unhappy* marriage. And the state of health they seek to regain is not singleness but *happy* marriage.

But the balance of personal gain and loss is not the only criterion by which to judge the phenomenon of contemporary divorce. No institution, whatever rewards it brings to individuals, is defensible if it destroys the society of which it is part. And we have often been told, and still are told by some neoconservatives, that divorce is a malignancy within the social corpus, a growth that will kill the host it feeds upon. The new ideal of marriage, we hear, with its emphasis on freedom to grow and change—and hence to divorce—ignores parental responsibility. The divorcing gratify their own needs but forget those of their children and their society. We divorce for our own sakes and, in doing so, heedlessly unravel the web of society, for unbroken home life is the means by which the young are socialized, culture is transmitted, and civilization survives though generations are born and die.

Such is the cry of doom. But it is based on emotional and philosophic convictions rather than evidence. Predictions of disaster based on objective data—the known rate of depletion of some natural resource, for instance—are likely to come true unless steps are taken to alter the trajectory of history. But predictions of disaster based on changes in customs, moral values, or social institutions are more likely not to come true; they reflect not the calculable future but the fear and dismay people feel when the ways they have always taken to be right, good, and necessary are replaced by others. Changes in religious beliefs or rituals, in sexual behavior, in standards of modesty, in male and female roles, or in marriage, divorce, and family patterns, have often led people—even thoughtful ones—to prophesy social disaster, but though history makes much of the few times they have been right, it makes little of the many times they have been wrong. Who remembers, today, Cato the Elder's prediction that the rise of women's rights would spell the end of law and order, and of the greatness of Rome? "The moment [women] begin to be your equals," he warned the Senate in 195 B.C., "they will be your superiors.... Our liberty, destroyed at home, is even here in the Forum crushed and trodden under foot." It was a false prophecy; women continued to win measures of legal and financial equality and family life continued to change, but Roman democracy flourished for another century and a half, and Rome's greatest period came still later, when women were freer than ever. Three centuries after Cato, Juvenal caustically portrayed the latest Roman manners and morals as infinitely decadent; to hear him tell it, the game was nearly up. But in fact there were two hundred years of Roman greatness to come.

The unbroken nuclear family may seem to many people the right, good, and necessary means of child socialization and of cultural continuity, but theirs is a parochial and ethnocentric view. Neither unbroken marriage nor the nuclear family is universal throughout human societies; many other systems of marriage and forms of the family have existed, and most of them have worked well enough within the societies in which they evolved. It is all a matter of fit. The marital relationships and family structures that well served the Homeric Greeks, the Point Barrow Eskimos, or the medieval Moors would surely not serve us well today.

But neither would the forms of marriage and family of our own grandfathers. The changes wrought by our technology, the women's movement, the sexual revolution, and the redefining of the meanings of masculinity and femininity have all made it impossible for marriage to survive as it was, for as it was, it could not meet the needs of modern men and women. And therefore it has changed in its internal structure, its balance of power, its allocation of roles, and above all in its expected duration—formerly a lifetime, now only as long as it fulfills its proper contemporary functions.

Divorce has thus become not the antithesis of marriage but an essential aspect of the marriage system: It is the only way an individual can remain happily married—by changing partners —as his or her needs change in the course of a lifetime. Divorce, which seemed to be the problem afflicting and eroding marriage, now appears to be the essential adaptation that permits marriage, in its new embodiment, to survive as an institution and to perform the functions we require of it.

And this can only redound to the benefit of the society as a whole. When marriage today succeeds—when it is an emotionally, sexually, and intellectually satisfying partnership of equals —it enables men and women to function effectively in the society around them. When it is not, it leaves them distressed, needy, and ineffective. Successful marriages tend to create successful members of society; unsuccessful marriages tend to do the opposite.

Thus both for the individual and the group, the value of marriage is not marginal but major. Marriage is not a doubtful blessing but a necessity. It has long been an individual and social good, and in its modern incarnation, having undergone a great metamorphosis, it remains so—but divorce is an essential component of it. As George Bernard Shaw once said, somehow seeing all this long before it became true, "Divorce, in fact, is not the destruction of marriage, but the first condition of its maintenance."

This book, which has dealt with the divorce experience, is, then, really a book about one aspect of modern marriage. It is about the death of love but its rebirth; about endings but beginnings; about change but continuity; about the passing of an old ideal but the emergence of a new one—an ideal that is as valid and as admirable in our time as the old one was in its time.

Notes on Sources

The following notes give sources of all data except our own, or those not fully identified in the text. We make no attempt, however, to give the sources of those ideas and insights that are, by now, incorporated in the lore of divorce. But it will be apparent to the knowledgeable that we have stood on the shoulders of many giants, among them Willard Waller, Ernest Burgess, Jessie Bernard, and William J. Goode.

A WORD ABOUT OUR SURVEY

There will be no references in the Notes below to our own national questionnaire survey. Wherever a statement is made about how formerly married people now behave or think or what they experience, if no source is cited here, the information comes from that survey or from a supplemental series of depth interviews.

The survey was conducted in 1975–1976; it yielded a total of 984 completed questionnaires from separated and divorced people (plus, for comparative purposes, 113 from widowed people). It is a non-random volunteer sample, but in most of its demographic characteristics it is quite similar to the national population of separated and divorced people: it includes, for instance, roughly representative proportions of individuals from most economic and educational levels, the major religious groups, the various age cohorts, and all regions of the nation. True, it consists one-third of men and two-thirds of women, but this poses no problem; the data are compiled separately for the sexes. The sample is somewhat low in childless persons and it is almost completely deficient in people below the poverty level and in blacks. Otherwise, there are enough people in every category to permit us to make comparisons—of the working class with the middle class, for instance, or the briefly married with the long married, or the young with the middle-aged, and so on; the findings of such comparisons tend to be valid even within a volunteer sample. And more generally, where our data could be compared with those obtained by sociologists and psychologists currently doing research in this field, the results were usually reassuringly close; this gives us confidence that the rest of our findings, which are not to be found elsewhere, are similarly trustworthy.

We gathered the sample by several means. Parents Without Partners, a national organization of separated, divorced, and widowed persons, published our questionnaire in its monthly magazine, *The Single Parent*; the bulk of our replies came from this source. But to fill in those categories of the formerly married population missing from, or underrepresented in, the PWP sample, we solicited replies by two other means: thirty members of the American Association of Marriage and Family Counselors, all of whom do divorce counseling as well as marriage counseling, and some two dozen other people—chiefly sociologists specializing in marriage and the family—distributed questionnaires for us to persons in the needed categories.

The questionnaire was long and detailed; individual responses contained anywhere from 150 to well over 300 items of information. All of it was data-processed, with eight major and ten limited cross-tabulations. In addition to multiple-choice questions, the questionnaire had a number of open-ended questions, and many of our respondents wrote replies that ran to a dozen or two dozen pages in length. These comments, too, were data-processed after coding; more important, they are the source of many of the case histories and first-person statements in the text.

The other major source of case histories and first-person statements is the series of nearly 200 depth interviews we conducted, but to avoid contaminating the survey data, we did not tabulate these interviews or mingle them with the questionnaires.

CHAPTER I (pp. 1-35)

1. This statement, and the rest of the paragraph, are documented in Hunt, 1966, *passim*, especially Chapters III through V.

2. The 1976 ratio of divorces to marriages: National Center for Health Statistics, *Monthly Vital Statistics Report*, Vol. 25, No. 10; for the divorce rate per thousand in 1976: *ibid;* for the divorce rate in 1962: National Center for Health Statistics, 1973(b), p. 22.

3. U.S. Bureau of the Census, 1977, Table 1; and on the larger total who have passed through: Norton and Glick, 1976, p. 13.

4. The one-in-two chance of breaking up: Weiss, 1975(a), p. 12; also, Dr. Paul C. Glick, Senior Demographer, Population Division, U.S. Bureau of the Census, personal communication.

5. Same as note 3, this chapter.

6. Marriage rate, 1957 through 1967: National Center for Health Statistics, 1973(b); for recent years, National Center for Health Statistics, *Monthly Vital Statistics Report*, Vol. 23, No. 12; Vol. 24, Nos. 5 and 12; and Vol. 25, No. 10.

7. Current ratio: U.S. Bureau of the Census, 1977, Table 1; the ratio in 1962: Hunt, 1966, p. 18.

8. Average lag between separation and divorce today: National Center for Health Statistics, unpublished worksheets for 1974; average lag in 1960: Monahan, 1962.

9. U.S. Bureau of the Census, 1977, Table 1.

10. National Center for Health Statistics, 1976, section 2, pp. 5–7.

11. Norton and Glick, 1976, p. 15; National Center for Health Statistics, 1973(b), Table 12; U.S. Bureau of the Census, 1976(a), pp. 14–15; and National Center for Health Statistics, 1976, section 2, p. 8.

12. Median age at separation: see note 8, this chapter; other data in the paragraph: National Center for Health Statistics, 1976, section 2, p. 11. Note, however, that somewhat younger median ages are given in U.S. Bureau of the Census, 1976(a); the Bureau counts persons whose divorces occurred in the past as well as those currently divorcing, hence we chose to use the National Center for Health Statistics data.

13. The figures in the table are compiled from U.S. Bureau of the Census, 1977, Table 1.

14. Same as note 13, this chapter.

15. Goode, 1956, pp. 46–53.

16. Norton and Glick, 1976, pp. 13–14; U.S. Bureau of the Census, 1972(b), Table 7.

17. Same as note 16, this chapter.

18. This is the inference one can make from data in the U.S. Bureau of the Census, 1972(b), Table 7, which deals with urbanized areas, and which can be compared with figures in same publication for all areas.

19. U.S. Bureau of the Census, 1972(b), Table 1.

20. National Center for Health Statistics: *Monthly Vital Statistics Report*, Vol. 24, No. 13.

21. National Center for Health Statistics, 1976, section 2, p. 19.

22. For 1962: National Center for Health Statistics, 1964, section 3, p. 3; for 1973: Norton and Glick, 1976, p. 15.

23. U.S. Bureau of the Census, 1973(c).

24. Baber, 1953, pp. 451–461; Bell, 1963, p. 402.

25. See detailed discussion and sources in Chapter VII of this book.

26. The lower figures: Norton and Glick, 1976, p. 9; the higher figures: Ross and Sawhill, 1975, pp. 40–41.

27. The figures are approximations; the surveys differ somewhat. The two most important are: Martin S. Weinberg and Colin J. Williams: *Male Homosexuals* (New York: Oxford University Press, 1974), and Marcel T. Saghir and Eli Robins: *Male and Female Homosexuality* (Baltimore: Williams & Wilkins, 1973).

28. Bohannan, 1971(b), p. 41.

29. Quoted in *Journal of Marriage and the Family*, Nov. 1971, p. 632.

30. O'Brien, 1971.

CHAPTER II (pp. 37–70)

1. In our survey sample, only 20 per cent said they and their spouses had both wanted the divorce, but U.S. Bureau of the Census, n.d. [1975(b)], pp. 10–11, cites Emily Brown, chairman of the Family Action Section of the National Council on Family Relations, as estimating that both parties desire it in about six out of ten divorces.

2. Hunt and Hunt, 1975, *passim*.

3. Holmes and Rahe, 1967.

4. Glick, 1976(a), p. 16; Gove, 1973.

5. National Institute of Mental Health, 1974, 1975(a), 1975(b), and 1976.

6. This statement and the rest of the paragraph: Hunt, 1966, *passim*, but especially Chapters I and II.

7. Raschke, 1976, working with a sample drawn from Parents Without Partners (but not national), makes a somewhat similar finding, namely, of a significant correlation between "sexual permissiveness" (in attitudes) and postmarital adjustment.

8. See, for instance, discussion in Bernard, 1975.

9. Raschke, 1976. See also note 7, this chapter.

10. Weiss, 1975(a), p. 236, reports a similar finding.

11. It was already on the way out a decade ago; see discussion in Hunt, 1966, pp. 275–280. But in our reading of more recent research literature, we found almost nothing of the older view.

12. Bohannan, 1971(b), pp. 60–61.

13. Glick, 1976(b), Table 8; also, U.S. Bureau of the Census, 1977, Table 6.

14. Same as note 13, this chapter.

15. Bureau of Labor Statistics, 1975(a), Table 2.

16. Same as note 15, this chapter.

17. *Marriage, Divorce and the Family Newsletter*, April 15, 1975.

18. *Marriage, Divorce and the Family Newsletter*, December 1, 1975.

19. Memphis: *The New York Times*, December 7, 1976; Newark: *The New York Times*, December 31, 1976.

20. Weiss, 1973(b); Raschke, 1976.

CHAPTER III (pp. 71–100)

1. For the usefulness of work as a partner-finding milieu a generation ago: Goode, 1956, p. 255; Hollingshead, 1952.

2. So we learned from our survey respondents and interviewees, but also from advertisements and feature articles in a sampling of newspapers, regional magazines, and singles magazines covering 30 major metropolitan areas, and from a limited amount of direct observation.

3. This and the details in the balance of section 3 are drawn from the same sources as in note 2, this chapter, plus interviews with a number of proprietors and managers of the new ways and means.

4. Howard Ryals, publisher, *Singles World* magazine, personal communication.

5. Three times as many today as in the early 1960's: we arrived at this by extrapolating from our sample to the national FM population (but adjusting for the sample's lack of the poor and blacks, few of whom use dating bureaus or marriage brokers); we get a figure on the order of 400,000. An estimate for the early 1960's, based on Vedder, 1951, and Hunt, 1966, p. 300, is 140,000.

6. *The Single Parent*, July/August, 1976, p. 37.

7. There are more than three times as many female FMs and widows aged forty-five or over as there are male FMs and widowers aged forty-five or over; see U.S. Bureau of the Census, 1977, Table 1.

CHAPTER IV (pp. 101–126)

1. Braudy, 1974.

2. Krantzler, 1975, among others, applies this view to marital breakup.

3. Hunt, 1966, p. 128, errs by implying that most men suggested sex on the first or second date; when we reviewed the original work-sheets

of the survey made for that book, it turned out that a little less than half the men said they usually did so.

CHAPTER V (pp. 127–156)

1. Goode, 1971, pp. 481–484; the highest rate he cites is 396 divorces per 1,000 marriages in Algeria in 1920. The U.S. 1976 rate is a little over 500 per 1,000 marriages, according to *Monthly Vital Statistics Report,* Vol. 25, No. 11, of the National Center for Health Statistics.

2. Hunt, 1974, pp. 152–153. This was a national-questionnaire survey of more than 2,000 adults, designed, conducted, and data-processed by a professional opinion-research organization; the purpose of the survey was to compare sexual behavior in the early 1970's with that in the Kinsey era (the 1940's).

3. Hunt, 1974, pp. 115–116.

4. Hunt, 1966, pp. 162–163.

5. Hunt, 1974, p. 244, and Patton, 1976, p. 60. Patton, working with a single chapter of Parents Without Partners in a relatively conservative area, found that 92 per cent of the males and 84 per cent of the females had had postmarital coitus. But since the sample included widows and widowers, whose rates are known to be lower than those of the divorced (Gebhard, 1971), the rates for the divorced alone would be still higher than those he found.

6. Kinsey et al., 1948, p. 284; Kinsey et al., 1953, p. 559.

7. Hunt, 1974, p. 245.

8. Comparing our survey data to those for married people in Hunt, 1974, and in Kinsey et al., 1948 and Kinsey et al., 1953.

9. Gebhard, 1971, pp. 101–103.

10. Hendin and others are quoted to this effect in "Narcissus Redivivus," *Time,* Sept. 20, 1976, p. 63.

11. The separation of love and sex, due to unresolved oedipal conflict, has been explored innumerable times in the psychological literature ever since Freud's first formulation of it in *Contributions to the Psychology of Love.* A good résumé of theory and clinical findings on the matter can be found in Winch, 1963, chapter 19.

12. The distinction between manifest functions and latent functions, widely used by sociologists, is to be found in Merton, 1968, Chapter III; his original paper was published in 1948.

13. Ford and Beach, 1951, p. 118.

14. Harlow, 1971; Lowen, 1972; Montagu, 1955; and many others.

CHAPTER VI (pp. 157–188)

1. We arrive at two and a half million as follows. The twelve-month total of divorces to November, 1976, is 1,084,000: National Center for Health Statistics: *Monthly Vital Statistics Report,* Vol. 25, No. 11. Num-

ber of children per decree, 1.2: National Center for Health Statistics, 1976, Table 2-9. Thus, a total of 1,300,800 children. But since only half of all separations result in divorces, according to Weiss, 1975(a), p. 11, the number of children affected in any year is twice the number indicated by the divorce data. Thus, 2,601,600 children were affected in 1976. The 1951 figure: National Center for Health Statistics, 1970(a), p. 16, 304,000 children; doubled, to allow for separations not ending in divorce, 608,000.

2. U.S. Bureau of the Census, 1977, Table 5; and total number of persons under eighteen, same source, Table H.

3. U.S. Bureau of the Census, 1977, Table 5.

4. This is inferred from the fact that four out of five divorced persons eventually remarry: U.S. Bureau of the Census, 1976(a), p. 3.

5. Kenneth Keniston, "The Emptying Family," *The New York Times*, February 18, 1976.

6. See Note 16, Chapter II.

7. McFadden, 1975, p. 34; Wheeler, 1974, p. 77.

8. Georgia Dullea, "Who Gets Custody of the Children?" *The New York Times*, October 14, 1975.

9. U.S. Bureau of the Census, 1977, Table 5.

10. As cited in Newsletter of the National Council on Family Relations, Task Force on Divorce and Divorce Reform, October, 1976, p. 7.

11. Weiss, 1975(a), p. 169.

12. Virginia Slims Poll, Vol. III, n.d. [1974], p. 60.

13. Bryant et al., 1975, p. 47.

14. Bryant et al., 1975, p. 43.

15. U.S. Senate Committee on Finance, 1974, p. 43.

16. National Center for Social Statistics, 1974, and unpublished 1975 data in press (personal communication from Louis B. Hays, Deputy Director, Office of Child Support Enforcement, Department of Health, Education, and Welfare).

17. Ross and Sawhill, 1975, p. 175; and Henry H. Foster, Jr., and Doris Jonas Freed, quoted in *Newsday*, September 10, 1975, p. 15-a.

18. *The New York Times*, April 7, 1976, AP dispatch based on HEW release.

19. Same as note 15, this chapter, but p. 44; and same as note 16, this chapter.

20. Personal communication from Louis B. Hays (see note 16, this chapter); and *Newsday*, September 10, 1975, p. 15-A.

21. Cost of rearing a child at low-income level: *World Almanac, 1976*, p. 206; at moderate living standard: Community Council of Greater New York, cited in *The New York Times*, September 20, 1976, p. 1.

22. Unpublished data from U.S. Bureau of the Census (personal communication from Arthur J. Norton), in press: 3,129,000 single-parent families headed by separated and divorced women with children under eighteen, in 1976. We add a little under 300,000 more for single-parent

families headed by separated and divorced fathers with children under eighteen, since U.S. Bureau of the Census, 1977, Table 5, shows 7.7 per cent as many children living with FM fathers as with FM mothers. For the ratio of single-parent families to intact nuclear families, see U.S. Bureau of the Census, 1976(b), Table 3, Table 6, extracting figures for those with children under eighteen.

23. U.S. Bureau of the Census, 1975(b), Table 6; Gongla, 1974, pp. 3–4.

24. Gongla, 1974, pp. 14–15.

25. Brown, 1975; see also Weiss, 1973(c).

26. Wallerstein and Kelly, 1974, 1975, and 1976, and Kelly and Wallerstein, 1976.

27. Weiss, 1973(c), p. 24.

28. Epstein, 1975, pp. 238–241.

29. Brandwein, 1974; Borenzweig, 1976.

30. Rosenthal and Finkelstein, 1976.

31. Weiss, 1973(c), p. 19.

32. Herzog and Sudia, 1971, pp. 3, 99–120.

33. Ross and Sawhill, 1975, p. 152.

34. Herzog and Sudia, 1971, p. 61.

35. Herzog and Sudia, 1971, *passim;* Ross and Sawhill, 1975, chapter 6.

36. Bieber et al., 1962; Hoffman, 1969; Saghir and Robins, 1973; Hedblom, 1973; and Manosevitz, 1972.

37. Weiss, 1975(a), pp. 219–220; Aldous, 1972.

38. Same as note 26, this chapter.

39. Herzog and Sudia, 1971, pp. 55–56.

40. Despert, 1953, p. 10.

41. Herzog and Sudia, 1971, p. 65.

CHAPTER VII (pp. 189–218)

1. Virginia Slims Poll, 1974, pp. 54, 56.

2. Weiss, 1975(a), pp. 117–118, reports this, too.

3. Weiss, 1975(a), pp. 11, 120–124.

4. One in eight: Rosow and Ross, 1972; twice that many: Wheeler, 1974, p. 100.

5. Two-thirds of the states, that is, still have fault law or optional (but not unilaterally available) no-fault grounds: Women's Bureau, 1975, pp. 375–379; Council of State Governments, 1976, pp. 238–239.

6. Philip F. Solomon, president, American Academy of Matrimonial Lawyers, personal communication; Johnson, 1977.

7. Wheeler, 1974, pp. 6–7.

8. Wheeler, 1974, pp. 155–157, 166.

9. Same as note 5, this chapter.

10. Nine-tenths in California: Mack, 1977. On the time required: Lenore Weitzman, personal communication.

11. Virginia Slims Poll, 1974, p. 58; Bryant et al., 1975, p. 48.

12. Quoted in Nemy, 1976.

13. Quoted in *Newsday*, Sept. 9, 1975, p. 4-A.

14. Lenore Weitzman, personal communication. The same points are dealt with in detail in Weitzman and Dixon, 1976.

15. Philip F. Solomon, personal communication.

16. Bryant et al., 1975, p. 41; the 1939 figure (29 per cent): National Center for Health Statistics, 1973(b), p. 19.

17. Philip F. Solomon, personal communication; *Business Week*, February 10, 1975.

18. *Marriage, Divorce and the Family Newsletter*, April 15, 1976.

19. Ivins, 1977.

20. Fisher, 1973.

21. Mack, 1977.

22. Johnson, 1977.

23. Bohannan, 1971(c), p. 285.

CHAPTER VIII (219–239)

1. U.S. Bureau of the Census, 1976(a), p. 3.

2. Among authorities who report that sexually open marriages (and hence, by extension, sexually open love affairs) are insupportable to most people are Paul Gebhard, director of the Institute for Sex Research; George and Nena O'Neill, authors of *Open Marriage;* and C. Ray Fowler, executive director, American Association of Marriage and Family Counselors. See Hunt, 1977.

3. The 660,000: U.S. Bureau of the Census, 1977, p. 5; the 260,000: Arthur J. Norton, Chief, Marriage and Family Statistics Branch, U.S. Bureau of the Census, personal communication.

4. Van Gelder, 1976.

5. Quoted in Van Gelder, 1976.

6. Quoted in Van Gelder, 1976.

7. The Creative Divorce National Counseling Center (San Rafael, California), for one, specifically lists this service in its brochures.

CHAPTER IX (pp. 241–264)

1. Campbell et al.

2. Gove, 1973.

3. Gove, 1973; Glick, 1976(a); National Institute of Mental Health, 1974, 1975, and 1976.

4. Gove, 1973.

5. A generation ago: sources differ somewhat, but thirty or more years ago the median time for those who remarried was somewhere around three to five years after divorce (five to seven years after separation). See Jacobson, 1959, pp. 69–70, and Goode, 1956, p. 331.

6. U.S. Bureau of the Census, 1976(a), Table O, shows 16.5 per cent of remarried men and 16.2 per cent of remarried women as having remarried within the first year; however, since only five out of six men and three out of four women ever remarry (same source, p. 3), we multiply each percentage by the appropriate fraction, and get about one-seventh of men and of women remarrying within one year after divorce.

7. U.S. Bureau of the Census, 1976(a), Table O, for medians; however, these medians refer only to those who do remarry, sooner or later, so we multiply median for men by five-sixths, median for women by three-fourths, as in note 6, this chapter. (N.B.: the National Center for Health Statistics, 1973(c), p. 13, reports the median time to remarriage as only 1.2 years for women and 1.0 year for men, but these are the findings of a single year and are based on data from only fifteen states.)

8. The figure for less than half a century ago: Waller, 1930, p. 335; Cahen, 1932, pp. 98–109; the figure for today: U.S. Bureau of the Census, 1976(a), p. 3.

9. Glick, 1976(a); Arthur J. Norton, Chief, Marriage and Family Statistics Branch, U.S. Bureau of the Census, personal communication. For trends, 1960 to 1969, see National Center for Health Statistics, 1973(c).

10. Estimate by Arthur J. Norton (see note 9, this chapter), via personal communication.

11. U.S. Bureau of the Census, 1976(a), Table R, from which median time to remarriage can be extracted for divorced persons in different age groups.

12. U.S. Bureau of the Census, 1971, Table 8.

13. U.S. Bureau of the Census, 1971, Table 4.

14. U.S. Bureau of the Census, 1971, Table 8.

15. U.S. Bureau of the Census, 1977, Table 1 (omitting the fourteen-to-seventeen cohort, and recalculating percentages).

16. U.S. Bureau of the Census, 1976(a), p. 8 and Table I.

17. See, for instance: Berelson and Steiner, 1964, p. 310; Bell, 1963, p. 146; and Cavan, 1969, p. 225.

18. The twenty-year age difference: National Center for Health Statistics, 1973(c), Table E. For the other median age differences: U.S. Bureau of the Census, 1972(b), Table 11.

19. National Center for Health Statistics, 1973(c), pp. 10–11 and Table G.

20. The best-known and most extreme exposition of this view was that of Bergler, 1948.

21. Westoff, 1977, pp. 32–33.

22. Westoff, 1977, p. 39.

23. Bohannan, 1975.

24. Campbell et al.; Bernard, 1972, pp. 67–75.

25. U.S. Bureau of the Census, 1976(a), pp. 13, 17.

26. Data in the next three paragraphs are derived from U.S. Bureau of the Census, 1976(a), Table G, by collapsing the two youngest cohorts

of each sex, and then taking an average of these so as to have one overall figure.

27. U.S. Bureau of the Census, 1976(a), Table H.

28. U.S. Bureau of the Census, 1976(a), Table F.

29. Using the method outlined in Glick and Norton, 1973, but with more recent data drawn from U.S. Bureau of the Census, 1976(a), Table G, we multiply chance of first divorce by chance of remarriage by chance of second divorce, for men and women aged twenty-five to thirty in 1975, and get a 9.9 per cent chance for the men, a 12.5 per cent chance for the women.

30. Paul C. Glick, Senior Demographer, Population Division, U.S. Bureau of the Census, personal communication.

31. U.S. Bureau of the Census, 1976(?), Table H; and see note 10, this chapter.

Bibliography

Since it would serve no purpose to name every work on divorce we examined, what follows is a highly selective list; it is limited to those works cited in the Notes on Sources plus a handful of others that we found particularly useful.

Aldous, Joan. "Children's Perceptions of Adult Role Assignment: Father-Absence, Class, Race and Sex Influences," *Journal of Marriage and the Family*, February, 1972.

Baber, Ray E. *Marriage and the Family*. New York: McGraw-Hill Book Company, 1953.

Bell, Robert R. *Marriage and Family Interaction*. Homewood, Ill.: The Dorsey Press, Inc., 1963.

Berelson, Bernard, and Gary A. Steiner. *Human Behavior: An Inventory of Scientific Findings*. New York: Harcourt, Brace & World, Inc., 1964.

Bergler, Edmund. *Divorce Won't Help*. New York: Harper & Brothers, 1948.

Bernard, Jessie. *Remarriage: A Study of Marriage*. New York: The Dryden Press, 1956.

———. *The Future of Marriage*. New York: Bantam Books, 1973. Paper.

———. "Note on Changing Life Styles, 1970–1974," *Journal of Marriage and the Family*, August, 1975.

Berson, Barbara, and Ben Bova. *Survival Guide for the Suddenly Single*. New York: St. Martin's Press, 1974.

Bieber, Irving, et al. *Homosexuality: A Psychoanalytic Study*. New York: Basic Books, Inc., 1962.

Blum, Sam. "The Re-Mating Game," *The New York Times Magazine*, August 29, 1976.

Bohannan, Paul (ed.). *Divorce and After*. Garden City, New York: Anchor Books, 1971(a). Paper.

Bohannan, Paul. "The Six Stations of Divorce," (1971[b]), in Bohannan (ed.), 1971(a).

———. "Some Thoughts on Divorce Reform," (1971[c]), in Bohannan (ed.), 1971(a).

———. "Stepfathers and the Mental Health of Their Children," Unpublished report, on grant RO1MH21146, to the National Institute of Mental Health, U.S. Department of Health, Education, and Welfare, December, 1975.

Borenzweig, Herman. "The Punishment of Divorced Mothers," *Journal of Sociology and Social Welfare*, January, 1976.

Brandwein, Ruth A. "The One Parent Family as a Viable Life Style." Paper presented at the annual conference of the National Council on Family Relations, St. Louis, Mo., October, 1974.

Braudy, Susan. "A Diary of the First 441 Days After the Marriage Is Over," *Ms.* Magazine, April, 1974.

Brown, Emily M. "Divorce and Human Growth." Paper presented at the national convention of the American Alliance for Health, Physical Education, and Recreation, Atlantic City, N.J., March, 1975.

Bryant, Barbara Everitt, et al. "American Women in International Women's Year." Detroit: Market Opinion Research, 1975. Mimeo. report of survey conducted for the U.S. Commission on International Women's Year.

Burchinal, Lee G., and Loren E. Chancellor. *Survival Rates among Religiously Homogamous and Interreligious Marriages:* Agricultural and Home Economics Experiment Station Research Bulletin 512. Ames, Iowa: Iowa State University of Science and Technology, December, 1962.

Burden, Susan, et al. (eds.). *The Single Parent Family: Proceedings of the Changing Family Conference V*. Iowa City, Iowa: The University of Iowa, 1976.

Bureau of the Census. *See:* U.S. Bureau of the Census.

Bureau of Labor Statistics. *See:* U.S. Department of Labor, Bureau of Labor Statistics.

Cahen, Alfred. *Statistical Analysis of American Divorce*. New York: Columbia University Press, 1932.

Campbell, Angus, Philip E. Converse, and Willard L. Rodgers. Untitled "quality of life" study, in progress; early results summarized in Institute of Social Research (University of Michigan) *Newsletter*, Summer, 1974, Ann Arbor, Michigan, P.O. Box 1248.

Cavan, Ruth Shonle. *The American Family*. New York: Crowell, 1969.

Cosneck, Bernard J. "What About Trying It Again," *The Single Parent*, November, 1972.

Council of State Governments, The. *The Book of the States, 1976–1977*. Lexington, Ky.: The Council of State Governments, 1976.

Despert, J. Louise. *Children of Divorce.* Garden City, New York: Doubleday & Co., Inc., 1953.

Epstein, Joseph. *Divorced in America: Marriage in an Age of Possibility.* New York: Penguin Books, Inc., 1975. Paper.

Fisher, Esther Oshiver. "A Guide to Divorce Counseling," *The Family Coordinator,* January, 1973.

Ford, Clellan S., and Frank A. Beach. *Patterns of Sexual Behavior.* New York: Harper & Brothers, and Paul B. Hoeber, Inc., 1951.

Foster, Henry H., Jr., and Doris Jonas Freed. "Marital Property and the Chancellor's Foot," a series of articles on divorce laws concerning marital property in the authors' regular column, "Law and the Family" in *New York Law Journal,* May 24, August 23, September 27, October 25, November 22, and December 27, 1974, and January 31, February 27, March 28, April 25, and May 23, 1975.

Fuller, Jan. *Space: The Scrapbook of My Divorce.* New York: Fawcett, 1975. Paper.

Gebhard, Paul. "Postmarital Coitus among Widows and Divorcees," (1971), in Bohannan (ed.), 1971(a).

Gettleman, Susan, and Janet Markowitz. *The Courage to Divorce.* New York: Simon and Schuster, 1974.

Glick, Paul C. "Some Recent Changes in American Families." (U.S. Bureau of the Census. *Current Population Reports:* Special Studies: Series P-23; No. 52) Washington, D.C.: U.S. Government Printing Office, n.d. [1975]. Same as: U.S. Bureau of the Census, n.d. [1975 (b)], q.v.

————. "Trends in Family Formation and Dissolution: Implications for Policy." Paper presented at the Groves Conference on Marriage and the Family, March, 1976(a).

————. "Living Arrangements of Children and Young Adults," *Journal of Contemporary Family Studies,* Spring, 1976(b).

————. "Updating the Life Cycle of the Family," *Journal of Marriage and the Family,* February, 1977.

————, and Arthur J. Norton. "Perspectives on the Recent Upturn in Divorce and Remarriage," *Demography,* August, 1973.

————, and Robert Parke, Jr. "New Approaches in Studying the Life Cycle of the Family," *Demography,* Vol. 2 (1965), pp. 187–202.

Gongla, Patricia. "Single Parent Families: Extended- and Extra-Familial Aid and the Socialization of Children." Paper presented at the annual meeting of the Society for the Study of Social Problems, Montreal, August, 1974.

Goode, William J. *After Divorce.* Glencoe, Ill.: The Free Press, 1956.

————. "Family Disorganization," in Robert K. Merton and Robert Nisbet (eds.), *Contemporary Social Problems* (New York: Harcourt Brace Jovanovich, 1971).

Gove, Walter R. "Sex, Marital Status, and Mortality," *American Journal of Sociology,* July, 1973.

Green, Maureen. *Fathering*. New York: McGraw-Hill Book Company, 1976.

Habant, John, and Patricia Gongla. "Single Parent Family Report." Paper presented at the annual meeting of the National Council on Family Relations, Toronto, October, 1973.

Harlow, Harry F. *Learning to Love*. New York: Ballantine, 1971. Paper.

Havens, Elizabeth M. "Women, Work, and Wedlock: A Note on Female Marital Patterns in the United States," *American Journal of Sociology*, January, 1973.

Heclo, Hugh, et al. *Single Parent Families: Issues and Policies*. Mimeo.; report prepared for the Office of Child Development, U.S. Department of Health, Education, and Welfare, 1973.

Hedblom, Jack H. "Dimensions of Lesbian Sexual Experience," *Archives of Sexual Behavior*, Vol. 2, No. 4 (1973), pp. 329–341.

Herman, Sonya J. "Women, Divorce and Suicide." Paper presented, in part, at the meeting of the American Association of Suicidology, April, 1976. Based on the author's doctoral dissertation, The Catholic University of America.

Herzog, Elizabeth, and Cecelia E. Sudia. *Boys in Fatherless Families*. Office of Child Development, U.S. Department of Health, Education, and Welfare, DHEW Publication No. (OCD) 72-33. Washington, D.C.: U.S. Government Printing Office, 1971.

Hoffman, Martin. *The Gay World*. New York: Bantam Books, 1969. Paper.

Hollingshead, A.R. "Marital Status and Wedding Behavior," *Marriage and Family Living*, November, 1952.

Holmes, T.H., and R.H. Rahe, "The Social Readjustment Rating Scale," *Journal of Psychosomatic Research*, Vol. 11 (1967), pp. 213–218.

Hunt, Bernice, and Morton Hunt. *Prime Time: A Guide to the Pleasures and Opportunities of the New Middle Age*. New York: Stein and Day, 1975.

Hunt, Morton. *The World of the Formerly Married*. New York: McGraw-Hill Book Company, 1966.

———. *Sexual Behavior in the 1970s*. Chicago: Playboy Press, 1974.

———. "Why 'Open Marriage' Failed," *Family Circle*, January, 1977.

Ivins, Molly. "E.R.A., Alimony, Child Care; The Outlook," *The New York Times*, January 22, 1977.

Jacobson, Paul. *American Marriage and Divorce*. New York: Rinehart & Company, Inc., 1959.

Johnson, Sharon. "California's Divorce-Yourself Brings a Backlash," *The New York Times*, January 6, 1977.

Kelly, Joan B., and Judith S. Wallerstein. "The Effects of Parental Divorce: Experiences of the Child in Early Latency," *American Journal of Orthopsychiatry*, January, 1976.

Kinsey, Alfred C., et al. *Sexual Behavior in the Human Male*. Philadelphia: W. B. Saunders Company, 1948.

————. *Sexual Behavior in the Human Female*. Philadelphia: W. B. Saunders Company, 1953.

Klein, Carole. *The Single Parent Experience*. New York: Avon, 1973. Paper.

Krantzler, Mel. *Creative Divorce: A New Opportunity for Personal Growth*. New York: Signet/New American Library, 1975. Paper.

Lowen, Alexander. "The Spiral of Growth: Love, Sex and Pleasure," in Herbert A. Otto (ed.), *Love Today* (New York: Association Press, 1972).

MacDonald, Steve. "The Alimony Blues," *The New York Times Magazine*, March 16, 1975.

McFadden, Michael. *Bachelor Fatherhood*. New York: Ace Books, 1975. Paper.

McKenney, Mary. *Divorce: A Selected Annotated Bibliography*. Metuchen, N.J.: The Scarecrow Press, Inc., 1975.

McKinney, Sally. "The L.T.A.—With Children," *The Single Parent*, July/August, 1976.

Mack, Gail. "For $59, a New Yorker Wins a Divorce without Lawyers," *The New York Times*, January 6, 1977.

Manosevitz, Martin. "The Development of Male Homosexuality," *Journal of Sex Research*, Vol. 8, No. 1 (1972).

Marriage, Divorce and the Family Newsletter, P. O. Box 42, Madison Square Station, New York, New York, 10010.

Merton, Robert K. "Manifest and Latent Functions," chapter III in his *Social Theory and Social Structure* (New York: The Free Press, 1968).

Monahan, Thomas P. "When Married Couples Part: Statistical Trends and Relationships in Divorce," *American Sociological Review*, October, 1962.

Montagu, M. F. Ashley. *The Direction of Human Development*. New York: Harper & Brothers, 1955.

Morrison, J. R. "Parental Divorce as a Factor in Childhood Psychiatric Illness," *Comprehensive Psychiatry*, Vol. 5, No. 2 (1974), pp. 95–102.

National Center for Health Statistics, Public Health Service, U.S. Department of Health, Education, and Welfare. *Monthly Vital Statistics Report*: various issues of *Provisional Statistics, Final Marriage Statistics*, and *Final Divorce Statistics*, Vols. 20–25 (statistics for 1971 through 1976). Rockville, Maryland: U.S. Department of Health, Education, and Welfare, 1972 to 1977.

————. *Vital Statistics of the United States, 1970: Volume III—Divorces*. Washington, D.C.: U.S. Department of Health, Education, and Welfare, 1964.

————. Series 21, Number 16: *Marriage Statistics Analysis, United States, 1963*. Washington, D.C.: U.S. Department of Health, Education, and Welfare, 1968.

————. Series 21, Number 18: *Children of Divorced Couples: United*

States, Selected Years. Washington, D.C.: U.S. Department of Health, Education, and Welfare, 1970(a).

——. Series 21, Number 20: *Increases in Divorces, United States—1967.* Rockville, Md.: U.S. Department of Health, Education, and Welfare, 1970(b).

——. Series 21, Number 21: *Marriages: Trends and Characteristics, United States.* Rockville, Md.: U.S. Department of Health, Education, and Welfare, 1971.

——. Series 21, Number 22: *Divorces: Analysis of Changes, United States, 1969.* Rockville, Md.: U.S. Department of Health, Education, and Welfare, 1973(a).

——. Series 21, Number 24: *100 Years of Marriage and Divorce Statistics, United States, 1867–1967.* Rockville, Md.: U.S. Department of Health, Education, and Welfare, 1973(b).

——. Series 21, Number 25: *Remarriages, United States.* Rockville, Md.: U.S. Department of Health, Education, and Welfare, 1973(c).

——. Series 21, Number 23: *Teenagers: Marriages, Divorces, Parenthood, and Mortality.* Rockville, Md.: U.S. Department of Health, Education, and Welfare, 1974.

——. *Vital Statistics of the United States, 1972: Volume III—Marriage and Divorce.* Rockville, Md.: U.S. Department of Health, Education, and Welfare, 1976.

National Center for Social Statistics, Social and Rehabilitation Service, U.S. Department of Health, Education, and Welfare. *Findings of the 1973 AFDC Study: Part I, Demographic and program characteristics.* Washington, D.C.: U.S. Department of Health, Education, and Welfare, 1974.

National Institute of Mental Health, U.S. Department of Health, Education, and Welfare. Statistical Note 100: "Marital Status, Living Arrangements and Family Characteristics of Admissions to State and County Mental Hospitals and Outpatient Psychiatric Clinics, United States 1970." Rockville, Md.: U.S. Department of Health, Education, and Welfare, 1974.

——. Statistical Note 120: "Marital Status and Age of Male Admissions with Diagnosed Alcohol Disorders to State and County Mental Hospitals in 1972." Rockville, Md.: U.S. Department of Health, Education, and Welfare, 1975(a).

——. Series D, No. 3: *Marital Status and Mental Disorders: An Analytic Review.* Rockville, Md.: U.S. Department of Health, Educaton, and Welfare, 1975(b).

——. Statistical Note No. 124: "Characteristics of Diagnosed and Missed Alcoholic Male Admissions to State and County Mental Hospitals, 1972." Rockville, Md.: U.S. Department of Health, Education, and Welfare, 1976.

Nemy, Enid. "Feminists Look at Alimony," *The New York Times*, February 6, 1976.

Norton, Arthur J. "The Family Life Cycle Updated: Components and Uses." Paper presented at annual meeting of the Population Association of America, New Orleans, April, 1973.

———, and Paul C. Glick. "Marital Instability: Past, Present, and Future," *Journal of Social Issues*, June, 1976.

O'Brien, John E. "Violence in Divorce Prone Families," *Journal of Marriage and the Family*, November, 1971.

Patton, Robert David. *Sexual Attitudes and Behaviors of Single Parents*. Dissertation presented for the Doctor of Education degree, University of Tennessee, Knoxville, March 1976.

Proulx, Cynthia. "Sex as Athletics in the Singles Complex," *Saturday Review/Society*, May, 1973.

Raschke, Helen June. "The Role of Social Participation in Post Separation and Postdivorce Adjustment." Paper presented at the annual meeting of the Southern Sociological Society, Washington, D.C., April, 1975.

———. "Sex Differences in Voluntary Post Marital Dissolution Adjustment." Paper presented at the annual meeting of the American Sociological Association, New York City, August, 1976.

Rosenthal, Kristine M., and H. Finkelstein. "Role Change and Role Continuity of Fathering." Paper presented at the annual conference of the National Council on Family Relations, 1976.

Rosow, Irving, and K. Daniel Ross, "Divorce among Doctors," *Journal of Marriage and the Family*, November, 1972.

Ross, Heather L., and Isabel V. Sawhill. *Time of Transition: The Growth of Families Headed by Women*. Washington, D.C.: The Urban Institute, 1975. Paper.

Saghir, Marcel T., and Eli Robins. *Male and Female Homosexuality*. Baltimore: Williams and Wilkins, 1973.

Single Parent, The, the journal of Parents Without Partners, Inc., 7910 Woodmont Avenue, Washington, D.C. 20014.

Spicer, Jerry W., and Gary D. Hampe. "Kinship Interaction After Divorce," *Journal of Marriage and the Family*, February, 1975.

Stuart, Irving R., and Lawrence Edwin (eds.). *Children of Separation and Divorce*. New York: Grossman, 1972.

U.S. Bureau of the Census, U.S. Department of Commerce. *Current Population Reports*, Series P-20, No. 223, "Social and Economic Variations in Marriage, Divorce, and Remarriage: 1967." Washington, D.C.: U.S. Government Printing Office, 1971.

———. *Census of Population: 1970. General Population Characteristics*. Final Report PC(1)-B1. Washington, D.C.: U.S. Government Printing Office, 1972(a).

———. *Census of Population: 1970. Marital Status*. Final Report PC(2)-4C. Washington, D.C.: U.S. Government Printing Office, 1972(b).

———. *Current Population Reports*, Series P-20, No. 239, "Marriage,

Divorce, and Remarriage by Year of Birth: June 1971." Washington, D.C.: U.S. Government Printing Office, 1972(c).

———. *Census of Population: 1970. Family Composition.* Final Report PC(2)-4A. Washington, D.C.: U.S. Government Printing Office, 1973(a).

———. *Census of Population: 1970. Persons by Family Characteristics.* Final Report PC(2)-4B. Washington, D.C.: U.S. Government Printing Office, 1973(b).

———. *Census of Population: 1970. Women by Number of Children Ever Born.* Final Report PC(2)-3A. Washington, D.C.: U.S. Government Printing Office, 1973(c).

———. *Current Population Reports,* Series P-20, No. 287, "Marital Status and Living Arrangements: March, 1975." Washington, D.C.: U.S. Government Printing Office, 1975(a).

———. *Current Population Reports,* Series P-23, No. 52, "Some Recent Changes in American Families." Washington, D.C.: U.S. Government Printing Office, n.d. [1975(b)].

———. *Current Population Reports,* Series P-20, No. 297, "Number, Timing, and Duration of Marriages and Divorces in the United States: June, 1975." Washington, D.C.: U.S. Government Printing Office, 1976(a).

———. *Current Population Reports,* Series P-20, No. 291, "Household and Family Characteristics: March, 1975." Washington, D.C.: U.S. Government Printing Office, 1976(b).

———. *Current Population Reports,* Series P-23, No. 63, "Premarital Fertility." Washington, D.C.: U.S. Government Printing Office, 1976(c).

———. *Current Population Reports,* Series P-20, No. 306, "Marital Status and Living Arrangements: March, 1976." Washington, D.C.: U.S. Government Printing Office, 1977.

U.S. Commission on International Women's Year. *See:* Bryant et al., 1975.

U.S. Department of Labor, Bureau of Labor Statistics. Special Labor Force Report 183: "Marital and Family Characteristics of the Labor Force, March, 1975." Washington, D.C.: U.S. Department of Labor, n.d. [1975(a)].

———. Summary, Special Labor Force Report: "Children of Working Mothers, March, 1975." Washington, D.C.: U.S. Department of Labor, August, 1975(b).

———. "Women in the Labor Force: The Early Years; The Middle Years; The Later Years." Reprinted from *Monthly Labor Review,* November, 1975(c).

———. Bulletin 1880: "U.S. Working Women, a chartbook." Washington, D.C.: U.S. Department of Labor, 1975(d).

———. Special Labor Force Report 181: "Work Experience of the Population in 1974." Reprinted from *Monthly Labor Review,* October, 1975(e).

U.S. Department of Labor, Women's Bureau. *1975 Handbook on Women Workers:* Bulletin 297. Washington, D.C.: U.S. Department of Labor, 1975.

U.S. Senate Committee on Finance. *Social Services Amendments.* Senate Report No. 93-1356, 93rd Congress, 2nd Session 42 (1974). Washington, D.C.: U.S. Government Printing Office, 1974.

Van Gelder, Lawrence. "Cohabitation and the Courts: The Stigma is Beginning to Fade," *The New York Times,* September 2, 1976.

Vedder, Clyde B. "Lonely Hearts Clubs Viewed Sociologically," *Social Forces,* December, 1951.

Virginia Slims American Women's Opinion Poll, The, Volume III. New York: The Roper Organization, Inc., 1974.

Waller, Willard. *The Old Love and the New.* New York: H. Liveright, 1930.

Wallerstein, Judith S., and Joan B. Kelly. "The Effects of Parental Divorce: The Adolescent Experience," in James E. Anthony and Cyrille Koupernik (eds.), *The Child in His Family—Children at a Psychiatric Risk,* Vol. 3 (New York: John Wiley & Sons, Inc., 1974).

———. "The Effects of Parental Divorce: Experiences of the Preschool Child," *Journal of the American Academy of Child Psychiatry,* Vol. 14, No. 4 (Autumn 1975), pp. 600–616.

———. "The Effects of Parental Divorce: Experiences of the Child in Later Latency," *American Journal of Orthopsychiatry,* Vol. 46, No. 2 (April, 1976), pp. 256–269.

Weiss, Robert S. "Helping Relationships: Relationships of Clients with Physicians, Social Workers, Priests, and Others," *Social Problems,* Vol. 20, No. 3 (Winter, 1973[a]), pp. 319–328.

———. "The Contributions of an Organization of Single Parents to the Well-Being of its Members," *The Family Coordinator,* July, 1973(b).

———. "Emotional and Social Issues in Single Parenting," in Heclo et al., q.v., 1973(c).

———. *Marital Separation.* New York: Basic Books, Inc., 1975(a).

———. "The Provisions of Social Relationships," in Zick Rubin (ed.), *Doing Unto Others* (Englewood Cliffs, N.J.: Prentice-Hall, 1975[b]).

Weitzman, Lenore J., and Ruth B. Dixon. "Alimony: A Quest for Justice in Changing Times." Paper presented at the annual meeting of the American Sociological Association, New York City, August, 1976.

Westoff, Leslie Aldridge. *The Second Time Around: Remarriage in America.* New York: The Viking Press, 1977.

Wheeler, Michael. *No-Fault Divorce.* Boston: Beacon Press, 1975. Paper.

Winch, Robert F. *The Modern Family.* New York: Holt, Rinehart and Winston, 1963.

Women's Bureau. *See:* U.S. Department of Labor, Women's Bureau.

World Almanac and Book of Facts, 1976, The. New York/Cleveland: Newspaper Enterprise Association, Inc., 1975.

Index